designing

designing

RADICAL THINKERS IN DESIGN

Expansion in practice and the global increase in numbers of those with design education or who study design has not brought with it increased understanding. On the contrary, despite the intelligence of many of those entering the field, reduced to the crudest understanding of vocation, depth of thought disappears; crises remain untouched; genuinely new practices and conceptions struggle to be comprehended in their implications.

Radical Thinkers in Design, a moment of the larger project *Designing in Dark Times*, seeks in a small way to try to address this situation by bringing back into circulation, as aids to thinking and praxis, some key provocative texts in contemporary thinking on designing.

TITLES IN THE SERIES

designing designing, John Chris Jones

Defuturing, Tony Fry

Wild Things, Judy Attfield

Design Noir, Anthony Dunne and Fiona Raby

designing designing

John Chris Jones

BLOOMSBURY VISUAL ARTS
LONDON · NEW YORK · OXFORD · NEW DELHI · SYDNEY

BLOOMSBURY VISUAL ARTS
Bloomsbury Publishing Plc
50 Bedford Square, London, WC1B 3DP, UK
1385 Broadway, New York, NY 10038, USA

BLOOMSBURY, BLOOMSBURY VISUAL ARTS and the Diana
logo are trademarks of Bloomsbury Publishing Plc

First published in Great Britain 1991
This edition published 2021

Copyright © J. C. Jones, 1991

J. C. Jones has asserted his right under the Copyright,
Designs and Patents Act, 1988, to be identified as Author of this work.

For legal purposes the Acknowledgements on pp. lix–lx constitute
an extension of this copyright page.

Cover image by Jonathan Moberly

All rights reserved. No part of this publication may be reproduced or
transmitted in any form or by any means, electronic or mechanical,
including photocopying, recording, or any information storage or
retrieval system, without prior permission in writing from the publishers.

Bloomsbury Publishing Plc does not have any control over, or responsibility for,
any third-party websites referred to or in this book. All internet addresses given
in this book were correct at the time of going to press. The author and publisher
regret any inconvenience caused if addresses have changed or sites have
ceased to exist, but can accept no responsibility for any such changes.

A catalogue record for this book is available from the British Library.

A catalog record for this book is available from the Library of Congress.

ISBN: HB: 978-1-3500-7197-1
PB: 978-1-3500-7067-7
ePub: 978-1-3500-7068-4
ePDF: 978-1-3500-7069-1

Series: Radical Thinkers in Design

Typeset by Newgen KnowledgeWorks Pvt. Ltd., Chennai, India
Printed and bound in India

To find out more about our authors and books visit
www.bloomsbury.com and sign up for our newsletter.

Human plurality, the basic condition of both action and speech, has the twofold character of equality and distinction. If men were not equal, they could neither understand each other and those who came before them nor plan for the future and forsee the needs of those who will come after them. If men were not distinct, each human being distinguished from any other who is, was, or ever will be, they would need neither speech nor action to make themselves understood. Signs and sounds to communicate immediate, identical needs and wants would be enough.

Hannah Arendt
The HumanCondition

A THOUGHT REVOLVED

This title, and those of the other sections, were taken from *The Collected Poems of Wallace Stevens*, Faber and Faber, 1955. The poems from which each come were selected by chance process using random numbers to pick a page and a position on it and then choosing a title or subtitle from the poem that had been selected. Having arrived at the titles in this indirect way I am not sure what they mean or how they may be seen to relate to the essays to which they have become names. Like our own names, or those of apples, of musical groups, of many common things, we are inside them. Not that we own them. My apologies, and thanks, to the memory of Wallace Stevens.

CONTENTS

list of illustrations   x
introduction to the new edition by Clive Dilnot   xi
foreword by C. Thomas Mitchell   liv
author's note   lv
preface to the 1984 edition   lvi
acknowledgements   lix
introductory essay: the future of breathing   lxi

1 A Thought Revolved   1
   Love, hate and architecture   3
   How my thoughts about design methods have changed during the years   13
   Now we are numerous   29
   Beyond rationalism   37
   Principles in design   73

2 The World without Imagination   83
   St Ives by chance   85
   Composing by chance   105
   Some reflection on chance   111
   Designing designing   125

3 It Must Give Pleasure   145
   Opus one, number two   147
   '... in the dimension of time'   169
   Continuous design and redesign   191
   Things   219

4 Things of August   241
   Is designing a response to the whole of life?   243
   35 wishes   257
   Voices at the conference conference   277
   The design of modern life   303
   Utopia and Numeroso   327

afterword by John Thackara   337

the illustrations before and after each essay were assigned by chance to the pages indicated, as described on pages 108–109

ILLUSTRATIONS

1. On waking, Salzberg, 1969   ii
2. Visual poem by Edwin Schlossberg, Blacksburg, Virginia, 1974   lviii
3. Visual poem by Edwin Schlossberg, Chester, Massachusetts, 1974   xci
4. Automatic carpark, Austin, Texas, 1974   2
5. Root from street excavation, Zurich, 1982   12
6. From the supermarket, Jones family, London, 1975?   28
7. Self-portrait, Blacksburg, Virginia, 1974   35
8. Airport, Roanoke, Virginia, 1974   36
9. View from Holland Park, London, 1976   71
10. Grass, Zurich Street, 1982   72
11. Sugar from a café, Zurich 1982   81
12. Cartop in desert, Arcosanti, Arizona, 1974   84
13. Steel ring from street excavation, Zurich, 1982   103
14. Metal turning, Zurich street, 1982   104
15. Blackberry leaves, Hampstead Heath, London   110
16. Metal foil, Zurich street   123
17. Piano keys, Chester, Massachusetts, 1976?   124
18. Street debris, Zurich, 1982   143
19. Plastic strap, Zurich street, 1982   146
20. Nail, Zurich street, 1982   168
21. Letter shapes, copied from hairs in rag paper, Joel Fisher, 1978   190
22. Label, Spitalfields market, London, 1982   217
23. T-shirt, chance location in house, London, 1982   218
24. Radio transmission towers, London, 1977   239
25. Ruled paper, London, 1977   242
26. Feather, Zurich street, 1982   256
27. Truck maintenance, Kilburn, London, 1976?   275
28. Lawn sprays, Austin, Texas, 1974   276
29. Holland Park, London, 1976?   302
30. Cows, barbed wire and prehistoric stones, Avebury, England, 1976?   326
31. On waking, Chester, Massachusetts, 1976?   336

other illustrations, not listed, are described within the essays to which they belong

introduction to the new edition

Not the least of the sins of the obsession with the 'research' in the contemporary university is that it unreflectively privileges the appearance of the new. Failing to see the extent to which its own thinking is thereby hobbled and limited, understanding turns in even narrower circles of concern. Design is not immune to this condition. Expansion in practice and the global increase in numbers of those with design education or who study design has not necessarily brought with it increased understanding of design. On the contrary, despite real attempts to counter these impulses, reduced to the crudest understanding of vocation, depth of thought disappears, crises remain untouched; genuinely new practices and conceptions struggle to be comprehended.

Radical Thinkers in Design, a moment of the larger project *Designing in Dark Times*, seeks in a small way to try to address this situation. The project is to bring back into circulation, as provocations and aids to thinking, some key texts in contemporary thinking on design(ing).

As acting in the world descends ever deeper towards instrumentalism, these books offer counter-views. In what they open towards, what they explore and present, above all in what they *anticipate*, they point to the concrete possibilities, as well as to the necessity, of paradigm shifts in design thinking and in our conceptions of what designing today can and should be. They offer approaches, concepts, modes of thinking and models of practice that can help not only in thinking how design can be re-thought and re-positioned in its internal momentum, but also in how it offers an integral mode and capacity of acting in the world. By showing how, at base, designing contains irreplaceable critical and affirmative moments, they point us towards ways of reversing some of the negative and destructive tendencies threatening to engulf the world.

*

John Chris Jones's *designing designing*[1] is the earliest of the books to have been published. It is perhaps the least read. The first edition of the work appeared in 1984 (under the title *Essays in Design*). It was republished, in a small edition, under the current title, in 1991.[2] Yet while *Design Methods*

---

[1] As is apparent from a first view of the text, Jones deploys lower case titles throughout the book. I have maintained this.

[2] *Essays in Design* was published by John Wiley & Sons. *designing designing* (the lowercase is intentional) was a reprint of this edition with a new cover by Jonathan Moberly and an additional introductory essay by Jones, 'The Future of Breathing' (London: Architecture, Design and Technology Press, 1991).

(1970),[3] Jones's acclaimed magnum opus, and the book whose reception was in many ways the provocation and occasion of these papers, is still in print, *designing designing* has been unavailable for many years. One of the most unexpectedly original volumes ever published on the subject of designing and the shaping of modern life and one of the most pertinent for today – anyone who picks up *designing designing* will be struck immediately by how many current issues, if in embryo, Jones takes an approach to – it remains essentially unknown. In a profound sense, it awaits its readers.[4]

There are various reasons why the book has remained all but invisible. Initially presented, in its original title, *Essays in Design*, in a way that conveyed almost nothing of the force it potentially contained, the first edition of the book had the misfortune to be published at a time when professional Design was booming, economically at least, but at a moment when critical thinking in design practice was at a nadir.

But the reasons that the book could scarcely be accepted at the time of its first publication are more than circumstantial. The product of ten years of reflection and experimentation, and offering a savage auto-critique of his own work on 'methods' as well as of the wider means and ends of advanced industrial societies as a whole, the book challenges the traditional product- and progress- orientated focus of Design.[5] Insisting that the world now coming into being *requires* designing to be understood as 'a response to the whole of life' – the title of the 1974 conference presentation which is catalytic for the whole volume – the book is a proposal for a profound reconstitution of design, a work therefore of design *thought* in the strongest sense.

But *designing designing* is also unique in its exploration of what writing – and therefore thinking – on designing might be. Forty years on, it remains an astonishing and unprecedented document. Combining essays, interviews, reflections, performances, plays, poems, chance procedures, photographs,

---

[3] Design Methods: *Seeds of Human Futures* (London and New York: John Wiley, 1970) revised edition 1980. Translated into Japanese, Russian, Romanian, Polish and Spanish.

[4] Software engineers and designers in more process-orientated and time-based fields have generally been far more sympathetic than mainstream designers to Jones's work after *Design Methods*, especially following the publication of *The Internet and Everyone* (London: Ellipsis, 2000). John Thackara has written very beautifully on the impact of the latter book in a tribute to Jones's 90th birthday. https://blog.p2pfoundation.net/the-internet-and-everyone-celebrating-john-chris-jones-at-90/2017/10/29. The blog is reproduced as the afterword to this volume.

[5] The shift in the title between the 1984 edition and the 1991 edition (and now this one) is significant. It is the shift from Design as noun (professional activity) to design as verb (by no means necessarily only a professional activity). In this essay I will use 'Design' capitalized to designate professional design. designing lower case designates designing as activity or capability, which may or may not take professional form and which is not a-priori or conceptually limited to 'Design'.

collages and quotes, Jones makes a book which, as the publisher's cover note for the 1991 edition has it, 'is not simply about designing but is instead itself an instance of the ideas and processes explored within it'. This is not inaccurate. It catches Jones's sense of trying to bring designing and writing closer together – as when he writes at the beginning of the paper 'designing designing' that although he has been 'asked to write [a] summary of some of the main aspects of "how to design", I am reluctant to do so unless I can make the paper itself an example of the methods I am to describe' (p. 128).[6]

What this account misses, however, is the sense of the book's initially at least, baffling compendium of ways in which thinking and writing about design can be re-construed. It is not only, though it in part is, the range of formats that Jones deploys – almost one for every chapter – but also that the book as a whole is a complex, even difficult, *composition*. Indeed the latter is a key term. The book is radically composed, even more, in a sense, than it is written and designed. Thus, for example, illustrations and quotations are profuse. But most of these – and not least, to readers' bafflement, the titles of the four parts of the book (which bear no relation to their content) – are chosen wholly or in part by chance.[7] More, the book is composed in a second sense, now using this term as it is used to describe writing-at-the-typewriter, because Jones insists on reproducing, so far as he is able, the sense and sometimes the actuality, of the manner and conditions under which many of the presentations were created, at times in part by drawing on chance procedures, in other moments as reflections composed in real time, in others again where what is presented is the product of spoken reflections and where Jones is seeking to preserve the experience of speech (p. 38). Added to this is Jones's deceptively simple language. In its subjective thrusts and reflections, its sometimes frankness and directness, Jones's modes of writing are at the opposite end of the spectrum from the language of 'research'. Most dominantly and paradoxically of all is the weight given in the book to chance methods and to performative scripts. Together, these represent half of the 'essays' in the book. But as readers discover, none of this is merely willful.

In any case, it is precisely this 'difficulty' with the books form and language which creates the force and distinctive character of the work. What establishes it as nothing less than a proposal for a new basis and direction for designing – a reconstitution of its place in the world of a very profound kind – is the conjunction between its substantive and its formal moments; between how it opens thought for designing radically beyond the limits normally permitted to it and the ways in which these moments of the possible expansion of

---

[6] All quotations with only page numbers refer to *designing designing*.
[7] For Jones's explanation of this, see pp. ix (section titles) and 108–9 (quotations and illustrations).

thought concerning designing can exist *only* because of this challenging and reworking of the norms of writing 'about' design.

*

This introduction will look at these two moments – that of the challenges posed by what Jones propounds concerning designing (challenges which exceed to a significant degree how design could be thought of in the 1980s and perhaps also today); and that of Jones's use of language, format and method – above all his use of chance and the performative. The latter are the moments which cause much of the difficulty that many readers find with Jones's writing, at least initially. But which are also the agencies that permit Jones to think beyond the permissible limits of that thinking – or which, better said, open the space through which designing, as against 'Design', can be *thought*.

I will look at both aspects at a length which is traditionally inappropriate for an introduction.

Yet, it seems to me that the work requires this, not because it cannot speak for itself but because the depths of what is caught within it are not necessarily immediately apparent to thought. *designing designing* is especially in the first instance, bafflingly elusive in what it presents and in how it presents it. For those familiar with *Design Methods* it stands at the opposite pole to the transparency of the latter. To get at what the book offers therefore requires two things: an opening up and an articulation of the substantive challenges to the norms and modes of 'thinking design' that it contains; and an exploration, necessarily sympathetic, of the necessity for, but also the challenges of, the book as an extremely radical piece of 'design writing'. The rest of the introduction will be structured around these two issues.

First, however, something more should be said concerning the book as a whole.

Consisting of nineteen essays – though as the reader discovers, the definition is stretched in some cases and it might be better to use a hybrid collectivity such as "things, statements, configurations, discursive fragments" – *designing designing* was written, compiled and composed across the decade of 1972–82. In many ways the book is Jones's reaction to *Design Methods*, especially to attempts to use what that book tried to articulate simply as 'recipes' or as 'answers' or an ideology of designing (p.18). But it goes much further than a simple 'response' to the 'failure' of design methods. It is both a questioning of 'what has gone wrong' and an attempt to take 'some responsibility for putting things right' (p. 149). The interest in the book lies in how Jones thinks the second point.

The brief background is this. In 1970, Jones, who had been designing and researching in industry and research since the 1940s,[8] and had been increasingly focusing on the question of 'methods', had seen *Design Methods* as 'a goodbye present to the subject' – from which he then proposed to retire (p.128). Retirement was not a matter of age (Jones was only 44 at the time) but from a sense of increasing disquiet with design and design methods: 'I was beginning to feel it was not such a creative or liberating activity as I had once fancied it to be. In fact, I was beginning to see design as not so much as a process of creation as of control' (p. 128). By 1974, 'feeling that academic life that too had become rigid and inhuman' (p. 149), Jones had resigned his professorship.[9] Once out of design, he worked in software, wrote,[10] studied time-arts: film, theatre, poetry, and especially (and the impact has never left him and continues in his work and life to today) the use of chance methods in composition developed by John Cage. But the 'escape' from design was never complete. Across the 1970s and early 1980s, Jones was continually asked 'back' (to conferences and the like) to reflect on design and design methods. *designing designing* is the product of these reflections.

In drafting these essays and performative scripts, Jones was juggling complex demands. By external audiences he is asked to reflect on present issues in design and designing and especially on design methods (which are always the sub-text if not the overt context of speaking). But these texts are also Jones's auto-reflexive analysis of his own practices of design. Moreover, as already noted, analytical self-questioning ('Where did we go wrong?' [p. 158][11]) has to be balanced by the equal impulse 'to put things right'. Jones's affirmative answer to his own question as to how this might be done – 'Designing a response to the whole of life' – necessitates designing with radically different aims and goals.

Therefore, his project is necessarily complex. If it begins from his central perception that professional procedures in Design are failing at some of their central tasks – above all, as Jones puts it, 'the failure of their 'inability to respond to life itself which [is] becoming the object of design as the extent

[8] The second chapter of the book, 'how my thoughts about design methods have changed during the years' (pp. 13–27) provides a useful biographical introduction to Jones c.1974.
[9] He had been appointed the first professor of design at the then new British Open University (OU) – the world's first national university organized for 'online' or distance learning.
[10] Most notably, the book *The Internet and Everyone* (London: Ellipsis, 2000), though also a host of other smaller publications. There is an excellent bibliography of Jones's work at http://www.indiana.edu/~iucdp/jonesbib.html.
[11] For all the auto-critique of design methods in *designing designing*, there is little defensiveness. Jones has a balanced view of the necessity, as well as the limitations, of methods. See, for example, comments on pp. 15–19, 32–33, 203.

of what is man-made grows and grows' (p. 150) the 'solution' (which must at once build from the 'revolutions' in industrial life but nonetheless go significantly beyond the given limitations of 'industrial' designing and thinking) is not immediately known.[12] It must be explored, and, because this is designing and not simply thought, it must be explored 'in practice' as it were, created as a demonstration as to what might be possible. Finally, all of this, to be more than utopian speculation, has to be objectively grounded in what is emerging and as what Jones will call, the 'new and expanded contexts for designing and acting' (contexts that he felt were already, by 1970, emerging).

It is out of this complex of issues that Jones fashions his essays. The essential question that dominates them is, in effect, *what are the modes of designing that might be adequate to respond to 'industrial life' in its emerging forms?* As already implicitly hinted above, his key to beginning to make an answer to this is to see the limitations of professional Design as he sees them, not as questions internal to designing, but as symptoms of far more fundamental problems in the traditional organization and mentalities of industrial society. And this failure is not just a failure in terms of traditional industrial concerns. It is more deeply a failure to respond adequately to the objective shifts that are already, by 1970, beginning to transform the artificial world. As Jones puts it in a strong equation, given that it is 'evident that we are now living on other side of [a] revolution in industrial life' (p. 149), this in turn demands what he calls a 'revolution-within-that-revolution' (p. 150). It is this second 'revolution' that, for Jones, is missing 'from [present-day] design methods, from software designing, from architecture, from industrial life' (p.150). This revolution is not merely a matter of methods. It is better thought of as the necessity for profound transformations in how we stand to ourselves, to the world, and how we respond to, and act in relation to – or, better, simply 'in' – life.

Without this 'revolution' Jones maintains, we fail to capture, not least through designing, the different sense of 'us', persons, mind, life, that is now *objectively* emerging: '"It", "life", is, among other things, a process not a progress, and so is design, or so it should be, can be. A process of remembering, re-making oneself, constantly, out of all of one's past, one's

---

[12] The term 'industrial designing' is used here not in the sense of the specific profession but of designing 'within the industrial' in general. In retrospect, we can see today how much the 1970s were in many ways the cusp decade between the older, still essentially nineteenth- or mid-twentieth- century industrial frameworks, and emergence of 'post-industrial', that is, contemporary societies. Daniel Bell's sociological *The Coming of Post-Industrial Society* (1976) was an early marker of this shift. Jones was prescient in his instincts concerning the *degree* of this shift, which he saw as going well beyond the notion of 'post'-(modern, industrial) that became dominant in the 1980s. In effect, he is writing *then* of conditions that apply more fully today.

world, a world in which I am the content of the worlds of others as they are of mine' (p. 187).[13]

designing designing is the exploration of how Jones tacks towards answers to these questions with respect to designing. The book is organized in four sections. The simplest way to grasp what is offered is to say that the first and third sections are largely substantive; the second and fourth largely methodological. Like all definitions, this one mischaracterizes the separation but is useful for first thinking.

- Broadly, the first five essays ('A Thought Revolved') including the very important preface and the 'Introductory Essay: The Future of Breathing', provide a useful introduction to Jones's thinking across the decade. (Chapter 2 offers a helpful biographical perspective.)
- The second group of chapters ('The World Without Imagination') break, to a degree, with substance and explore chance: first as a case study of an experiment in using chance methods ('St Ives'); then as a method (including delineation of how chance is used in the composition of the book, pp. 108–9), and finally as an exchange of letters and as 'applied' in the composition of an academic paper.
- The third section ('It Must Give Pleasure') returns to substance. It includes the two most reflective and most critical essays in the book: 'Opus one, number two', and '… in the dimension of time'. The other two papers are a quasi-poetic meditation on 'things', and a broadly academic paper – 'Continuous design and redesign' – which extends many of the concerns of 'designing designing'. These last two papers provide an overview of Jones's sense of the design process in the mid- to late-1970s with the latter paper doing so in relation to designing long-life software.
- The last section ('Things of August') then takes up again 'method', now focusing on the performative. It presents five highly varied scripts for (usually academic conference) performance – including, most importantly, as the first of these, the 1974 'paper', that is, the script for a conference play ('Is designing a response to the whole of life?'), which was Jones's first, and in some ways his boldest, statement using chance methods of composition to break the norms of academic design writing and which was catalytic, in many ways, for the whole volume.

[13] There is an echo here in this last phrase of some comments by the young Marx on James Mill: 'As I anticipate the others' enjoyment and use of my object, and as I concretize those anticipation's in an object that I choose/create then I get the immediate pleasure and consciousness of having satisfied a real human need through this creative work.' See, e.g. David McLellan, *The Thought of Karl Marx* (London: Papermac, 1995), p. 23.

This then is the book as one receives it. The question now is to apprehend what it *shows*[14] – which does not mean simply what the book means 'for the present', nor does it mean to offer a critique (in current terms) of what is presented. It means something more like to comprehend its challenge; to ask, at least implicitly, how we stand in the face of what it asks of us – which is encapsulated in the astonishing (and not infrequently genuinely peculiar) 'originality and range of reflection' on designing that he offers. This means that the first task is to read Jones, which means to be able to take hold of what the work is attempting to comprehend; to try apprehend what it is that Jones is seeking to comprehend in these reflections and experiments.

I

Some challenges of *designing designing*

Having said this, it now becomes possible to go back to the questions from which we began: the substantive reasons why the book could scarcely be accepted at the time of its first publication. These were not only circumstantial. More profoundly, the intellectual, and one suspects the emotional, difficulties of grasping the book, went beyond even the critique it offered (which, in some of the later papers are very severe indeed). The real difficulties then – and now – lie in what the book affirmatively proposed, in what, concerning designing, it was driving towards.

Perhaps the best way to see this is take a sampling of some of Jones's key propositions. Here are five. They are deliberately brought out in some depth to catch a sense of Jones's use of language and his modes of argument.[15] They are also called out here because one of the peculiarities of the text is the manner in which, and as the very opposite of a declarative, systematic work, some of the most profound propositions Jones advances come almost unbidden in the midst of arguments. A frequent experience in reading the text is to encounter these moments and then later be unable to locate the precise source of the sentence or paragraph one read. In

---

[14] Not, note, what it *tells* us. Jones wishes, as far as possible, not to 'tell' but to 'show' – that is to exemplify, to manifest, to demonstrate that which he wishes to make evident.

[15] There is an interesting question around the distinctive manner of Jones's language. Deceptively simple and straightforward in vocabulary, the syntax, the play of ideas, the rhythm and relation of the propositions advanced, both analytic and rhetorical (and often in the same moment at once statement and proposition, abstract and concrete) are highly complex. As previously noted this makes Jones's prose eminently quotable, but all but impossible to paraphrase well. To use a term that is of some importance in the book, the language is performative – or better, it performs, it acts. And the only way of grasping how it acts is through reading and sensing the connections, the processes of thought, that are embodied within the statements he makes, be they in snatches of a line or in passages of some length.

Jones, substance is not presented for the taking, it is *found*. And then as frequently, lost again.

Here then are five moments. They concern the survival of design, its real subject matter, its limits, its aims, its work.

1. Particularly in the 'Preface to the 1984 edition', Jones presciently pre-figures what today we could call the 'expanded field' of design. He insists on drawing from this however uncomfortable implications for how we need to re-understand and practice designing. Thus, after presenting 'how far reaching' are the ways he sees designing already transforming beyond expectations

> as the process of devising not individual products but whole systems or environments; ... as participation, [with] the involvement of the public in decision-making processes; ...as an educational discipline that unites arts and sciences and perhaps goes further than either; ... as creativity potentially present in everyone; ... and now the idea of designing WITHOUT A PRODUCT as a process of way of living in itself ...
> a way out of consumerism?[16]

He comments, in the light of these developments:

> Looking now at my earlier definition of design as the initiation of change in man-made things, I still like the emphasis on change but not the assumption that design is limited to the thinking of a few on behalf of the many. Nor do I like the assumption that it is to do with change in things but not in ourselves. In my re-thinking of the nature of design in these pages I have moved far from the picture of 'it' as the specialized activity of paid experts who shape the physical and abstract forms of industrial life which we all as consumers accept or adapt to. That notion cannot possibly last forever - it's too limiting, too insensitive to the reactions it provokes. It's too inert. Designing, if it is to survive as an activity through which we transform our lives, on earth, and beyond, has itself to be redesigned, continuously. As do other false stabilities that we construct ... as stepping stones, no more. (p. ix)

[16] This listing, remarkable for its time, should be compared with the one Jones offers in the opening to the first chapter of *Design Methods* (pp. 3–4). The movement between these two listings is indicative of a sea change in the perception of where design (and industrialization) 'was' (c. 1960) and where (post the 1970s) designing in Jones's view is moving towards.

2. Concerning design, the book nonetheless does not confine itself to Design. An instance is where Jones is reflecting on his original hopes for design methods:

> Whatever may have become of design methods in recent years the original intentions of those of us who tried to improve design processes, ten or more years ago, was to respond to the connectedness of everything. To cease splitting life into fragments, particularly when it is people and the experience of life that is being fragmented … to overcome the limitations of professional procedures in all the design professions. Their inability to respond to life itself, which was becoming the object of design, as the extent of what is man-made grew and grew. To make what Thomas Kuhn has called a paradigm-shift, in the nature of designing. To change the objectives, the criteria, the procedures. To abandon specialization, which pre-supposes that products, buildings & the like can be adequately designed by separate groups of professionals, in isolation, leaving the connections between designed things and what exists to take care of itself. (p. 152)

There are a whole range of issues laid out in this passages that are central to *designing designing* as a whole, but what most powerfully connects Jones's critique of 'design methods' (and of design in general) to the larger problem of grasping and responding to 'changes in context' is *also* what is missing 'from design methods, from software designing, from architecture, from industrial life', namely the understanding that the proposition, 'It is ourselves, not our words, that are the real purpose of designing' is not merely a slogan to be nominally attached to designing as-is, but is the logical outcome of the fact that as the extent of what is man-made grows and grows, so by *objective necessity* 'life itself … becomes the object of design.'

3. If the aspiration of designing in its full sense is to address this scale and scope of issues, can design remain Design? Or, do we need a wholesale transformation in our understanding of what designing has to become, in how it must be thought? In how it envisages what its purpose, its roles, are?

> I realize that, in attempting to change the processes of design, in trying to increase the scale, the scope, of the man-made, we failed to change the aim, the goal. Design-as-process, design at the scale of being, does not have a goal. Its non-instrumental. It's a question of living, not of planning life-not-yet-lived. Design without a product. The idea seems nonsense if applied to designing by professionals, but seen as part of a historic shift from product-thinking to process-thinking isn't it what we overlooked? Designing disappears: becomes a way of using, an enlivening of how we live. There is no outcome. It's a question of being, without stop. (p. 158)

4. But is designing even the issue? Is not thinking and acting already impelled *through* design to what is 'beyond' it (even while it contains it)?

> More of Edwin's letter to Gregory Bateson. I like so much that little jolt to my thinking by the notion, new to me, that 'things' do not evolve but context does. Is evolution, then, the process of seeking to re-establish harmonies with context, a context that spontaneously changes? And is design this same seeking, or should it be? Intention, in designing, according to this view of things, would then be appropriate only as the means to get to the state of accord with context, the state of harmony, bliss perhaps, which intention destroys? … Is designing, then, a dangerous weapon to be used only when things have got into a mess, and something to be avoided when life is going well? The context of design, according to this apparent reversal of the usual view of it as positive, is 'problem', life gone wrong. And, in particular, the splitting of mind from matter, persons from nature. The underlying problem of modern times? In this light, 'bad' design is that which perpetuates this fundamental split, or alienation, between each of us, as persons, and 'the world', as we so destructively describe our situation. And 'good' design is that which tends to heal the split, and, in doing so, to make designing unnecessary. (p. 183)

5. But if we begin to think of designing in this way, can design continue to renounce the ambition of changing the world?

> So to me now, as in the past, the purposes of making changes in methods not only in design but in all departments of life, is to change the pattern of life as we make it, artificially and collectively; not to support the status quo and the inhumanities we inherit but to permit the composing of a form of life that is free of the errors of specialization and alienation … to make a way of living that is beautiful (can laws be beautiful? can work?) … [and] to attempt the best we can imagine and to use all intelligence to make it real. … It's time to change our aims, to see ourselves collectively as different, as able to respond to the conditions of human life. (p. 32–4)

There is a fundamental, even ontological, shift in these reflections, particularly the last. Turned towards the practice of designing, it means that design has no function, no role, no meaning, if it is not primarily the *enlivening* mediation of emerging relations and patterns of life. This is the essence of the single paragraph in the book that comes closest in feel to a manifesto of Jones's thought. The passage is at once outrageous – what is the status of the beautiful? – and eminently practical: it names the conditions by which this aspiration could be realized. Read today, it reads less as a utopic statement and more as the *minimum* realistic demand that we can put on ourselves in order to avert disaster.

*

What is most immediately obvious in reading these five moments is that almost nothing in the quoted instances could have easily – or even at all – been adopted into professional designing in 1984. To repeat a point made at the beginning of this introduction, in offering trajectories of thinking, views of what designing might be, propositions that are still heretical from the standpoint of professional Design, they anticipate questions that, at least in the main, we have scarcely satisfactorily encompassed let alone answered.

The second observation follows from the first. It is that what is intimated in these instances is nothing less than a series of proposals for reconstituting designing's place anew. Moreover, it is clear that this redirection of designing is done on the basis of a profound break with the norms and limits of industrialization seen in 'traditional' ways. In these theses Jones is proposing a redirection of designing of a far deeper kind than *Design Methods*, for all its systematic organization, could conjure. Even if, in that book, Jones took the model of designing at its then professional limit, and even if *Design Methods*, in some of its moments, hints at a wider comprehension of designing and of 'methods' in general,[17] it still it remains essentially tied to the model of the industrial system as-then-was.[18] By contrast, *designing designing* is no longer within this orbit. What it proposes in instances, and what the book conveys as a whole, is the necessity for construing a *wholly*

---

[17] In the preface to *Design Methods* Jones discusses how he sees the changes in design methods as occurring in parallel to new methodologies of planning and acting developing in a whole range of industrial and non-industrial fields. In a statement of considerable importance for what later emerges as core elements of *designing designing*, he notes:
Together, these new methods suggest we are collectively seeking, not only new procedures, *but new aims and a different level of achievement*. Whereas the aim of traditional methods was to make local improvements and changes, the new methods seem to be directed at the *total situation*, both *outside the boundaries of traditional expertise and within the personal experience, or 'inner world', of individuals.* (*Design Methods*, p. x., my emphasis)
designing designing is in many ways the realization of those three emphasized moments taken into a 'methodology' of designing that can no longer have the form of methods per se. See also in general chapter 5 of *Design Methods*, pp. 69–73. Note also the book's sub-title: 'Seeds of human futures'.

[18] And in so far as problems of this nature remain it retains its potential within those limits.

new orientation towards designing, one that is unprecedented with respect to industrialization.[19]

What Jones sees already in the 1970s is a more fundamental change in the structure of the 'ever-growing' man-made world, one which in turn forces a reappraisal of the ethos of acting in this world as a whole, including designing and its professions:

> There is a morality in widening the scope of life; what was before inevitable now becomes conscious choice. And once this widening, this prior liberation has occurred it is no longer realistic but insulting to refuse the new ideals and purposes that are now possible. Industrial life HAS changed its nature in recent years and this includes the means of pursuing aims never tried before. Of course, the enlargement of what is possible includes the enlargement of what is bad as well as good, that is the risk, unavoidable. A new responsibility for which the institutions and professions and roles we inherit are surely unable by their form and nature to respond. (p. 33)[20]

This is where the contrast between *Design Methods* and *designing designing* becomes most sharply evident. The role of *Design Methods* was understood as inducing change to, but within, Design.[21] The reflections gathered in *designing designing* still proffer change as occurring through designing but through a far more radical reconstruction of its operation, scope and thinking[22] – such that through this change in direction, this breaching of the limits, it becomes capable of a far more radical, ontological, subjective and experientially grounded orientation towards acting in the world.

The third point that begins to become apparent in reading these moments follows from this last observation on the desired capability of designing. Reading the book as a whole, and sensing from the quoted passages, it becomes clear that Jones is working on the basis that there is an underlying grounding or objectivity to what he is sketching – namely that already by the late 1960s and 1970s, and certainly by the 1980s, the context of designing and

---

[19] Though not, and this is key, as a simple rejection of industrialization. Jones is not William Morris redux.

[20] See, for example, p. 80, where Jones discusses this problem.

[21] And more widely within technological thinking, as when Jones speaks in *Design Methods* about the need to open designing to 'reliable' (proven) knowledge and methods 'gained from fields like computer programming, psychotherapy, behavioral science, electrical circuit theory and communications' (p. xii).

[22] And we might add, apropos of the last line of the quotation, that 'designing' here necessarily includes 'responsibilities' and the 'institutions and professions and roles' (ibid.). The *designing* of designing necessarily includes the re-designing of both sides of this equation.

of 'industrial life' as a whole is already radically transforming. This in turn changes the context of designing particularly, though not only, of what we assume the contexts, objective and subjective of designing to be. Epitomized by, as Jones puts it, 'the change from products to processes, from hardware to software, from architecture = buildings to architecture = the way life is organized' this 'revolution' in industrial life impels a shift from 'product to procedure to process' (p. 150).

He captures the sense of this in two successive examples he gives in the essay 'Opus one, number two'. The first draws on Jones's experience with the Open University:

> The Open University's buildings are a small and irrelevant part of what it offers to students whereas the teaching programs, and the papers and broadcasts by which they are transmitted, together with the odd corners of houses and technical colleges where the learning takes place, are what the university consists of. This change from the university-as-place to the university-as-procedure (which can occur in almost any place) is the revolution I am talking about. (p. 150)

This is a shift that we might term as 'software' (but which Jones more interestingly calls 'context design' – see the key passage on p. 279) but, in any case 'procedure' in Jones sense, which slips rapidly towards 'process', has a far deeper experiential, even ontological content. This becomes clear in the second example Jones gives, where he moves backward in time to posit a forward-looking model of process in relation, simultaneously and inextricably, to design and life.

Jones quotes from the Tang dynasty poet, Pei Ti:

> In front of the balcony,
>> As the expanse of water
>> Fills with ripples.
>
> The solitary moon,
>> Goes wandering without pause.
>
> From the depths of the valley
>> The cries of the monkeys rise;
>
> Borne by the wind
>> They reach me in my room.

'The building itself' continues Jones,

is barely mentioned. Yet its presence is felt. What is described, recreated, is the experience. Of being there, and of what else is there. The state of mind. Consisting of all these things. This … so delicate awareness, is closer …. to 'life', to what I'm now calling the new architecture, the architecture of being, of being here, making the connections, for oneself? When we design interconnections what becomes of this? … The architecture of process. Of life as process. As process designed. (pp. 153–4)

The shift is clear. The opening to 'procedure' as Jones calls it, leads logically into an awareness of process understood as experience but not in the instrumental sense, in something closer to 'states of mind'. It is the 'delicate awareness' of situation, context, processes, above all – and this is thrust of the argument, and really the fourth element we can pull from these instances – the sense of our *implication* in these processes.

In fact, the real indictment that Jones makes of 'design methods', in the hardest critiques that he offers (see, e.g. but not only, pp. 152, 155, 159, 174) is that of our absenting of ourselves at precisely the point – above all, though not only, as mind – that we most need to enter and accept our implication in the processes of designing and making.

> Aims, purposes, requirements, functions: these are words for how we see what is needed. But when we name them we tend to exclude the main part, the least predictable: ourselves, our minds, and how they change once we experience something. It is ourselves, not our words, that are the real purpose of designing. The biggest mistake is to take the product alone as the aim. It is always secondary. (p. 212)

In fact, as the reader discovers, much of *designing designing* was written, in one way or another, as the rescue of mind – which means that it is written against its denial and with a counter-determination to create within design and within industrial society, the necessary spaces for mind. A summary quotation that captures some of this sense occurs in a continuation of the points made in the second of the passages given above, where Jones was speaking of the necessity of a paradigm shift in designing:

> But the paradigm change was resisted. We still have design professions, and we still have the old idea that what is being designed is 'objects.' The designers persist in acting as if they themselves are objects and the people whose lives are being shaped by this objective process are being treated as objects. Without minds of their own. We have yet to face up to the changes needed in everyone's role, self-images, procedures, and ways

of life… [to understand that] what makes us people, and not objects, is that we *are* the interconnections … as objects we interconnect to a large degree, but as minds we interconnect far more than that. If we design for interconnection only at the object level (limiting ourselves to what can be calculated and neglecting what can only be imagined, and felt, but not measured), we are bound to create a way of life which is experienced as inhuman. (p. 153)[23]

The counter-force to the limitation of interconnection is that in fact there is an inescapability to our experiential and mental as well as physical involvement in the world.

Jones's instance – and it applies sharply to designing – is how we understand 'world':

As soon as I catch myself typing that deadly word 'it' I realize that the world is not an it, is not a thing, detached from ourselves. It is ourselves. The world is not just the earth and sea and sky and plants and animals and houses and roads and cities and cars and farms etc. It is also our lives, our experiences and memories, our minds. When we say 'the world', and when we call it an 'it', we are making a false distinction between the things we perceive and the processes of perception and recognition by which we learn to see and act. It is obvious, as soon as one stops to think about it, that an abstract word like 'world' is not the name of an object. It is the name of a great mass of shared experience out of which we infer the existence of the planet earth and of all the things upon it. For everyday living it is of course necessary and appropriate to use this verbal convention as if it were a fact, but when we are designing, when we are trying make a change, or an improvement to what we call world, it is surely right and necessary to understand what it is we are really doing, and not base our decisions on words that we know to contain a false picture. *Designing, as I see it now, is, or could be, the process of unlearning what we know of what exists, of what we call the 'status quo', to the point where we are able to lose our pre-conceptions sufficiently to understand the life, and lives, for which we design.* (p. 172, my emphasis)

[23] A point that Jones makes even sharper a few pages later when he talks of the deadening notion of representing the whole of life by a rational block diagram which is limited to those aspects of life that are capable of measurement and of calculation. Which, of course, (though we did not see it at the time) excludes much, or all, of what makes life worth living. That which is incalculable. That which cannot be put into words, unless they are used poetically, with real feeling. (p. 176)

What Jones is really calling for is both an increased weighting to perception – by which he means comprehension of situations (at one point he characterizes his activities post-1970 as, in part, 'trying to find ways of increasing perception, and of reducing action, in design, so that what's new is more sensitive to what's already there' [p. 22]) – and a sharper awareness of the interrelation of action and perception.

> Technology is not just an idea: its action. It's the making of physical changes to the world, its altering nature, to an extent at least. And such changes, such actions, create reaction. A social reaction, when we see for ourselves what the changed world is really like. Seeing it, and experiencing it, changes our perceptions. I'm sure of that. It tells you things you didn't know about yourself and leads you to act in new ways. Ways that are not predictable from a theoretical model, or concept. (pp. 322–3)

Jones posits the same notion of desirable *exchange* between methods and to designing in general, between industrial life and technical change and society.

> I guess that the big fault of industrial life is that relationships operate in only one direction but should operate in two. We now expect technical change to cause social change as a matter of course but attempts to make social change influence technology are still thought of as revolutionary They should be normal. If they were, both 'technology' and 'society' should cease to be fixed objects or false gods, they would become ever changing elements of a new kind of living. This two-way relationship should be one of complementarity. (p. 6)

He extends this reciprocity to theory and practice, though with an ontological twist that redefines the aims of the process:

> To me theories are safe but temporary stepping stones across the dangerous waters of life, the unknown. But it is the unknown, not theories or principles, that are the source of the new. The whole point of transformation, the central part of the design process is to change what already exists, and this includes both theories and practices. Each should influence the other. To make theory the master of practice is surely a form of repression. It is like being against one's children, one's ideas, one's unrealized potential. To make each responsive to the other is to create the conditions for love not hatred. (p. 7)

✻

If we were to try and summarize where Jones is pushing to here we might do it, somewhat paradoxically, by returning to a quotation from the introduction to *Design Methods*, which I gave earlier in a footnote (n.17):

> Together, these new methods suggest we are collectively seeking, not only new procedures, but *new aims and a different level of achievement*. Whereas the aim of traditional methods was to make local improvements and changes, the new methods seem to be directed at the *total situation*, both *outside the boundaries of traditional expertise and within the personal experience, or 'inner world', of individuals*.

Three propositions are contained in these sentences. They run through *designing designing*, which is in fact, much more so than *Design Methods*, the place where Jones realizes these propositions.

The first, and in the end perhaps the deepest in the book, is that the question of methods and procedures, and therefore of designing, is always also, and in practical and not merely theoretical terms, *centrally* a question of ends and aims and that this question *precedes* and does not follow practice:

> Though we saw the need to change the processes of designing we did not see the need to change its aims. We retained the concept of 'product' as the outcome of designing. We did not see that we were accepting only a part of the challenge which we took up: the challenge to transform the idea of progress, which presumes a specific goal, into the idea of process, which does not. This transformation is, I now realize, a main event of the twentieth century, though it may have started earlier. A change which is happening in many areas of life, not only in design. (p. 159)

The second proposition or insistence is that it is the 'total situation' – the context in Jones's language – that is today the crucial site of designing. This echoes an understanding that others were exploring at the same moment[24] (as well as anticipating crucial developments in ethics and politics) but Jones gives the insight a radical twist. In *Design Methods* the insistence is that the real task of designing today (the real site of the applicability of 'methods') is in 'the design of "all-things-together"' – meaning, he says, the successive levels of 'the function and use of things, the "systems" into which they are organized, the "environments" in which they operate … [and] the *operating*

---

[24] Most obviously, Herbert Simon's famous line from c.1980: 'Everyone designs who devises courses of action aimed at changing existing situations into preferred situations' (*The Sciences of the Artificial*, 2nd edn [Cambridge: MIT Press, 1981], p. 111). See also Horst Rittel's concept of 'wicked problems' in 'Dilemma's in a General Theory of Planning', *Policy Sciences* 4 (1973), pp. 155–69.

wholes of which modern life is being formed and made'.[25] The key issues here are, one, the scalar movement *between* these levels, and, second, the implication that methods and procedures of designing, *no less than of any other major field of action* (e.g. technology) must today extend to addressing the 'operating wholes' of which life is made. This is the necessary scale of design today.

In *designing designing* this sense continues, but it is now placed in a deeper context – as when Jones asks himself at one point, 'What IS the context of design?' and answers (in an all too brief phrase), 'It is our minds … it is also evolution … of all things, natural and artificial' (p. 182). The twist is that when today we speak of 'expanded fields of design' (or, more outrageously, make the claim 'design is all')[26] then, even if not fully intended, the direction of movement is outward: Design (as-is) *expanding* into ever larger contexts of action. But in Jones the movement runs in the *opposite* direction. In the face of the realization of these 'expanded' contexts of design, it is not the expansion of Design into ever greater spheres of operation ('from the teaspoon to the cathedral') that is key but the *transformation* of the understanding – and practice – of what designing might be.

In contending with what is concretely emerging – the 'revolutions in industrial life', all that today we would call the artificial – as well as with the understanding that designing is *itself* the engagement of mind[27] and of the 'evolution of all things, natural and artificial', then designing is the act of both dealing with the un-schematized (artificial) Real and is itself, as designing, *beyond* given schema. In this context, practice and thought cut through established limits (break with inadequate reflection) and offer, against limit, a realm of possibility which can only be approached but never fully encompassed. This excess – the infinite moment – is the capacity or capability of designing, that which 'acts' within finite practices of designing but which is never completely circumscribed by these.

The third insistence picks up this last point. When Jones speaks of the new methods acting 'outside the boundaries of traditional expertise and within the personal experience, or "inner world", of individuals', he breaks emphatically with the professional concept of designing as a kind of neutral zone. He is pushing against the view of Design that neither

[25] *Design Methods*, pp. xxv–xxvi.
[26] Most notably Victor Papanek, in the introduction to *Design for the Real World* (London: Paladin, 1974).
[27] The concept of 'mind' in *designing designing* is of paramount importance. The term reappears continually in the arguments Jones advances. Here it stands for the essence of subjectivity, but it also stands, not only as that which is applied to, or drawn on, designing but also as that which designing itself *explores*. Cf. here the hint in Herbert Simon as the possibility of thinking designing not only as a mode of acting on the world but of understanding (Simon, p. 164).

overreaches its *assigned* limits,[28] nor explores too far within the 'inner world' of individuals (be they of the designer him or herself, or of the persons he or she is designing for). Against this, the dissolution of limits permits the concept of an open field of designing whose boundaries – both objective and subjective – can be neither known or set a priori, and cannot be subject to Law.[29] *designing* is then a field both more 'subjective' and 'objective' than we might have supposed, and a field that is no longer simply so, that is, it is no longer simply autonomous and defined.[30] If, today, we in part concede the understanding that designing is *itself* the engagement of mind, the idea that it is the 'evolution of all things, natural and artificial' remains to be realized – and, as we are beginning to accept – a task of some emergency.

II

WRITING, SPEAKING, PERFORMING

So far, I have largely been writing on the concepts developed in *designing designing* as if the text was a kind of transparent membrane through which the ideas emerge. It is, of course, in part, just that. All texts to a degree are. Prose prides itself on just this. But the assertiveness of propositions and the logic of connections between concepts that the reader gradually makes in reading a text are only one part of the story. The other is what happens within and through the language(s), the voices, the strategies and tactics, the forms and the modes, deployed.

[28] That is externally assigned limits. Professional design imagines its autonomy is self-selected. It is not. This is seen most clearly in architecture, whose functions, including most emphatically the places where it is permitted some autonomy, are today dictated by the political economy of development and construction. See, for example, Kenneth Frampton, 'On the Predicament of Architecture at the Turn of the Century' in his *Labour, Work, and Architecture* (London: Phaidon, 2002), pp. 8–19.

[29] Configuration cannot be subject to Law. All configurations, natural and artificial, obey local laws, just as all contend with circumstances and with the configurations of the situations with which they engage. However, none, in their totality can be a priori encompassed by Law. In designing we are necessarily engaging with uncertainty. A philosophy of designing is a philosophy of uncertainty. Jones's passing remark, 'If you wish for certainty you might as well leave this subject alone/because design is to do with uncertainty' (p. 20) is of deeper significance than might be thought.

[30] There is a perhaps a parallel here to Barthes's insight that true interdisciplinarity only begins from the encounter of practices and disciplines 'in relation to an object which traditionally is the province of none of them' (Roland Barthes, 'From Work to Text', in Stephen Heath [ed.], *Image Music Text* [London: Fontana, 1977], p. 155). Today, 'designing' could be conceived as such a field, that is, as a 'truly interdisciplinary' realm which is no longer simply owned by 'Design' and is a justified object of interest for a whole range of fields and disciplines.

In *designing designing* the relation between 'content' and 'language' is particularly close. Rather than pre-existing its expression, content – thinking what designing *might* be – emerges in and *through* the writing. The essays in the book are instances of the conscious exploration of how these moments can be intertwined; where the interaction between reading, writing, thinking and designing (and of imaginatively experiencing the performative moments of some of the texts) becomes the principle both of the understanding that the work offers, and of how the work, as a whole and in its complex and varied parts, is organized. What the work 'says' – its specific content concerning what designing might be – cannot be dissolved from the modes through which it is said. In *designing designing* this interrelationship is taken to high degree. The work is in this sense profoundly experimental; a decade-long attempt at exploring how understanding can be pushed beyond the boundaries and limits of what-is.[31]

Problems in language

There is nothing willful about this act. On the contrary, it is a *designed* solution to a real problem that Jones faced at this point. One illustration of this is wholly practical – as when he says at the beginning of the essay 'The Future of Breathing', which is in part a reflection on his own practices as a designer, that he hopes these reflections 'will throw light on the reasons for the less familiar kind of writing I have been led to in my attempts *to improve the processes through which things can be improved*' (p. lxi) . The marker here is that Jones is feeling that the existing languages of design are inadequate not simply for 'design thinking' or methods but *for designing as a practice.*

A second aspect of this exploration is at once critical and affirmative. In order to mount and drive the critique of design methods, where it needs to go and to begin speaking of designing as it 'should, and can, be', Jones feels that he needs a language of thinking, conceiving, articulating and exploring designing that is flexible, rich and resonant; one that is capable of exploring designing in the directions which appear at this point to be necessarily opening up for it.

But in the 1970s, no less than today, such a language did not exist. If Jones 'leaves' Design after 1970 because he feels it has become 'rigid and inhuman', part of the reason for this is what has happened to language. As he put it in one of the sharpest critiques in the book:

> We sought to be open minded, to make design processes that would be more sensitive to life than were the professional practices of the time. But the result was rigidity: a fixing of aims and methods to produce designs that

---

[31] This explains why, as noted earlier, although Jones's texts are eminently quotable, they are almost impossible to paraphrase (because paraphrase becomes, in effect, a translation, and in this instance a highly reductive one).

everyone now feels to be insensitive to human needs. Another result was that design methods became more theoretical and many of those drawn to the subject turned it into the academic study of methods (methodology) instead of trying to design things better. The language used to describe designing, and to describe the aims and purposes of things designed, became more and more abstract. The words lost touch with how it feels to be a designer and how it feels to inhabit the systems being designed. Abstract language can often be a release from the status quo. It was a release in the beginnings of functionalism, and in the beginnings of design methods. But it can so easily become fixed, in which case it turns, overnight, into a tyranny. (p. 159)

Abstracted, disconnected from its 'right place as a practical way of enlivening design' (p. 182), essentially *depleted* in their capacity for resonance, the languages of design and design methods can no longer serve through which to *think* design *and therefore, to repeat, are no longer adequate to practice.*

But there is also a third, equally acute, problem that Jones faces with language. By contrast to *Design Methods*, where the content, that is, the methods, were known in advance – they largely pre-existed Jones's masterful synthesis and organization – *designing designing* faces the opposite problem. The content, the putative 'answers', even the answers to critique ('Where did we go wrong?') are *not* known. When Jones says that, vis-à-vis design methods and more widely vis-à-vis the problems of designing (and living) in industrial society, he wants 'to take some responsibility for putting things right' (p. 149) the 'what' – the means by which things can be 'put right' – are not transparent to thought, not given to hand, nor reachable for 'off the shelf'. They have to be *discovered*. But what is 'discovered' must first be *experienced* as that which might be capable of being named. However, when one does not know with certainty of what one speaks, when what one wants to get to is *not* given, *not* ready to hand, when it must be brought out, named, won – and won from what obscures it, what blocks it, prevents its thought (i.e. the existing modes of speaking 'about' design) then to bring matters to voice, to speech, it is necessary to have to push beyond the norms of existing language.

What Jones is understanding here is the degree to which the norms of writing and speaking concerning designing *themselves delimit what can be said, and therefore delimit the range of what can be thought and hence of the forms and modes that practice can take.*

Against this, as we've seen, the entire thrust of *designing designing* is to open design to a reconstitution and a redirection far more radical, in real terms, than he had proposed in *Design Methods*. But this cannot be done within the given limits and modes of speaking about designing.

Shattering and challenging

What this means in practice is that to go forward, Jones has to shatter – first for himself, and then in terms of the wider agenda of the norms of thinking designing – the modes of writing for and about design, which the existing languages of design delimit and restrict. This is why the papers, reviews, exchanges of letters, scripts of performance and so on that Jones assembles in the book have to take the form or have to be configured (designed) as experiments in ways of breaking with and reconstituting these spaces. These 'essays' have to try to do two things at once.

- Substantively, to work towards offering a critique of designing and design methods-become-abstract-and-inhumane, a critique which at the same time can lead to and become the site of explorations of 'another way' of designing.
- In terms of the languages they deploy – formally, methodologically, in terms of format(s), and most importantly of how they address experience (and not least the experience of thinking) – they have to try to break through the incapacity of existing languages of design to adequately comprehend designing and its real contexts of operation.[32]

It is this mixture of answer and question, substance and language that gives the work its force.

But it is also a combination which produces, at least initially, some genuine difficulties for the reader. It is telling in this respect that in their cover notes to the book, the publishers of the 1991 edition unusually conceded that if 'ultimately enriched' the reader will also be 'challenged' and even 'at times frustrated'. The reasons for this are multiple (if so too, equally, are the joys of the text – difficulty does not necessarily mean the absence of pleasure). But while we need to look at these moments – language and format, the question of system and anti-system (and design and anti-design) and above all at the peculiar role that chance and performance play in Jones's thinking and writing in the works that make up *designing designing* – we need also to look in more detail at the problem Jones was

[32] Both moments are significant. There is a strong argument to be made – and Jones explicitly and implicitly makes it in *designing designing* – that the language of Design (professional Design) becomes inadequate to grasp designing today in part because in delimiting the contexts of designing to 'Design', it artificially limits comprehension of the true range of the capacities or capabilities (and limits) of designing. What *designing designing* constantly hints at, in ways redolent for its own times, is the potential shape and range of what is opened here.

faced with when he began publicly to reflect on design methods and the possibilities of designing.[33]

The difficulty of the project Jones was involved with

To understand this, we have to go back to the difficulty of the project that Jones is involved with in the early 1970s. As he tells in the second chapter, Jones has spent the decades of the 1950s and 1960s working on projects in engineering, designing and design-related research; on developing 'design methods' and in beginning to teach design (pp. 15–21).[34] Appointed first professor of Design of the Open University as he completes work on Design Methods in 1970, all seems set for Jones's extended career in design and academia. Yet, this does not happen. As early as 1966, he was already voicing serious doubts about the design professions (p. 179). By 1974 he has left the Open University, moving from design to working in software and interesting himself in what he calls 'the time arts (music, film, theatre, poetry) and in Indian and Chinese philosophy' (pp. 173–4). With respect to design methods then, Jones 'votes with his feet'. But at this point the criticisms he has of methods (including his own work) do not quite come into focus. To do so requires – as we will see – a precipitating event.

But before looking at this we need to grasp some of the conditions which apply to the kind of critique Jones can launch. In fact, a whole series of problems confront Jones as he begins to think how to articulate both his unhappiness with professional Design and with design methods and his alternative sense of the possibilities of designing designing. Each is a tension present when Jones begins to try to publicly address the crises and possibilities of Design and designing. They are not the only factors, but they are, in effect, the initial considerations concerning writing about design, that Jones could not, at some level, c. 1973, *not* be concerned with.[35] I give a listing of these below, because to comprehend fully what *designing designing* is attempting to do, it is necessary to grasp the difficulty of Jones's position in the 1970s – which in retrospect seems far simpler, far less difficult than in fact, analytically speaking, it was.[36]

[33] 'Publicly' because all of the essays in the book, without exception, were made for public contexts, the vast majority as talks or conference papers. (See the first line of Jones's acknowledgements, p. lix.) The book is a public pronouncement twice over. This makes a difference to language and presentation. And to the notion of risk.

[34] C. Thomas Mitchell gives a useful summary (Mitchell, this volume, p. liv).

[35] I put it in the format of a double negative because it expresses the fact that these face Jones as close to objective requirements.

[36] I am neglecting here – because it would extend this introduction much too far beyond its already excessive length – the historical circumstances and the wider context of attitudes in designing and design methods and theory across the 1970s. These are equally complex.

Eight elements are involved. From Jones's perspective they fall into two groups: questions and tensions around the issue of control, and question and tensions around the issues of power. The first moments are largely, but not wholly, negative. The second group are largely, but not wholly, affirmative.

    1.   System/anti-system/discovery/question

Design Methods was avowedly a systemic work. It was explicitly a proposal for new systems of designing, at least for complex entities. Jones sought to reconstitute designing at its then-highest level of dealing with technical complexity.[37] He laid out the book systematically to attain these ends. That was why it was taken up as a work of design thinking and methodology in the strongest senses of the term. But *designing designing*, and the papers he writes as critique of methods, cannot be a systemic work in that sense. Jones's needs are not for the synthesis and presentation of that which is known but for the opposite, the *discovery of what is not yet known*, first from the side of critique and second from the side of the *question* as to what, affirmatively, designing might designing be, for us, in our increasingly man-made world. This means that there can be nothing static or final or closed in the inquiry as to what designing might be. Any answer is at best provisional. Hence, Jones cannot make a new system to deal with what must be dealt with.

    2.   As Design/As anti-design

One of Jones's deepest critiques of design methods and especially the language of methods, is that it is anti-practice; that it has divorced itself from what it should be – 'a practical way of enlivening design'. Conversely, there is a need then to try to bring language and writing on design closer to designing itself – or as Jones puts it in the quotation already given at the start of the paper: 'Now that I am asked to write this summary of some of the main aspects of "how to design", I am reluctant to do so unless I can make the paper *itself an example of the methods I am to describe.*' (p. 128). This follows through to the idea that while these papers are written (or written/spoken), they can also/should also be/ configured (or, if you take the standpoint of time, composed). So writing takes on a configurative as well as a designing dimension. And this implies that not only the individual essays or performances should take on some aspects of designing

---

[37] 'Architecture, engineering, industrial design, but also software design, artificial intelligence, creative psychology'– or as revealingly said in the publisher's notes to the 1980 edition, 'particularly relevant to the designing of compositions in time, e.g. traffic flow, TV and radio programs, educational courses, tourism, exhibitions, communication systems, self-help schemes and the like'.

but also the book as a whole, in its deepest sense, should be configured and designed in its entirely, as a work. But this sets up a paradox. Because, what Jones also opposes in the application of design methods is that 'methods' replace designing (i.e. *conventions* of designing replace actual designing). On the reverse side therefore, if the book has to be designed, it cannot be as 'Design': it must, to a degree, be anti-design; it must shift from Design as a merely external element applied to the text to a sense of the work designed internally as it were, in its structure. It follows then that writings on design must be both 'more' and 'less' designed: This explains the peculiar quality of *designing designing* as a book at once designed and 'un-designed' or even as anti-design (e.g. Jones's deliberate use of chance methods in its composition).

    3.   No unitary format

As indicated, *Design Methods* was systemic. The work was designed after all as a handbook. The thirty-five methods were presented in uniform manner. For *designing designing* no such uniformity is possible. Experiential, the works presented designed (or at least configured, composed) *responses to situations.* While utilizing format, they cannot privilege a single model. This is why *designing designing* presents the oddity of a book that utilizes almost as many formats as there are presentations.[38] The listing in footnote 38 has about it almost a sense of comedy. But what it speaks to is the flat refusal to systematize. Inventiveness of format is an essential aspect of the thought of the book, and not least the experimentation to see the ways in which writing, thinking, speaking, performing concerning designing can be given something of the responsiveness and transducing quality of designing – of how configuration and composition can be given greater weight in the manner in which we attempt to voice designing.

    4.   The problem of control.

But what must absolutely be opposed against the vulgarization of methods is the whole ideology of control. The very first paragraph of the book rails against it: that is, against the impulse to see designing as a means of control,

[38]   In approximate order of appearance: a long reflective letter-as-essay; an invented question-and-answer dialogue; a biographical reflection; reflections on past practices coming close to a new manifesto; an extended interview; a 'book review'; a case study on chance and its reflection; a poster and commentary; an exchanges of letters; two academic presentations created in part through use of chance procedures; an extended reflective composition on the typewriter executed in real time; poetic reflections on objects and processes; a dramatic presentation of imaginary conversation (created in part through chance procedures); the script of a performance; a play with voices composed in part in spirit of John Cage's 'Silence'; a presentation handed over entirely to other voices; a play-with-video performed largely as dialogue in a conference.

that is, to see it technocratically. 'I hate the idea of controlling, even a hostile environment . . . control implies lack of respect for something' (p. 5). But the opposition to control has to extend to writing. Against construing writing as controlling, 'as a message meant to control our future thoughts and acts' (p. 279), Jones has to discover ways of doing the opposite, of 'letting go' and of creating forms of presentation as experiences which are open in the reflections they induce.

But, again paradoxically, at the same time as Jones rails against design as control, he also recognizes that in practice designing (and individual designers) consistently suffers from *lack* of control. Usurped by interests (economic, technical, conventional – even the fear of designing) then, just as writing on design is forced into narrower, behavioristic models, so today designing works in ever narrower parameters. There is a need therefore to recover a degree of real 'control' over designing and over writing and thinking on designing. 'Real control' means here breaking with the assigned limits and expectations of what should and should not be 'designed'. It implies recapturing 'control' over designing rather than designing as a means of control.

5. Not power/a different kind of space/for re-learning

The yearning for control is a yearning for power. And if control is eschewed – at least as an ideology – then the language he deploys must also participate in this necessity. It cannot take refuge in the ease of fact. Crucially, it must ensure that it eschews power. (One of the 'accidents' of design methods was that to readers they appeared to promise the power that comes not only with access to 'truth' but also to method.) The language – and perhaps, even more, the *structure* of the book – must neutralize the possibility of its being appropriated in this way.

To put this more affirmatively, what it seeks is not power but the space of opportunity, for author and listener/reader alike, 'to re learn, to develop, to grow' (p. 158). The aim has to be to offer 'not so much a message meant to control our future thoughts and acts' but something closer to the provision of experiences – of reading, writing, voicing – 'in which we are freed from the anxieties and purposes that often close the mind to all but self-interest. A context in which our thoughts may be unexpected . . . to . . . ourselves' (p. 279).

6. From space to time

If *Design Methods* was declarative – 'spoken about in clear language/such as the scientist uses when he writes a paper about how people do this or how metals do that' (p. 16): an attempt to make the design process logical in the technical sense of the term – the aim of *designing designing* is not illogicity (not a simple opposition) but the expansion of what is logically required of designing with respect to acting in the artificial: the reworking of the logic of designing as at once more experiential, less abstract, more connective, more allowance of slippage and composition, more attuned to relations, to what emerges in the process.[39] Put very simply, this logic has to be the counter-point to the essentially spatial conditions of systemic methodologies, black-box representations and the like (p. 174). In Jones's view – and it is one of the strongest underlying propositions of the book – it is the insertion of *time*, the place of becoming rather than Being (p. 279) into the language of designing allows designing to recoup its relation to experience – and not least because it is only through time that we can recoup and envisage, and hence potentially realize, other futures.

7. Risk/wager

The desire for control, for certainty, for the recipe, for the total model, for the answer – all of these erode the capacity (the necessity) for risk. This was one of the lures of design methods. But it is only in acts of risk and in highly improbably wagers that thinking (and designing) can occur – whether in practice or in writing. Putting risk at the center of presenting is therefore a *necessary* counter to the behavioristic desire to control every outcome. As will be said at the end of this essay, one quality of *designing designing* is that it constitutes, in effect, a guide to acting-in (and thus living with) uncertainty. A guide to so doing has itself to manifest risk – even as it simultaneously demonstrates what it is that risk/uncertainty can achieve.

8. 'Design methods' versus life

Finally, in this listing of conditions – and in relation to a question with which we began – what weight, even in a book on designing, should be given to 'design methods' or even Design? To ask how does either stand to life? Is there not, conversely, a need to look 'outside the world of methods, which once seemed larger than it does today'? (p. 151) and hence a need to bring into the discussion other voices? In short to bring life back into Design, which at extreme, threatens to exclude it? – not by asking, yet again, about 'design and society' (where the conjunction defines the separation) but (say) by the direct interjection of other voices, other sensibilities, other logics. Is it possible to create a genuine polyphony around and *for* designing?

*

[39] An instance of this, which comes appropriately when Jones is most doggedly and openly (consciously, in real time) pursuing the processes of his thinking, attempting to discover in, through and during the processes of writing, comes in the passage at the end of the essay 'Opus one, number two'. He is thinking about what constitutes 'purpose' and 'process' and records his processes of thinking-as-discovery as register of the *incomplete moment* of that discovery (pp. 162–4). The passage, which is too long to be quoted here, needs to be read in full because it captures Jones's shift in writing and thinking from the declaration of 'what-is' to the discovery of what might be.

xxxix

What this listing tells us – or should tell us – is that for Jones in the 1970s the ways of beginning to speak otherwise concerning designing, both as critique and as affirmation, are not obvious. The conditions are complex. The circumstances are not propitious. That difference can emerge requires a precipitating event – almost, one mighty say, an accident. Something that provokes an event to occur.

The precipitating event: EDRA 1973, chance procedures and the performative

The event that matters for Jones was an invitation, in 1973, to give a paper at a conference for the Environmental Design Research Association (EDRA). It is his reaction to this invitation which opens the possibilities for much of his subsequent work. At first glance it is easy to miss that the paper which emerges – 'Is designing a response to the whole of life?' (whose title in itself summarizes the ethos of what *designing designing*, as a whole, pushes towards) is the catalytic moment for his thinking and writing. Buried away at the beginning of the final section ('Things of August', pp. 244–55), the reader tends to comes across the paper 'too late' in their reading of the book. In fact, it should in many ways be the first 'paper' the reader confronts. A hint of the import of the paper comes in the largely biographical second chapter where Jones gives a succinct account of the process he went through in 'composing' the paper (pp. 22–4 – and he augments it further on pp. 182 and 244–5). What becomes clear in these pages is that the EDRA paper was the decisive event in terms of opening Jones's thinking and writing.

The gist of the development of the paper is this.

The invitation Jones receives to submit his paper is accompanied with a sheaf of technical instructions, twice as long as the five-page paper requested. Already beginning to react against impulse towards control in design, and – as we've seen – feeling increasingly opposed to both the abstraction of language and the behaviourism inherent in the languages of design theory, Jones determines that he won't participate: 'He'd adopted the whole language of behaviorism,' he says of the conference organizer, 'to describe to his … authors exactly how they should do their papers. I felt how insulting … that we have this mass of machine language instruction we send to each other in a bureaucratic manner … I thought to myself I won't give this paper, I'm damned if I'm going to' (p. 23).

But then he reconsiders. The turning point is an observation Jones remembers reading in John Cage, whose work had begun to interest Jones by this point, especially 'about how to use chance to compose music and to compose lectures. He says in there, if you receive a nasty instruction, you could refuse it … or you could do what John Cage does which is, apparently, to obey the instruction and then do more. It's tedious and arduous but a nicer way of responding' (p. 23).

This is what Jones does. In his words, 'stomaching the instructions', he obeys, to the letter, the conditions for submitting a paper. But he does more. Drawing on the chance procedures that he was learning from Cage, Jones composes what he calls 'an imaginary conversation of different voices' (p. 244), a small drama involving five figures – EDRA, who represents the bureaucratic voice of the conference; Immanuel Kant, 'who speaks a far better kind of abstract thinking than we designers seem to be capable of'; Walt Whitman, who speaks, as 'antidote, about his feelings and of more everyday concerns'; Carl Jung, 'who says that no method is any good unless the right person uses it' and Graham Stevens, a real-life artist-designer (pp. 182, 248).

As Jones describes in the preface to the paper, the characters speak sentences taken from their works by chance procedures. 'Nothing was left to the decision of the writer once the choice of voices and texts had been made' (p. 244). Accepted by the conference – how, given Jones zealous conformity to the instructions could it have been refused? – the 'paper', meaning the script for performance, is then presented, that is, *acted out* in the conference.

The script can be read. Its elliptical relation to its title can be pondered.

But there is no doubt of the catalytic importance to Jones of the process of the coming to be of the paper. He refers to it four times in the book.[40] More significantly, he felt the model to be successful and he repeated it. As he says, 'By 1976, writing conference plays [often by deploying chance methods] had become a habit' (p. 259).[41]

From EDRA to 'writing'

But what, precisely, did the EDRA paper achieve for Jones? Why did it have this catalytic role – in terms of his ability to write and think, concerning designing?

---

[40] Biographically (pp. 22–4); how it was impelled by the 'sterility' of the languages of academic conferences (p. 182); with respect to the procedures he deployed (pp. 244–5), with respect to how it was interpreted (pp. 254–5).

[41] *designing designing* gives us several examples of varieties of performance or plays, most of these drawing in some way on chance procedures, as well as instances of Jones using chance procedures in the composition of academic papers (see especially 'designing designing' (pp. 125–44) and 'continuous design and re-design' (pp. 191–217) as well as in more reflective essays and presentations ('how my thoughts on design methods have changed during the years' (pp. 13–27) and 'in the dimension of time' (pp. 169–89). In fact the element of the performative, which runs through the book as a whole, including in many of the writings which are not ostensibly 'performance' pieces at all but in which the voice, the mode of presentation and the estimation of experience matter.

Experiences are notoriously difficult to break apart. And one loses much in the process. But if we focus less on the paper 'itself' and more on its consequences, we can see a number of aspects, more than we might at first expect.

1. The work – the 'small conversation' is first of all an act of *necessary* violence, a freeing act

We've seen that, for Jones, c. 1973, the critique of methods, and the disengaging from within designing and industrial life of what is affirmable in both, has to be waged also as a war on the ways in which language, expressed as in methods, in 'fixed terms of reference' (p. 128) is capable of destroying reflection. In the EDRA performance, a space for the possibility of other languages in speaking designing is *violently* created. Violently because it breaks absolutely with the shibboleths of academic conference writing.[42] So the paper – the play – is a *gesture* – now using this term in its most serious sense.[43]

2. Second, and somewhat paradoxically, as an act of 'letting go' the work is also a re-assertion of control

These two things are bound together. Jones, as we've seen, detests 'control'. The paradox of the EDRA process is that as a letting go of authorship and decision – the use of chance procedures, the deliberate distancing of authorial control – the act is actually an assertion, by Jones, of the *double* capacity, first to refuse the 'bad rule' (Kant) and second to reassert (self-)control over procedures designed to remove autonomy and self-control. In the EDRA piece, chance was both a way of letting go – a point that finds its strongest affirmative expression in the extract from Jones's diary given on p. 278 – and a way of recovering control. What Jones is in effect saying in EDRA – and then across *designing designing* as a whole – is that the very worst way of 'letting go' is not consciously, not when you deliberately choose procedures which entail a degree of letting go and constraint, but in the passive

---

[42] Clearly of 1974 but no less clearly also of today. In an age of 'peer review' it is worth considering whether any of the essays in *designing designing* could survive such a review – even though, as pointed out above, five of them were published in early issues of *Design Studies* between 1979 and 1984.

[43] See the last pages of the chapter 'Beyond Action' in Giorgio Agamben, *Karman: A Brief Treatise on Action, Guilt and Gesture* (Stanford: Stanford University Press, 2018), pp. 60–85. On p. 84 Agamben defines 'gesture' in the sense he means it and which has some reference to Jones's sense of designing, in which those who deploy it in acting 'are not limited to acting, but in the very act in which they carry out their action, they at the same time stop it, expose it, and hold it at distance from themselves'. The analogy is by no means exact. But it suffices to suggest a model of acting where, if instrumentality and operationalism is necessarily present, it is not *only* so. Jones's ability to see designing as that from which we may also step back from (e.g. p. 183) resonates with the emerging sense that, for us in the future, we require, to live well in the world, views of acting-in-world that cut between the traditional divide between acting and not-acting. See also n. 50 in the present text.

acquiescence to bureaucratic and methodological control. 'Control implies lack of respect for something' (p. 5); for the person or thing or the process to be controlled (p. 5). Conversely, to deploy chance against the given is to paradoxically reassert one's own capacity, not to 'control', in the behavioristic sense, but to give some autonomy back to one's decisions. It is contesting of obedience to rule, to method thought merely instrumentally.

3. The work – and we can only really call it this, something that stands as a performance – is a creative critical event which is also an affirmative intervention

Agreeing with the lessons he was then absorbing from John Cage, Jones makes the situation he is placed in through the invitation for the EDRA paper into the site of a creative intervention. Given the invitation, Jones's choices are to reject or capitulate. He does neither. Instead, obeying the rule he 'does more'. There is of course critique. But if the work arrives out of protest *it does not stay there*. Obeying instead the 'law' of interventions – that to resolve a paradoxical situation or a relation that is not a relation, a new framework of thought or experience must be proposed, 'on condition, of course, that a certain number of parameters be abandoned, a certain number of novelties introduced'[44] – Jones both introduces novelties (the voices of Kant, Jung, Whitman, Graham Stevens, the use of chance procedures, the conversion of the paper format to a dramatic event) while the parameters of the academic conference presentation, 'obeyed' on one level, are abandoned on another. The 'relation that was not a relation' of the bureaucratic instructions for the conference papers versus the theoretical aspiration of the conference as an open space for thought is lanced. The result is to at least indicatively weaken the norms of the existing frameworks of academic papers in design conferences. Far more importantly it creates space for the possibility of other experiences, other dialogues concerning thought on designing, to emerge – even if, at this stage, these are scarcely known in any precise sense.[45]

---

[44] The line comes from Alain Badiou, in a passage in a conversation where he insists that the real work of philosophy (thought) is not critique (negative) but intervention – which can only be affirmative. Why? Because if you intervene with regard to a paradoxical situation or to a relation that is not a relation, you will have to affirm that it is possible to think this paradoxical condition (to propose a new framework of thought) on condition, of course, that a number of parameters be abandoned, a certain number of novelties introduced. Consequently, the determinant element of intervention is affirmation. It should be lost on no design reader that what Badiou describes here describes also design. Alain Badiou and Slavoj Žižek, *Philosophy in the Present* (Cambridge: Polity, 2009), p. 81

[45] The vast majority of the papers in *designing designing* come from 1978 to 1980. What in retrospect appears inevitable – the depth of the auto-critique of design methods; the articulation of design-as-process – is in practice far more difficult to arrive to than later perspectives make us think. This is one reason the book has to take the form of an emergence of critique and affirmation.

xliii

4. The work – the paper, the performance – is closer to design than to writing in the usual sense. It is a refusal of 'academic' discourse

Reference has already been made to Jones's desire for forms of writing design that are closer to being able to 'enliven' design. This can also be expressed as the desire to exemplify the design process in writing. Later, Jones will make explicit the analogy of constraints in writing and constraints in designing, talking at one point, for example, about his use of chance processes:

> Like the others which I have already chosen for this article, [this quotation] was picked by a chance process … and, like the other quotations, has been pre-typed on the page at a position which has also been picked by chance. Thus, in composing the article, I am faced with a task that is in some ways similar to that of a designer who has decided to make his design process, and the resulting design, sensitive not only to his present ideas but to his past, and to the past activities and lives of others. A deliberate attempt to compose something not so much by conscious intention and control, but by letting what already exists arouse the ideas that are being given form and substance here. (p. 171)

5. It follows that what Jones creates is both a 'paper' and not a paper: It is also a risk and a wager

While formally fulfilling the requirements of the conference, the work is not in any manner a 'paper' in any conventional sense. The break with the *norms* of academic writing is absolute. In this respect it acts like an event – that which obeys all the formal rules of a situation, but which also takes the form of a wager or a proposition that can push thought beyond the present limits of that situation. This reference to 'wager' reminds that, as noted already, the work is a *risk*. The retrospective publication of the EDRA paper, in a volume that dares to put chance and performative center stage again dulls the sense of the work as ris*k* – *chance* in the literal sense. And this is risk in the serious sense. It is attached to *wager*.[46] The heresy from the side of the academic conference is Jones's wager that 'work performed to a tempo thus not so much a message … as an experience of the moment' – a means of opening thought to the unexpected trumps explanation: that

---

[46] This finds its strongest expression in the statement, which occurs in the introduction to 'Voices at the conference conference'. The wager concerns what the experiential might do. The premise, or the risk that Jones offers, is that the ostensible subject matter Jones is aiming at – what he calls 'context design', the idea that we should be designing and 'seeking to make beautiful not only the results of human and industrial processes, *but these processes and the conditions under which they occur*', all that which has been neglected so far by the 'imagination, the artistic mind' (p. 279) – can be caught through a part chance-created drama (similar in structure to the EDRA paper), which itself will seek to 'exemplify context designing *and perhaps to explain the idea too*, if that is possible' (p. 279).

the creation for the space of what I will call later an 'originality and range of reflection' on the part of the listener no less than the author, is at least as valuable as a more didactic work. The reason for this is not that he is unaware of the limitations of this position vis-à-vis understanding design as is. The point is that he is after a different level of understanding as to what designing can be. The wager is of course a colossal risk. But that in itself is important. The risk is a testament to *the risk of thought*. It risks failure (and Jones partially concedes as much [p. 278]). But is also an attempt to put into being a different conception of what comprehending the possible range of designing can be; an attempt to speak – even allegorically – about that which, at the moment in which Jones spoke, could not be spoken of in Design. What Jones is maintaining – drawing here in effect on the whole lineage of avant-garde experiments – is that *an event of this nature is something that potentially brings to light a possibility that was until then invisible or even unthinkable.*[47]

These five moments are not insignificant for Jones. As has already been said, the EDRA paper was catalytic. In effect, it breaks him decisively with what-is (in terms of academic norms) and it opens, for him, writing in the fullest sense – that is, the translation of experience into formats *though which he could present, succinctly a series of experimental propositions for thinking concerning designing.*[48]

The rest of the book is a presentation of these possibilities.
Many of these essays would bear the weight of extended reflection themselves – especially perhaps the two most reflective essays in the book ('Opus one, number two' and '… in the dimension of time' [pp. 147–68 and 169–90]).

But from the readers' perspective there are two other issues that must first be confronted, for these are the peculiarities of Jones's book and the issues that cause initial problems with simply 'reading' the text. The issues are those of chance and the performative.

Why does Jones gives so much weight to each of these – such that, in effect, more than half the book is given over to the question and deployment of chance and of performative scripts?

[47] The question in all creative thought is what is thought that could not previously have come to mind. Milan Kundera, the Czech novelist, has a line that is worth quoting here: 'The sole raison d'être of a novel is to discover what only the novel can do. A novel that does not discover a hitherto unknown segment of existence is immoral.' Milan Kundera, 'The Depreciated Legacy of Cervantes', in *The Art of the Novel* (New York: Harper and Row, 1988), pp. 5–6. See also the introductory chapter to Alain Badiou's seminar *The Century* (Cambridge: Polity Press, 2006).

[48] This can be seen very well in simple terms in the first paper in the book where Jones *translates notes from a seminar* notes into a new format (invented dialogue as question-and-answer) which allow him to articulate with more force the points he wishes to make.

The use of chance

The background to Jones's use of chance and its first substantive application has already been hinted at. In the book too, one can read in part two of Jones's first experiments with, and some of his rationalizations concerning, the use of chance methods. The broadest case for chance is that, for Jones, in the early 1970s, 'chance' (exemplified above all in the writings of John Cage) was the means to open method. By method is meant here both literal methods of composition and methods of writing *and thinking*. Jones's use of chance is complex and probably deserves a paper in itself. Here I will note just two points. The first is that chance in its applied form – what Jones calls 'systemic' chance (as against the more radical indeterminancy' of Cage) (p. 101) – has the capacity *to turn text into event*. The instances of this are in the essay and in the volume itself – which as a whole constitutes itself as less of a 'book' and more as an event in its own right. In the language of the 1970s, this would be the work as 'text'. And indeed *designing designing* could be read profitably through the lens of Barthes's short essay, 'From Work to Text'.[49] In this sense, although chance is used as a 'method', it becomes, in effect, a device, a means towards opening experience.

But, we can also see chance as Jones in fact uses it, as a way of both metaphorically and literally of 'letting in the world'. There is a crucial sentence in Jones where, speaking of how he has grown weary of design methods and theory, he talks of the need to look 'outside the world of methods, which once seemed larger than it does today' (p. 151). Designing, in other words, requires for its vitality a constant and complex interchange not merely with itself but with the world, its contexts and its voices. If this is 'obvious', the fact is that, in practice, the disciplines of Design (thinking here especially of architecture perhaps) are often remarkably internal in their range of reference. In the EDRA paper, the use of voices from outside, no matter if brought in as chance quotations, act as initial starting points for insisting that the languages and mentalities of design have today *by necessity* to look outside their own world – and that only in so doing is design thought in its real contexts, that is, though in relation to life. To give this a slightly more technical cast, one of the reasons that chance has this capacity to help thought move beyond or to challenge the limits of the givens in a situation is that it acts as an intermediary which disturbs pure intention. Chance deployed allows the intrusion of the unexpected, of that which does not 'fit', that is, of all that stands for the world outside of formulations – the un-schematized real. It is not that chance *is* that content – in some ways 'chance' itself is a red herring – it is that chance 'speaks for' all that cannot be incorporated into the limitations of representations. Jones is sensitive to this problem: to the danger that representations, particularly in their technical 'black box' forms, can so easily work to exclude all that is incalculable,

[49] In *Image/Music/Text* translated by Stephen Heath (London: Fontana, 1977).

that is, 'most, or all of what makes life worth living' (p. 176). Chance is, in this view, a way station on the way towards more adequate ways of thinking and writing on designing.[50]

To summarize then, we can say that Jones *values* chance. He asserts its possibilities in the essays, and he deploys it wholesale in the book – first in the reflective 'biographical' essay, 'how my thoughts about design methods have changed during the years'; then in performance pieces ('35 wishes'; 'Voices at the conference conference'; 'The design of modern life') and then in application to academic papers in designing. In terms of writing, chance is the provocation of composition, it is, as with designing, the forcing of creative work within constraints. It is itself a value, and it is valued, for what experientially it is capable of evoking (see, e.g. Jones's evocations of the 'work' of chance on pp. 177–8).

Performance and the Performative

But EDRA is also a performance. And: the performative is central to *designing designing*, not only for all five of the papers in the final section, but because, in different ways, so many of its essays depend on it, at least to a degree. There are a number of aspects to this. Some have already been referred to in terms of the wager of the possibilities of the experiential. The latter includes the proposition that the expression of ideas is not confined to the apparently logical proposition; that the performative in itself theatrically *strikes* the spectator, *and that this striking is not absent of* ideas.[51] In other words, the performative is that which can present ideas and which in their experience of being 'struck' by them, escapes and evades the given limits of thought (see p. 279).

[50] A further aspect of the deployment of chance that cannot be explored here could be called the 'metaphysics' of chance. See Vilém Flusser, the chapter 'Our Programs', in *Post History* (Minneapolis: Univocal Publishing, 2013 [1983]), pp. 19–26, especially pp. 22–3. See also the essay by Giorgio Agamben, *What is Real?* (Stanford: Stanford University Press, 2018). Both Flusser's and Agamben's essays suggest a deeper *historical* 'metaphysic' of chance than we are used to thinking. In many ways we can now see that 'chance' is a form of expression in the last century of what we now tend to express as the radical contingency and interdependence of existence both of natural and artificial systems.

[51] Cf. Alain Badiou: that in the case of the theater, it is always 'explicitly a question of ideas'. The public comes to theater, Badiou asserts, not to be cultivated 'but to be struck. Struck by … ideas whose existence it did not suspect … [to leave] stunned, fatigued (thought is tiring), pensive'. What is 'pensive' in what is produced in performance is not an 'x' per se but a sense of encountering, and later recollectively reflectively examining, some facet of experience that we did not previously know – something that has extended our experience of what we *thought* we knew. Alain Badiou, 'Theses on Theater', in *Handbook of Inaesthetics* (Stanford: Stanford University Press, 2009), pp. 76–7.

If ideas are one side of the performative, the other is how it necessarily projects the embodied subject into the act of presentation, both in terms of speaker and by extension the listener/reader. It is the insistence that thought and action on these matters have to run *through* or via and not outside of, the subject. Attempts, conversely, to erase the subject, to make discourse 'objective' can be all too successful. But in Jones's argument we pay a terrible price for this, not only in academic and design discourse, but in life. Conversely, it is through the performative (which includes voice of course) that both the subject per se *and what the subject knows as a subject*, can be recovered.[52] Jones is implicitly arguing here that the intelligence of the subject contains understanding and modes of knowing that can be erased or lost when that knowledge is subjected to representational and configurational rules and systems. Such rules can delineate 'knowledge' but always at the potential price of rigidity, insensitivity and the like (p. 174). In terms of current systems and processes which *require* qualitative sensitivity to contingent circumstances and possibilities (and not merely to probabilities or recurrent Law), lack of such sensitivity can be fatal. Voice, then is the reassertion of the subject in dialogue, but it stands also for the re-introduction into the understanding of situations of that which purely 'objective' systems and methods can so easily miss.

In regard to performance, we can summarize its implications for writing in this way.

First, it invades writing in terms of a double influence: at once constructive – weigh given to composition and configuration; and experiential – above all in writing as voice ('beyond rationalism') and 'in-time' ('Opus one, number two'). That is, Jones begins to see writing (and speaking writing as well as translating speech into writing) itself as performance – in the volume even in the insistence on typescript as the reminder of this, of the craft of writing, here literalized.

Second, format is the occasion for event. In Jones, writing is emblematic. *It is itself the demonstration of its own process;* the apparent obverse of the (theoretical) aspiration of clarity and neutrality demanded by 'scientific' writing (p. 17). It is in fact an attempt to 'show' rather than 'tell' – to take the risk of showing.

[52] An instance of this in Jones comes where he introduces the published version of the long interview 'beyond rationalism' (pp. 39–70) explaining:
The typing of this version was a little experiment in trying to find a form of writing that retains some of the liveliness of speaking-while-thinking and does not impose on it the order of grammatical texts. In all but a few lines, I have retained as much of the informative pausing, hesitating, and revisingwhile-saying that I could perceive in the transcript. I was surprised to see how much more intelligent speech appears when one reproduces its accidents than when one edits it into grammatical form. (p. 38)

Finally, the performative moves directly into writing. Reference has already been made to the qualities of Jones's language, above all the deployment of a relatively simple 'common-sense' vocabulary in syntactical arguments whose flow and reference have something more in common, especially in the later papers, with poetics. Much of the pleasure – if also the challenges – of reading Jones comes from here. The wager is that, as with poetry and literature in general, we may be made or enabled to take in more than we consciously register. Particularly in the later papers, the drawing on poetry and on quasi-poetic moments extends the permissible range of thought and reference. For example, in '… In the dimension of time', at one point Jones segues from the critique of 'black-box' representation to quoting from the prologue to Frederico Garcia Lorca's comedy *The Shoemakers Wife* (pp. 176–7) to the evocation of chance to quotations from a previous interview. What is folded together here at once expands the field of thought of designing and draws the writing and thinking involved here closer to the processes of 'designing' in its creative and searching moments. That, at least, is the proposition of the work, the wager it is making.

III

There is, as I have said, much missing from this already far too long introduction. Absent for reasons of space is the logic of what Jones opposes and of how and why he creates his (auto)-critique of methods and design. Absent also, but this is deliberate, is critique. It is deliberate, because critique can so often come too quickly. Reading – meaning to stay with the book, to think through what is argued for – is in some ways harder. Anyone who opens this book understands that it is already quite a task simply to read through *designing designing*. Less forgivable is the absence of context. No work arises *sui generis*. It emerges out of wider patterns of thought, shared problems, signs read in differing but still connected ways. The reconstruction of the context is a significant absence. The double focus here – on challenge and on language – is by no means the full story. It is perhaps sufficient if it enables reading – thinking – to begin.

But having said this, what are the lasting implications of the book? What, in a way, matters, *from* it, not only substantively, but 'methodologically', that is, what it tells us concerning thinking designing?

I think three things can be said.

1. 'Originality and range of reflection': This phrase, which seems particularly apposite to describing what Jones manifests in *designing designing*, comes from Heidegger. Already referenced above, the full sentence from which it

comes is, 'The modern age requires, however, in order to be withstood in its future, in its essence and on the very strength of its essence, *an originality and range of reflection* for which today we are perhaps preparing somewhat but over which we can never gain mastery.'[53] The sentence has its own resonance in the context Heidegger deploys it, but simply to take up the postulate of the necessity for our times – and particularly for the modern world to be 'withstood in its future' – then we can see that what Jones offers us, in no matter how initially seemingly strange a manner, is precisely this, that is, an originality and range of reflection that is directly addressed to the problem, at least as seen in the context of the 1970s, of how we might 'withstand' (well) the modern age in its future. The astonishing variety of 'papers', the cornucopia of inventive constructs that make up the book, constitute this reflection. And this reflection is not passive but active. It is constitutive – constructive. It is the originality of these constructs – and the range of their scope (at least indicatively) that allows them to slip the limits of thought and therefore allows Jones to reconstitute the basis of designing. *designing designing* can perhaps then be best thought of, in the first sense, as an inventive construct attempting an 'originality and range of reflection' in relation to designing.

But we should also reflect further on Heidegger's point that an originality and range of reflection that is necessary to 'withstand' the modern age in its future. The term 'withstand' has special resonance for us today when 'withstand' means to make possible a future *against* the destructive trajectories of the age. We tend to forget the fact that the technological world – and by extension the professional world of Design insofar as it models itself on and partakes of this world (and this was particularly true of the architectural, ergonomic and engineering worlds Jones inhabited in the 1950s and 1960s) – is essentially defined by its *refusal* of depth reflection. Heidegger again offers the neatest, and the most devastating, formula of this state of affairs: 'In the will to will, technology (guarantee of stability) and the unconditional lack of reflection ("experience") first come to dominance. Technology as the highest form of rational consciousness, technologically interpreted, and the lack of reflection as the arranged powerlessness, opaque to itself, to attain a relation to what is worthy of question, belong together, they are the same thing'.[54]

[53] Martin Heidegger, 'The Age of the World Picture', in *The Question Concerning Technology and Other Essays* (New York: Harper, 1977), p. 138. The phrase comes, appropriately where Heidegger is reflecting on reflection and the relation of reflection and action at the beginning of the essay.

[54] It should escape no one's notice that this combination of 'experience' *without* reflection and technology (which *includes* the economic and the political system, itself organized as 'the guarantee of stability [grounded on] a constant form of using things up') describes the underlying economic and political context of today. Martin Heidegger, *The End of Philosophy* (Chicago: University of Chicago Press, 2003). pp. 99, 103.

But if the technological (and economic) domination of the logic by which the world is made is secured by denying, or at least limiting, reflection, then confrontation with the destructive moments of this logic cannot be done on their basis as given. It can only be done – and here we come back to Jones – by *inventing* forms of reflection that are at once unafraid to encompass this logic *in the same moment that they articulate, theoretically and practically, all that is denied in the technological lack of reflection*. It may be in fact that reflection in this (literally) inventive sense is the *only* methodological approach which can secure this understanding.

Such reflection, needless to say, cannot remain disengaged from action. On the contrary, the necessity is practical as well as theoretical. 'Practical' here means with a view to transformative action, that is, with an ability to model how we are capable of passing backwards and forwards between critique, affirmation and action.[55] Designing, in the expanded sense, is a potential moment for such reflection. As a process through which there occurs reflection-in-action on the artificial, it both *encompasses* the technological (it is not as current arrangements have it, merely marginal moment to it) *and* takes reflection beyond critique – to critical affirmation.

There is a methodological point here of some importance today. There is a much longer argument to be made but in essence it would be that it is not representational critique that secures the actuality of what, today, matters most. The greater claim is offered by reflexive designing. The truths – meaning the possibilities – of the artificial are *only* discovered reflexively, through forms of critical affirmation manifest in interventions. All this is already at some level understood in *designing designing*. It is why the book points in the directions it does. The difficulty for the reader is not in seeing this – Jones makes it remarkably explicit – but in daring to give it weight; in daring to think *with* Jones, and then beyond, to what is now required.

2. A reconstitution of the place of designing in the world: It was clear from the first section of this introduction that the views presented in the text constitute the basis of a 'new design philosophy' in the strong sense of the term.[56] The book is in fact nothing less than a proposal for a new

---

[55] 'Recognizing our transformative or productive activity has a special claim as a mode of acknowledging actuality which transcends the dichotomies between theoretical and practical reason, between positing and posited. Transformative activity acknowledges actuality in the act and does not oppose act to non-act.' Gillian Rose, *Hegel Contra Sociology* (London: Athlone Press, 1981), p. 204.

[56] The term belongs to Tony Fry. It comes from his book *A New Design Philosophy: An Introduction to Defuturing* (Sydney: UNSW Press, 1999). (To be republished as *Defuturing: A New Design Philosophy* [London: Bloomsbury, 2020].)

direction for designing, a reconstitution of its place in the world. It is this second point that is significant. *Design Methods* proposed new approaches *within* designing. *designing designing*, by contrast, is already pointing *through designing* to a wider sphere of acting – seen, for example, in the conclusions to 'now we are numerous', or in the extraordinary wager that Jones makes at the beginning of the paper 'Voices at the conference conference' (p. 279). This is why it constitutes, in the most rigorous sense, a new design philosophy and *not* a 'philosophy of Design'. It is at once a philosophy *for* designing and a philosophy in which 'designing', understood in the widest sense of the term, as both thought and action (a circularity of thinking-acting) has a central and *generative* place. Designing in this sense is crucial and generative for philosophy (meaning by this how we think of our places in the world) because the world-made is the site of mediation and negotiation between contexts and persons through the media of artifice. As such this mediation – for which designing is a crucial agency – constitutes for us the Real and hence a site of (our) truth. It is this site that is capable of generating a philosophy adequate to the condition of the artificial.[57]

A surprise of this philosophy is that it is also a philosophy of history. The point is this: If 'designing' is an innate human capacity, it only manifests in particular historical forms – and most often in ways that are never called 'design'. *Design* in the overt sense is a historical formation of the modern period and specifically of industrialization.[58] *designing designing* takes as its key moment the break in history represented by the ending of the dominance of the industrial in its traditional forms (i.e. where the industrial loses its formative capacity, economically, socially, politically). But it does not merely accept that what is then emergent simply 'is.' In its refusal to concede that the given trajectory of industrialization is the only available (that what-is can be reduced to 'sheer actuality without potentiality') and in its counter-insistence that what-now-is and what is now emerging, *objectively* contain the possibility for qualitatively *other* opportunities and futures, *designing designing* pits itself against the dominant argument that what-is is the only possible version (the only

---

[57] Note also here Herbert Simon's proposition that 'sciences of design and the sciences of the artificial' are co-terminus. See the preface to the second edition of *The Sciences of the Artificial* (Cambridge: MIT Press, 1996), pp. xi–xii.

[58] *Design Methods* was scarcely understood as a work of history even though it was, in a fundamental sense at the very least informed by a historical trajectory. It understood designing to be fundamentally historical in the forms that it takes. That is why *Design Methods* could never be what so many of its readers wished it to be, that is, a historically transcendent model of designing. *designing designing* is not a work of history but it lays out the basis of a *philosophy* of history of the artificial and the industrial.

form, the only configuration) of what could-be, not only in design, but in existence as a whole.[59]

3. An ethic: Finally, although the word almost never appears in the book, save briefly in its very last pages, the book constitutes an ethic. It is essentially an introduction to how to act (and by extension how to live) in uncertainty. It is so also a guide in embryo in how to *trust* in the absence of the illusion of external control – over the future, over nature, over ourselves.

> A theory is meant to predict. To control. To create certainty. But what you're saying is that ideas, if acted upon, do the opposite. Your belief as I understand it, is that we should accept not knowing what the future will be like and that we should trust in the abilities of ourselves, and of everyone else, to be surprised at what happens, to be changed by it, and to be able to react in new ways that at present we do not know? To seek to fix the future into a predicted form is, by this ethic … a wrong thing to do. It is to deny us our humanity, our ability to be. Life will change beyond our expectations. (p. 333)[60]

So, the book is asking, in effect, how do we deal with the fact – and the morality (p. 33) – of possibility? How do we deal with, live (well) with this potentiality? Now that production is no longer, in effect, an end but only a means (and not necessarily the only means at that) how can ends be re-construed not outside of acting but from within it? How can connection, in the deep sense that Jones intends it – close to what we speak of as 'relationality' today – be established? The way that one does that is to grasp the responsibility (the morality, to repeat the word) of possibility. Jones therefore sketches an ethic of possibility, but now concretely, through the medium of actions, not as abstraction and thus that which is antithetical to action and must deny the latter in its actuality.[61]

[59] The book thus pits itself against blind fate, against the identification of what-is with 'What-is'; against the view that sees only quantitative actuality without qualitative potentiality. Jones does not put it in this way – for one thing, as is already clear, the language of *designing designing* is deliberately conversational. It eschews philosophical jargon. There is a use of 'common sense' even in its poetic moments. But it is intuited, and made analytically evident, in the seriousness of Jones's critique of 'method' in relation to industrial life, and in the radical nature of what, against this limitation, and against what he opposes, he proposes.

[60] This comes from the script of the dialogue 'Utopia and Numeroso', the final 'essay' in the book.

[61] See Gillian Rose in note 55.

How then to finally summarize this book – an anyway impossible and perhaps unnecessary project? Perhaps we might say something close to how the project of another enigmatically composed volume of reflections on life was summarized: that in undertaking it and completing it to this point, Jones had succeeded in disengaging for us what was potentially affirmable in designing, and had affirmed that.[62]

Clive Dilnot

[62] I am here playing off the final sentence of Richard Ellman's unsurpassed lectures on Joyce's Ulysses: 'Having completed his plan, Joyce might well feel that he had succeeded in disengaging what was affirmable in existence, and had affirmed that' (*Ulysses on the Liffey* [London: Faber & Faber, 1972], p. 185).

foreword

When I first encountered John Chris Jones' work while a student of architecture I was baffled by his view of "designing WITHOUT A PRODUCT...as a process or way of living in itself", a view which differed so markedly from the professional training I was receiving at the time. I had, however, been struck in my studies by the abject failure of visually oriented designers to address even the most basic human requirements in their designs and became increasingly fascinated by Jones' approach which, at least potentially, could meaningfully incorporate people's wishes in the design process. Through repeated readings, I unravelled the ideas in Jones' writings and have found them to have immense relevance, not only to design, but also far beyond design, to the organization of life itself.

Designing Designing is a collection of recent writings by Jones, who is perhaps best known for his work in founding the design methods movement. He co-organized the first conference on design methods in 1962 and wrote the standard textbook on the subject *Design Methods*, which was published in 1970 and in a revised edition in 1980.

Designing Designing can be seen as a clarification and development of Jones' earlier work with design methods. In *Design Methods* he justified the need for new methods of design by demonstrating the inapplicability of traditional approaches, craft evolution and design-by-drawing, to new, large-scale design problems such as urban traffic systems and computer systems. In his new book Jones is even more explicit about how he views the design process to be changing. Jones challenges the traditional product-orientation of design with a process-oriented approach. The title *Designing Designing* is chosen to emphasize that the book is concerned with the design of the design process itself, rather than with the production of objects.

Jones developed his interest in process during his widely varied experience in engineering, industrial design, ergonomics, design methods, architecture, design education and research, and the futures movement. In each of the many fields in which he has worked Jones has been concerned with finding a way to rectify the misfits between people and machines, people and systems, which are so often the legacy of professional specialization. Such perennial and seemingly insoluble problems as traffic accidents, the failures and inadequacy of low-cost housing, and the continuing spectre of environmental pollution, Jones has long pointed out, result from the piecemeal application of product-type solutions to situations that are by nature process-oriented. Jones has now developed a much-enlarged, extra-professional vision of designing which he terms "design at the scale of modern life". This vision of design is the focus of *Designing Designing* and some examples of design at this scale are listed in the preface.

Designing Designing consists of essays, interviews, plays, poems, photographs, collages and quotes. Initially the presentation of the book seems unnecessarily obscure, with many of the writings being more akin to poetry than to prose. However, in producing *Designing Designing* Jones intentionally experimented with both form and content in an attempt to make a book which was not simply *about* design, but which was instead *design itself*, an example of the ideas presented within it. The patient reader of the book is rewarded with an abundance of insights into the nature of the design process which derive from Jones' broad experience.

Designing Designing should be of interest to those people in the professions, such as industrial designers and architects, whose work Jones addresses. The book is especially relevant to those in the newly emerging process-oriented design fields, such as software engineering, to which traditional product-oriented design methods, such as design-by-drawing, are inapplicable. The scope of Jones' recent work, however, goes far beyond the traditional bounds of design. Anyone with an interest in "the design of modern life" will be challenged, at times frustrated, but finally enriched by the unique and comprehensive vision of the future set out by Jones in *Designing Designing*.

C. Thomas Mitchell

author's note

This is a new edition of a book previously published as *Essays In Design* by John Wiley & Sons in 1984. It appears here under a new title with an introductory essay, "the future of breathing", written in 1987. The original essays are reproduced as a facsimile of typewriting, as they were in the first edition, because, being written "camera ready" (straight out of my head, like a letter to a friend) they lose something if typeset. Some parts of my meaning, or intention, are visual, not literary. For instance to read the essay "designing designing" (page 125) in which each page was composed to fill the spaces between pre-positioned quotations chosen by chance, you need to see the typescript itself.

j.c.j.
london, 1989

preface to the 1984 edition

What has become of design?

As I sit here on a Sunday afternoon looking at the titles of these essays and wondering what they have in common I'm struck by the extent to which the notion of design has changed.

Alongside the old idea of design as the drawing of objects that are then to be built or manufactured there are many new ideas of what it is, all very different:

> designing as the process of devising not individual products but whole systems or environments such as airports, transportation, hypermarkets, educational curicula, broadcasting schedules, welfare schemes, banking systems, computer networks;
>
> design as participation, the involvement of the public in the decision-making process;
>
> design as creativity, which is supposed to be potentially present in everyone;
>
> design as an educational discipline that unites arts and sciences and perhaps goes further than either;
>
> and now the idea of designing WITHOUT A PRODUCT, as a process or way of living in itself ... (a way out of consumerism?)

I suppose there are other views too but these are enough to let one see how quickly the notion has been changing and how far-reaching are its newer implications.

In my earlier book I defined design as the initiation of change in man-made things. Looking now at that definition I still like the emphasis on change but not the assumption that design is limited to the thinking of a few on behalf of the many. Nor do I like the assumption that it is to do with change in things but not in ourselves. In my re-thinking of the nature of design in these pages I have moved far from the picture of 'it' as the specialised activity of paid experts who shape the physical and abstract forms of industial life which we all as consumers accept or adapt to. That notion cannot possibly last for ever – it's too limiting, too insensitive to the reactions it provokes. It's too inert. Designing, if it is to survive as an activity through which we transform our lives, on earth, and beyond, has itself to be redesigned, continuously. As do the other false stabilities, ideas of order, which we inherit or construct, as stepping-stones, no more, useful as they may be in the moment. The turning of creative activity upon itself, attempting to change its nature, our own, is to me the most surprising, the most promising, of the changes to be noticed now, not only in design but as a general tendency:

the science-of-science;

learning-how-to-learn;

the technology of assessing technology;

"the composer as listener" (in the music of John Cage and other modern composers, poets, artists);

the think-tank;

the self-development movement;

what else? I see these as the turning of the objective and outward tradition of Western progress inwards towards itself as we try to correct the by-now-bad effects of having looked outwardly for centuries ...

It's time to look in the mirror as well as through the window. Soon it may be time to leave home. But first, a better picture of ourselves.

August, 1982

acknowledgements

These essays would not have been written but for the invitations of the people mentioned at the start of each. They would not have taken the forms that they have but for what I've learnt from the works of John Cage, Edwin Schlossberg and others whose example may be evident in the text.

Previous publication of the essays, sources of quotations, and acknowledgements of permissions to republish here, are indicated in the notes or references attached to each essay. The sources of the opening quotation, and those before each section-title, are:

page vii
Hannah Arendt, *The Human Condition*, University of Chicago Press, Chicago & London, 1958, pages 175–176.

page xciii
Annetta Pedretti, *The Cybernetics of Language*, Princelet Editions, London & Zurich, 1981, page 87.

page 82
John Cage, *Empty Words*, Writings '73–78, Wesleyan University Press, Middletown, Connecticut, 1979, page 61. This quotation is from fragments of the writings of Henry David Thoreau, recomposed as music to be spoken aloud.

page 144
Edwin Schlossberg, "For My Father", in *About Bateson, Essays on Gregory Bateson*, edited by John Brockman, E.P. Dutton, New York, NY, 1977, pages 146–147.

page 240
Gertrude Stein, *Mrs. Reynolds and Five Earlier Novelettes*, Yale University Press, Yale, Massachusetts, 1952, reprinted by Books for Libraries Press, Yale, Massachusetts, New York, 1969, pages 242–243.

The visual poems on pages lviii and xci-xcii are by Edwin Schlossberg and are reproduced with his permission. The letter shapes on page 190 were copied from the accidental shapes of hairs in rag paper by Joel Fisher and are reproduced with his permission. The photographs are from colour slides I made in the last ten years or so and the xerox pictures are of objects I found at chance-locations in Zurich and London. The process of selecting and positioning the quotations and illustrations is described on pages 108–109. The choosing of the section titles is described on page viii.

Much of the text of the essays was retyped by Charlie Boxer following the original typescripts.

The essays were written between 1971 and 1987.

The cover was designed by Jonathan Moberly. The numbers on the cover are from *A Million Random Digits with 100,000 Normal Deviates*, The Rand Corporation, The Free Press, Publishers, Glencoe, Illinois, 1965. They are from one the sheets of random numbers I used to determine the placing of illustrations and titles throughout the book.

This edition would not have appeared but for the actions of David Fulton of David Fulton Publishers and Tom Neville of Architecture Design and Technology Press.

introductory essay : the future of breathing

This essay was written in 1987 when Erwin van Handenhoven asked me to write something for an exhibition of *art and the automobile* at Le Centre d'Action Culturelle de Montbeliard in 1987 at the invitation of Pierre Bongiovanni.

The essay begins with an account of "my life with the car" and becomes, as it proceeds, a rethinking of what I have been doing in design and of how I now see it. It hope that it will reveal connections between life as we all experience it and the less familiar kind of writing to which I have been led in my attempts to improve the processes through which things can be improved...

My thanks to Erwin van Handenhoven for provoking this piece and for permission to reproduce his reply.

The French translation was published in *Penser L'Automobile*, Jean-Paul Curnier et al, Montbeliard: Centre D'Action Culturelle, 1987.

lxii

We are not provided with wisdom, we must discover it for ourselves, after a journey through the wilderness which no one else can take for us, an effort which no one can spare us, for our wisdom is the point of view from which we come at last to regard the world.

Marcel Proust[1]

Dear Erwin,

Thank you for inviting me to write.[2]

This is my story of my memories of the car. Is. Was. Earnestly.

When I was a child my parents did not have a car but they had friends who did. In particular there was Mr Bassett, an elderly architect, who used to take my mother, my sister Jennifer and myself for a drive on Sunday afternoons. I cannot remember why it was that my father didn't come, perhaps he used to sleep – he was a good deal older than my mother. Or perhaps he went for a walk? On afternoons when we didn't go for a drive he took us for country walks and taught us the names of the birds and the trees and the wild flowers. Some of them, anyway.

On our car trips we usually headed east into the mountains. We more or less had to because in the other direction was the sea. The only other choice was the coast road, north or south, but this we seldom took though we sometimes hit it on the way back. That's one rather odd thing about going for a drive in a private car – you have to come back to where you started from, you can't just abandon it when you get out. With public transport someone else takes the vehicle back and you are free to stay for as long as you like at the place you have reached. Much better. Transport should be a convenience, not an encumbrance, don't you think?

But I'm forgetting the thing that brought my childhood motoring to mind: I hated it because I was usually sick in the car, or else on the roadside immediately after shouting stop I'm going to be sick. But worse than being sick, which was a relief, was the driving miles and miles, up and up the mountain roads with their nauseating bends, while trying to keep my mind off the sensation of Sunday lunch (meat, gravy, vegetables, and one of my mother's delicious tarts or puddings) transformed inside me into a horrible-tasting substance threatening to fill up my mouth from the mysterious point beyond the tongue where one's outside ends and one's inside begins.

Eventually I got over car-sickness but while it lasted any suggestion that we were going in a car or a bus or a coach left me feeling awful. Once, when my mother and sister went on holiday by coach, my father took me by train to avoid the agony. Having to get a coach driver to stop while you're sick on the roadside, and then to wait while your parents get you some soda water and barleysugar sweets (which were supposed to make it alright for you to get back into the petrol-smelling atmosphere of the coach) is even worse.

When I was about eighteen I read of a competition to design the Car Of The Future and something made me very keen to try. To arrive at the design I examined quite closely the car of a friend, asking myself, for each of its features, how will this change, how will that? The car I examined was a Standard Eight (or was it Nine?) of about 1945, grey, with separate headlamps and mudguards and no projecting luggage compartment.

The design which came of reacting to what I saw as the faults of existing cars was a "double bubble", influenced I suppose by my strong interest in aeroplanes. The roof and windows become a moulded glass enclosure and the body was a streamlined egg-like shape with the mudguards, headlights, door-handles and other lumps submerged within it and the rear wheels half-enclosed. The twin headlamps were replaced by a single inset strip light.

The rear axle, engine, and luggage compartment comprised a detachable section that you could exchange at the garage for another when needing a service. This detached engine unit was very accessible and would put a stop to car mechanics having to work from underneath the car and having to struggle with nearly unreachable nuts and bolts.

The car was three people wide at shoulder level and could easily accommodate six with very adequate legroom at front and rear. To achieve this the wheels were reduced in size. By this means it became much more comfortable and could use less roadspace per person.

The car, which I modelled in balsawood and plastic, was one of the winners.

Looking at cars as they've evolved, closer and closer to my naive prediction of forty years ago, I've wondered why our future, automotively at least, was so predictable? Not only my entry to the competition, but the other entries which I remember, approximated quite closely to the subsequent history of car shapes. Had we been asked to predict social rather than technical events I guess I would have been completely wrong. I don't think anyone would have predicted the rebellions and changes of the sixties, still less the rise in oil prices or the new conservatism and conformity of the present. The futurologists didn't. Or the end of the car.

Technology, as we've known it so far, seems not yet to be historical, or fully human. Is that because it is stuck in the natural, the determinable, the spiritually and politically dead? What am I saying?

The first car I owned was a Riley Nine, of 1931, black, made of canvas and aluminium. It didn't rust. It had a crash gearbox and to learn to drive it you first had to master the art of "double de-clutch". Neither my wife Jeanne nor I learned to drive it properly, though we did manage the de-clutching, to shrieks of laughter and much danger to the others on the road. But usually the ignition wouldn't spark, despite frequent attempts to dry the magneto by putting it in the oven. The car spent nearly all its time in the garage until, after a few months, our first baby Susan was due and we had to sell the car for twenty pounds to pay for the pram, which cost twenty-five. No more cars until about 1957 when I began to earn more and Jeanne wanted relief from being housebound.

The next car we bought was a converted Ford van with side windows and plenty of space at the back for children and carrycots. Later we had a Ford Zephyr, and at the same time an Austin Westminster, lent me by the car seat maker for whom I was carrying out tests of seat comfort.

Then we bought the first of our Volkswagen campers, largely because they were the only cars with room for our five children. These became school buses for them and for some of the children living nearby. Also a series of little Fiats and Polos for Jeanne when later I commuted to work in the van. As we by then lived near the city centre, and my work was outside the city, this was "commuting in reverse", avoiding the congestion.

I have been running the last of the campers "into the ground" since 1972. It's still working well and gets occasional use, sometimes to help friends move their flats, or their children, or to serve as a mobile bed or work space. It's now fifteen years old and was last cleaned, and repainted, in 1982. But now I usually travel by train or by bus. I like looking at the people.

Why am I writing all this? I intended to be writing of the DESIGN of cars, and of traffic systems, not their individual use. But I guess that these reminiscences will turn out to be as relevant as the technicalities, possibly more so. Too much abstraction is perhaps what's wrong, and something is very wrong, with "the car" and with everything else that "we use". Or is it that the "it" is using us?

At the time when we had the Ford van and our second daughter Sarah was on the way I was working on the ergonomic design of one of the early computers. My employer, Harry West of AEI Ltd, left me free to explore widely before deciding how to tackle each new project. Hearing of this Michael Farr, the editor of Design, asked me to visit other computer makers and to undertake a wide-ranging study of the effects of computers on design.

I began this study by looking closely at "the industrial system as a whole", thinking, I suppose, that as the computer is a flexible and integrated thing its applications would be also. I imagined that the logic of this would bring about of its own accord the end of specialization and the beginning of a new kind of technology in which humanity prevailed and the mechanization of life would be over.

Perhaps the saddest bit of learning I've had to do in my life is to admit that this is not the case. Thirty years later most of the computer applications I see about me seem to have broken the promise of what I still see as the "gentle" nature of computers. The computers are being used to increase mechanization, not to supersede it.

But back to my investigation. "Why commuting?" That was the question from which I began to study the industrial system, and of the likely place of computers within it. Looking at the whole process of industrial work, in both factories and offices, I thought that this, the daily shuttling of large populations back and forth between polluted industrial areas and denatured suburbs, was the most stupid and contradictory thing in the whole picture, and the one most likely to be affected by computing. I saw it as a keystone which, once displaced, would permit the undoing of the whole mechanistic mistake.

And what happened? In trying for a precise answer to the question "why do we commute?" I was obliged to work out a new theory of manufacture,[3] comparing the structural differences between craftwork, mechanization and automation. My main finding was that the essential patterns in both craftwork and automation are compatible with the scale and tempo of the human body but the patterns in mechanization are certainly not.

My vision of "automation", as the way not only to "improve design" but to undo the mechanized inhumanity of centuries of misplaced industrial effort, was published in *Design*[4], where it attracted the opposition of liberal humanists. I felt then as I do now that this view of new technology as good is treading on sacred ground. Sacred to humanists perhaps? A point at which our culture might be revealed. Our actual beliefs.

Yes, this dream of a benign automation, if dream it is, is strangely unsupported by the realities of automation as I've seen it so far. Why? To answer that question is perhaps my present purpose. For the moment I still cannot say.

In 1959, I entered a competition to design "new roads for London". The sponsors of the competition wanted designs for a new road network to cope with the growth in the number of cars and other vehicles, already exceeding city road-space.

My approach to this was to look at traffic congestion, parking, and accidents (which I saw as the central problems of city traffic) and to ask myself "why, precisely, do they happen?". Only with proper answers to this question could a way be found to "remove the causes". (I didn't look as far back as to say "why not have fewer vehicles?" though today I might.)

To get at the causes of traffic congestion I looked for examples of dense traffic in other spheres of life, hoping to find some in which congestion and the other problems didn't happen. Then I might learn something.

The precedents I took were the movements of people on a piazza, swarms of bees, and flights of birds. I concluded that in each case the reason why congestion does not occur is that each pedestrian, bee or bird has sufficient advance information to anticipate the movements of the others and sufficient freedom of action to act on this anticipation, i.e. birds fly together as close as they can but not beyond the point where they infringe upon each other's freedom of movement. Each one keeps at such distance from the others that "congestion" does not arise.

When cars and other vehicles move on city roads this freedom is lost. The pattern of movements of the other vehicles is partly hidden. Drivers are prevented, by the road pattern, by the traffic rules, by low acceleration and braking power, from being able to use their intelligence to foresee congestion, and to act before it brings traffic to a crawl.

I gave similar thought to the questions of parking, accidents, and other horrors of city travel, in each case finding what I thought to be the principles for the design of "a perfect system".

So what can be done in practice? Plenty, I quickly discovered, as soon as you can see the way to end congestion and other traffic problems is not by pouring concrete and adding prohibitions but by providing information channels (to give the effect of "seeing round corners" and of "letting the others know where you want to go, how soon, etc, etc").

Of course this meant that my entry to the competition would be unlikely to please the judges for they were from the professions with an interest in fixed solutions and central control. "Trusting people" was not on their agenda.

So here it comes again, my recurring problem: what I saw as the inherently right solution was entirely compatible with the newest technology but it put me at loggerheads with the people in control. And, I'm sorry to say, with everyone else, for the assumptions of the rulers are also the assumptions of the ruled. Or most of them. For the moment.

The essentials of the plan (which I do not have space to describe properly here) were these:

A gradual evolution, in easy stages, each preparing the way for the next, over the twenty years 1959–79, from hopeless congestion to free-flowing automation. In the final stage of this all vehicles on city roads are automatically controlled for speed and route, and passenger-controlled for destination. Everyone, including children, old people, and those who are disabled can use the system as well as anyone else. Private cars, taxis and buses are replaced by driverless cars and minibuses which can be called to any pavement either by phone or by pressing destination buttons on converted parking meters. Everyone requesting a trip is given accurate predictions of journey time before the trip and during it. The time to a destination will of course increase unacceptably if too many people request it. My assumption was that when this happened some would defer departure or otherwise change plans until the predicted time fell to an acceptable figure. In this way the basic cause of congestion (the impossibility of knowing that it is there before you're engulfed in it) is removed, and intelligent behaviour becomes possible! Or so I assumed.

In this I am presuming that it is the presence of each of us that is accepted as "the real" and that "the system" is taken as variable, a fiction, a story that is being re-written all the time to suit the convenience of everyone. But not the convenience of the professionals who run it. That was the snag.

Other features of the system were these:

There is no parking problem because the automatic vehicles move off to respond to another call as soon as the last passenger gets out. And there are far fewer vehicles (most cars at present being stationary for more than nine-tenths of the time).

Nearly all traffic accidents are avoided because vehicles are automatically kept at safe distances and at moderate constant speeds (but double the present average traffic speed of about ten miles per hour at best) in single lanes with no overtaking. And all roads are fenced, or at a different level from the traffic.

(Thinking of this now I see that I did not give road-crossers the same rights as those in vehicles. That might be possible if the fencing is hinged, and openable according to pedestrian demands from push buttons at any point in the fencing, which slows the approaching vehicles to create a crossing space.... But this addition sounds as if it might bring everything to a stop and/or cause accidents. Is this a basic fault? If so, back to square one – it's a place I know well!)

There is no need for traffic lights as each vehicle keeps far enough from the one in front to allow crossing streams to pass through each other without stopping at intersections, just as do people walking in an open space.

There was much more to the scheme than this but I think I've remembered its essentials. The main practical point is that this solution to the problem of city traffic (still unsolved in every city in the world) was feasible with the electronics of the nineteen-sixties and could have been accomplished with the same effort and know-how that went into the moon landing. If that had been done then every major city in the world would have been free of congestion, of parking problems and of traffic accidents for the last ten or twenty years.

But what happened? Almost nothing. My entry to the competition was rejected and when it was published[5] ten years later, at a conference on technological forecasting, there was no response whatever. Why was this? That is a question I've often asked myself. My present guess is that this kind of scheme, though not particularly difficult to grasp or to carry out, called for big changes in self-perception, and in vested interests, that were not possible at the time. The difficulties, then, are "social".

One of them is that the scheme called for the abolition of private cars. It also means the closing down of some of the car factories (as only a fraction of the existing car output is needed if cars keep moving). It means a complete stop to the building of urban freeways, the scheme being feasible without making any change at all to the historic road plan of any city. This is the character of the new technology, properly used. It's localized, silent, and completely invisible. Nice. But it does not suit people who have adapted themselves to "the mechanical way of life". We have to change to get its benefits. The question is, can we? I sometimes think that adaption to mechanized living is "tragic", irreversible. If so, how are we to proceed with the post-mechanical?

There is one consolation I suppose. Many of the "bits" of what I take to be the perfect system for traffic automation have indeed appeared, piece-by-piece, in a much slower and more spontaneous evolution than the one I planned. For instance there are seeds of the ideal system in such things as air-radio reporting of traffic jams, linked traffic lights, tidal wave traffic flow, mini-cabs and mini-buses, electronic roadmaps, and electronic devices to control the distance between vehicles. And even in the growth of parking meters, road fencing, and one-way systems, if these are seen as temporary prohibitions, pending more flexible solutions.

I suppose I should have felt pleased at this, the capacity of "the world" to slowly and intelligently adapt to changes, outside the limits and stupidities of central planning. But I saw it as pathetic, compared to what seemed possible.

I was uneasy because I knew that to make my scheme work some people, somewhere, had to impose their ideas on others, "for their own good". That didn't seem right.

I wonder Erwin, what you now think about this question? It's something we've disagreed about, I seem to recall.

In 1962 I was asked to write something for a conference of lawyers talking about road accidents. My paper[6] was an attempt at a general theory of traffic collisions and was written with the aim of being able to see clearly, in a given traffic situation, what was dangerous about it and how to make it safer.

I began by asking myself why it is that traffic collisions occur? My answer was this: because, for one reason or another, vehicles or pedestrians fail to take avoiding action while there is still time to do so. (Considering this now I see that I was using the same strategy that I used to tackle congestion, but I didn't see that at the time. Only the scale is different.)

Looking more closely, I realized that normally each person in traffic keeps up a running prediction of the likely trajectories of moving objects (including their own bodies or vehicles) and of the capacity of each to take avoiding action. Each moves in a way that keeps everyone outside what I called the "withdrawal points" ("invisible safety envelopes" is a better name) around each vehicle or pedestrian. Within these envelopes collisions are unavoidable; outside them everyone has time to change to trajectories which do not collide.

Accidents are most likely to occur when these invisible envelopes move unexpectedly to new positions beyond which approaching vehicles or pedestrians have already traversed, as when the car in front stops unpredictably and you are too close to stop before colliding (though, for the expected deceleration of the car in front, you could have stopped in time). The invisible envelope of the car in front has jumped so that you're now inside it and bound to crash.

At this point Erwin, I'd better tell you my assumptions about "skilled performance" because, unless you know them, my theory may seem a nonsense. I'm not sure if we've ever discussed it.

My main assumption is that "only learners know what they are doing – skilled people do it unconsciously".

Learning a skill consists of teaching your nervous system to operate without your conscious intervention, as when you automatically look in the mirror, signal a turn and change gear while paying conscious attention to something else, perhaps to a conversation with someone in the car. You can drive for miles and not recall having stopped at the lights, turned corners, avoided pedestrians, etc, while driving safely all the time with your unconscious skills in control.... Safe driving (and safe road-crossing also) depend on everyone acting much faster than conscious thought.

If something happens outside the range of the skilled predictions you have taught your nervous system to make then your reactions change to those of a learner. Suddenly you make mistakes, become frustrated, over-conscious, and much slower. You have lost the pattern of predicting, and of readying actions before you need them. Then you can no longer look ahead but have to give all the attention you have to try to invent actions "in real time" while events are going too fast for you.

That's what happens in an accident, that and the attempts of your nervous system to snatch, from its repertoire, a series of sub-routines that may or may not fit the suddenly unfamiliar conditions. What we call panic.

Often, under stress, you will revert to an earlier skill. For instance, when angry you may speak in a local accent, or a mother tongue, that you have overlaid with a different way of speaking. What you have most recently learnt is the first thing to go.

Given these assumptions, and the "safety envelope theory", it is possible to look at a traffic situation (eg motorcycles in traffic, fog on motorways) and spot the kinds of accident to which it is certain to give rise. It is also possible to say which kinds of safety measures will remove the danger and which will not.

There is a lot more to the theory than I am saying here. There is for instance a categorizing of safety measures into four types: regularizing traffic, increasing perception, increasing manoeuvrability, and diverting impact energy.

This last of course includes the "soft car" option which you pursued in your thesis, and which I was astonished to see so well received by, was it, the Peugeot Company? I suppose it's the success of that which put you in the position to ask for this piece of writing and to get me back into the swim?

When I began to explain the logic of this to the lawyers (meeting in the incongruous Gothic rooms of the Law Society in London) some were angry with me because, according to my theory, "legal penalties" are as likely to increase accidents as to reduce them (because the laws assume conscious action in situations that in reality depend for their safety on everyone being skilled, ie acting unconsciously).

Therefore the responsibility for accidents does not lie with drivers or pedestrians but with those who make cars, roads, traffic laws and the like.

Given a particular traffic situation, and the unconscious nature of skill, certain kinds of accident are inevitable. And given a particular kind of road, eg a motorway or a city street, it becomes possible to see what has to be done to keep the speeds, the perceptual aids, the traffic rules, etc, so well matched to the skills and motions of drivers and pedestrians that the accident rate will be much less. That's what the details of the theory are about.

But as yet nobody has done this very fully though many of the well-known safety measures (eg traffic lights, rear-view mirrors and brake lights) fit the theory exactly. But still millions are killed and injured when, with thought and care in system design, nearly all accidents could I believe be avoided.

Though this paper aroused more interest than did my other attempts to do something about "the car", and the problems it creates, the people responsible for traffic and roads took no notice of it. At the time I used to think that, once something had been published in the technical literature, it was sure to be read and acted upon by those whose job it was to do so. But now, as I contemplate the reaction, or lack of it, to much that I have been doing all my life, I can see that I was wrong.

Ursula Huws said to me recently that new proposals and policies will not be effective unless those proposing them have a clear idea of how to get them adopted. For instance, you should know who, in a power situation, are the effective actors, the people who can influence events. And you should also know the pressures to which THEY are responding. In other words, without practical politics, ideas are dead.

But for a long time I've stopped trying for results. I've come to think that that way of thinking is part of what's wrong, part of the mechanical picture. What I'm describing here has to work without that conscious push, if it's to be true to itself, true to life. Done for its own sake. For the love of doing it.

As it says in *The Book of Changes*[7]

Nature creates all beings without erring: this is its straightness. It is calm and still: this is its foursquareness. It tolerates all creatures equally: that is its greatness. Therefore it attains what is right for all without artifice or special intentions. Man achieves the height of wisdom when all that he does is as self-evident as what nature does.

The plot thickens.

My last encounter with the design of cars was in the nineteen-sixties when I was asked to give advice on sitting comfort to John Cox, a manufacturer of car seats. For a start he asked me to forget about the seats they were making and to attempt a usable definition of "comfort". The only criterion in use at that time was, he said, "the managing director's bottom". Apparently this very shaky test was what the car companies relied upon approve or to disapprove of the seats which John Cox's company supplied. Occasionally "the managing director's wife" had a say also.

No-one in the industry could predict the comfort of a seat before it had been mass-produced and sat on by all the people who used the cars. And even then it was likely that no record of that great experience of mass sitting got back to the makers.

When I was asked to do this research I had worked for years on the size and shape of industrial seats and I was well aware of the excellent research done by R G Morant in the RAF, Ettienne Grandjean at Zurich and by my friend Alain Wisner at Renault (the first car maker to pay proper attention to ergonomics). But I had no idea of the specially arduous kind of sitting that is done by the many people who spend time cooped up in cars.

In response to this request I read a large proportion of the available literature on car seats, and on comfort. But even then I could see no way of defining comfort in a way that might be useful to the designers and the sitters. So once again I tried, from what information I had (and from journeys made in various kinds of cars, to observe my own sensations) to perceive the pattern of variables affecting comfort, as a prelude to devising a way of measuring it.

To augment my efforts I asked Ray Gray, Tony Ward, Gladys Moss, and others, to assist me by observing their own sensations in cars and in analysing the data.

The report[8] which emerged from all this took into account about 450 pieces of information which, when classified, formed an amazingly coherent picture.[9] The main variables became apparent as did many promising ways of improving the seats.

This time my report was well received, perhaps because it had been commissioned by a single person who was in a position to act on it without having to get the agreement of committees or having first to influence opinion.

His response was to ask me to proceed from this to making a usable technique for measuring comfort. This I did, with the help of Ray, Tony, Gladys and the large seatless Austin Westminster which the company bought for us to experiment with. In this car, fitted with experimental seats, we drove dozens of five-hour journeys up and down the motorways recording muscle sensations in various parts of our legs and backs. The result was better than I'd hoped. Despite the vagueness of the term comfort we found that there was reasonable consistency in the "discomfort ratings" assigned to different seats and plenty of indications of how to improve seats.

We found that the main influence on comfort is not the shape or softness of the seat but the size of the car. This is because, in a bigger car, your body is less crunched-up, ie the angles of the limbs at knee and hip are 90 degrees or greater. We also found that an upright posture, as in a van or coach, is much less fatiguing than is the cramped posture in a car. This is especially so for the driver as the nearly horizontal steering wheel in a van can act as a support which allows occasional changes from leaning forward to leaning back.

Sitting comfort comes of change, not static posture, no matter how well the seat fits the body.

As so often the result, once found, seems obvious, but, before we began, there had been nothing much to go on. Just rather weak theories, or hunches, which contradicted each other.

So how was THIS piece of work received in "the real world"?

lxxiii

Well, as I said, John Cox completely approved and he had only to instruct his colleagues to use the seat-testing technique for the results to reach the car makers and the public.

That is what did begin to happen. But then he sold the company to a larger one and I thought that that was the end of it. But, after the new owners had reorganized things I was approached again and began to give advice on their use of the testing method, and on the design of new seats, based on it, which they were supplying to various car makers.

During this phase I realized that even the owner of a company, though free to accept or to reject a new development from outside, cannot easily or at all control the speed or the intelligence with which the others put the idea into effect, or fail to do so. The "social obstacles" to one person controlling many are still there, even if the wished-for control may benefit everyone. Just as well I suppose. Was it my upbringing, in the capitalist culture, where the individual is hero, that led me to expect otherwise?

My learnings from this, and from other attempts to improve seats, were published in *Ergonomics* (as my goodbye present to the subject) in 1969.[10] I've not been in touch with the field since then so I don't know if the method of measuring comfort has been widely used or whether it's simply lying there, in the literature and perhaps in a few people's minds.

Still possessing the ancient VW camper, but for twelve years retired from the worlds of industry and academia, from the roles of designer, ergonomist and academic, this is the third time I've looked back in this way at my previous life, free now to write what I choose. The first was in *How My Thoughts About Design Methods Have Changed During The Years*,[11] in 1974, and the second was in *Writings Remembered*,[12] in 1976.

I come now to the nineteen-seventies and eighties, to my period "in the wilderness".

In these years I've made no more attempts to "improve the car", or any other part of industrial life, but have turned instead to art (especially poetry, music, film, theatre – the "time arts" as I call them, as antidote to design, which is largely spatial).

This is the period when I've despaired of doing anything "within the system" and tried instead to do what I can in smaller ways, with few resources but with greater freedom. It's also the time when I left job, accepted much less money, and left family life.

The gist of what I've been about can be read in two books from this period[13, 14] and will I hope appear in other books, written but as yet unpublished, or barely so.

Why did I turn away from "the world" and what has it to do with "the future of the car", the apparent subject of this long long letter?

Before answering, a pause, while I recall two incidents, in cars, that come to mind.

Because, for the moment, faced with those questions, I find no answer.

First: the Giraldus trip.

I'd always resisted reading *A Journey Through Wales*[15] (the account by Giraldus Cambrensis of his journey in 1188, ostensibly to recruit people for the Crusades). My father had urged me to read it and, when one day I saw it on a table in a London library, I opened it to the page where Giraldus describes my favourite place, the Dyfi estuary, near Borth, the village where I once lived and THE place to visit when we were children. The village was built on a storm beach.

I was charmed immediately. I set out in a few days in the camper, with a camera and a tape recorder, to travel his route – intending to read what he had to say about each place when I was at it.

On the way across England I'd decided to stop at the first recognizable place mentioned in each of his chapters, and, while there, I'd simply wait for the first person to come. Then I'd ask this person to read, for the tape recorder, the paragraph about that place, written nearly eight hundred years ago. And I'd also take photographs of the speakers and of the places where they stood. And of course I'd write an account of the trip,[16] just as Giraldus had done.

Everything worked perfectly. All kinds of people read the paragraphs and I had seven exhausting/exhilarating days seeing parts of Wales I'd never known and meeting so many people as I hurriedly tried to find "the spot" to which Giraldus had referred in all those places.

This was I think one of the nicest uses of "car" I have ever managed. (I am by now a lover of driving, never so happy as when on the road, and moving moving, over long distances. I don't like houses very much.)

Giraldus did the trip with packhorses. They were a large group, led by the Archbishop. Giraldus was intermediary, his father being a Norman baron and his grandmother a Welsh princess. Princess Nest, "the Helen of Wales".

At two points on the route I mailed taped accounts of the trip to my friend Edwin Schlossberg, in Massachussetts. I remember something he said on the tape in reply:

(This is a transcription of Edwin's voice into writing. When I listened there were many pauses, conveying the sense of "thinking happening". And driving too. In this version some of that is lost. It's best read slowly, and perhaps aloud.)

I'm driving along on the road
and
I always have a sense of
gratitude
that the road continues

it was an amazing moment for me in my life driving across America for the first time
and realizing that
"I kept going"

that no one

that the road didn't stop because
people went to have dinner

or
it didn't stop because people got tired of digging and hauling
and living for other people

it just continued

and I was able to follow that
just like that
old image of the king

being

walking down the path
that is unrolled for him by
the servants

the amazing thing about life is that
when it functions best each of us is a king
for all the other servants

and each of us is a servant for all the other kings

(long pause)

it's one of the reasons that I've gotten
very sensitive to the thought that

lxxvi
the only goal worth really pursuing
is to

love people very much

and that

requests for
new ideas

and new ways of thinking

and new things to make

is just part of
breathing

part of my biological process

but that

the thing
that isn't part of my biological process

which is most human

and the most difficult to ascertain
and to attain

is this feeling of being

really loved

being in love

by someone else

with someone else

that
most old idea
seemingly
of being in love

probably is
the newest idea

and not an idea at all

(pause)

I feel a
little bit
disassociated
talking

and not

and knowing that these won't be
words printed on a page
as a result of what I say

I'd like this to be words on a page written
so that I could read what I said

yesterday

just before I left where I was
I spent some time speaking with a little child who was describing a drawing that she had made

and her description of it
and the way she made that drawing

reinforced that sense about being in love

not only with one another

WITH one another

but with one's self

being totally accepting of
the dreams
that one puts together

lxxviii
chris you tell me a story

you told me a story once about the man whose coat kept changing parts

and yet it was still called a coat

it's funny that I never heard that story
in the way that I hear it now

which is that

it's a story about the living
it's about a person

and that each of us is that coat
more than the coat is

because

it's   uh

like Whitehead's old story
about how a rose is

should be very grateful to human beings for being here

because otherwise no one would know it was beautiful

and that coat wouldn't exist
or
wouldn't have that sense about its continuity without the living continuity of someone paying attention to it

this is some mysterious sense also

and I don't know any other word but mysterious to describe it

which has to do with

um
suddenly finding ourselves doing what we do

independent of
the
independent of the larger patterns that exist on earth

when I was younger I was overwhelmed

constantly

by the larger patterns
that existed on earth

not the small patterns

and
now
I'm weaving
I think both of them

my hand

my feet

are in coordination with my eyes

to steer this car down the road

and
the things
that

all the effects of all that

are in a sense
unconscious to me

but part of what allows the rest of me
the real
thing
to continue

lxxx
on my right I've
just passed a

house

that is called a mobile home

and

it's
it doesn't move

and I
used to think about that
and think about how awful it was that that existed

and then

and now

I start thinking about that
only in relationship to what I think could be the case

and what could be the case
is never

nearly never

as interesting
as what is the case

known
in relationship
to what could be the case

Well! I didn't mean to transcribe all that but now I have I can see it's relevance, to this, to everything. "Future of car", "wilderness", "comfort of seats","traffic", "accidents", "automation", none of these seems as real as it did. None of them is me, or you, or any of us.

And that is the question. Why are "we" so out of it, so uncentral to what's going on, in this century, this time, this world of objects, systems, goals (but always economic, never for the love of it, the love of our selves, of each other)?

If THAT'S the future of the car – you can have it! Take it away.

But the road, that's what I'd recalled, what Edwin said, about how it unrolls, for all of us. The invaluable substructure as Brecht called it, referring to the drains, the services, as well as the roads, which remained in the bombed cities of Germany though almost everything else was destroyed.

That's enough. That's what "the car" should be, no more than that. That's what it was in my traffic automation. A convenience only.

My favourite thought about "the road" is to do with the white line between the traffic streams. How IS it that this, and this alone, or even no line at all, is enough to keep very nearly every pair of cars (driven by us all at our most fallible, passing each other so close at double the speed of each) from crashing into each other? It seems a miracle.

I like to think of this as a nice example of "anarchy that works", of ordinary people, no matter who they are, being able and wanting of course to "act responsibly", once each is given "equal powers".

It's not the law or safety devices that make nearly every car pass the other safely on a two-way road, it's us, our immense capacities, normally unused, not certified or approved of, coming into play, in a situation which, though apparently very dangerous, is close enough to the human rhythms of the nervous system, and the senses of preservation and mutual respect, to bring out the best.

The car, being almost the only powerful machine that is open to everyone to use without prohibition, without central control, without professionals getting between us and it, is a freedom, yes.

A good precedent perhaps, in what we're heading for?

But to my second memory, the desert trip.

This was in 1985 when Annetta Pedretti, realizing that we both wanted to make the trip from Austin to California by land and not by air, looked up the costs of rental and provided the courage for us to travel by car. Over the deserts. About a dozen of them, by the time we'd driven back to Colorado to get on a plane for the opening of Eddie's exhibition in New York.

What a week, about nine days actually. And each day on the road was the same: several deserts to cross, each about 100 miles or more, with the distant hills or mesas visible up to about half that distance, as we slowly moved across those long straight roads of route 10, and others. In the Buick, a maroon one. Annetta called it The Buick Of Sighs, after Simon Usher's theatre group (the name is from a poem by Frank O'Hara).

The places. Fredricksburg, Sonora, Oxona (those two were I think just places to stop for coffee in low buildings with electronic games and car parks and real sheriffs and little else). Then Sheffield, Fort Stockton, Kent, Van Horn (more coffee), El Paso, Deming, Bowie, Tucson, Eloy, and on through Phoenix (where we left the route to go north and see Soleri's desert city, Arcosanti), then Glendale (with empty streets marked in the desert – 100th street, 400th street, etc, just signposts, nothing yet built among the cacti).

Quartsite (a new desert town perhaps 10 years old, composed only of mobile homes, some with gardens, with just a few schoolhouses, etc, in brick), Blythe, more deserts, and then to Palm Springs and the outskirts of L.A. Then we travelled through a valley planted with hundreds of standing windmills, an electric farm, perhaps one of the first serious efforts to switch to the wind, the sun, directly.

Days and days on the road.

Where are we heading for in L.A., it's about seventy miles across, I asked. The only place I know of is Sunset Strip said A, can we get there by sunset? Yes, and we did. Finding nowhere cheap to stay we slept another night in the car, parked on a piece of waste ground behind an illuminated sign. No blankets, a little uncomfortable. It was early summer. Our destination was the campus at San Luis Obispo, to take part in the architecture course, for a day or two.

And the driving? We shared that, each fighting for the wheel or else sitting back stunned at the sights, the distances, the dry air, the heat, the empty spaces. We wanted to stay. This is the earth.

Much more, but that gives the flavour.

It was not on that trip but another when Annetta, hearing me speak of my traffic automation scheme, said that she preferred the spontaneous growth of bits of it and asked why I hadn't tried to do something to encourage those, rather than plan the whole thing myself. She left me thinking that I was mistaken to give up because "the system" hadn't adopted it, and that I was behaving like an aggrieved designer, not as an active person.

I'm sure she's right but until I came to write this I couldn't see how to do otherwise, with any confidence.

I couldn't see how any such schemes as mine would work without there being first a plan, and also a public change of mind, of culture. A change in ourselves. That's why I turned to the arts and went "to the wilderness". Why I've subjected my recent works to the processes of chance,[13] as in the Giraldus trip, and out of that have begun to respect the ordinary more, you and I, everyone, and the amazing connections we overlook when pursuing goals derived from the centre.

But today, after rethinking all this, I've changed my mind.

The last step, in this journey through the past, was when I thought about my own use of the van, in London, and way that other city dwellers, and particularly taxi drivers, use their cars.

I realized that some drivers simply avoid travelling at the most congested times and on the busiest roads and one-way systems. If they are compelled to cross the city at peak hours they do so skillfully, using their slowly-acquired knowledge of which turns are banned and which roads are congested, and when. They travel mainly on the smaller roads, computing in their heads a route that avoids the many prohibitions of the official traffic plan (which forces nearly everything on to a few congested routes, and involves compulsory returns to where you were before, like snakes and ladders, if you depart from it).

As I contemplated the way skilled drivers get round this, I realized that it is very close to the way I expected the minicars and minibuses of the traffic automation scheme to operate....

And with that, I suddenly saw everything falling into place. Many of the details of the scheme, which are opposed by the static measures of the planners, re-appeared in my thought as extensions of what people try to do for themselves, despite the rules.

I remembered how impressed I'd been when I found that industrial systems come nearly to a halt when the operators are working to rule (rules made by the designers). And how well things run when the operators are able to cut corners and act on their own initiatives. So much so that "working to rule" has become a substitute for going on strike.

This week I had to walk up a long staircase from the underground because one of the new automatic lifts was not working. I asked the man attending to it why are they so often out of order. He said it was because there are so many safety devices and that these often jam when people hold open the doors to let in late-comers. "They're not designed for people" I said, as I've said so often of almost everything...

So then, out of these memories, and others like them, I saw it at last: the way to make sense of all this, to transcend the many conflicts between what I'd been proposing and what I'd seen happen.

THE SYSTEMS COULD BE "PEOPLE-DEPENDENT".

That was it. Everything came alive again. Slowly I began again to see that, if the machine parts, and particularly software, are designed on this principle, and if computing power is completely decentralized, the thing would work BECAUSE of people, not IN SPITE of.

No longer would designers try to make things "fool-proof". They'd have to find how to do the opposite.

A new world opens.

At each point the designed parts would be "incomplete", depending on anyone at hand perceiving what exactly is needed, just then, and getting the machine parts to do it. As when, in a severe traffic jam, someone gets out of a vehicle, sees what's needed, and then gives the instructions which enable everyone to become unstuck.

I'm enjoying this.

But I cannot plan it. No minority can. It depends on "everyone", on all of us. Not in our roles, paid by the centre, but in the new/old role of being what we are: "capable of anything", given the permission, given a technology that supports and enhances what we think and do.

How to do it?

That's a wrong question. It's not up to me, nor to any "designer".

It begins with the improvisations that happen anyway (the "not working to rule"), making these the precedents for how the technology is to be made and used.

Thus we the users, the public, become the designers (kings?). And in our paid roles (as public servants?) some of us follow those precedents in making the machines. Parts of the "people-dependent decentralized technology". (Whew!) The bits.

Or the breathing, as Eddie calls it. That's what engineering was meant to be, wasn't it? A service to everyone.

But now I remember something I wrote "from the wilderness" (actually I was on Hampstead Heath) in 1982:

...I was sitting on the grass above a little wooded valley...The sky was grey, the air warm, the grass and trees wild-looking, uncut, they had been growing fast. As soon as I began to listen I noticed three sounds: the leaves rustling in the wind, in gentle gusts, the birds, many, singing and calling all about, and the harsher more sustained sounds of traffic in the distance. I felt that in the difference between these natural and artificial sounds is the difference between the 'poetic' life on earth as it is, or was, and the 'enframed' life, as Heidegger sees it,[17] that it has become. What, I asked myself, is the difference, exactly? I wrote in my notebook:

"Traffic noises, so different, you can feel they are purposeful, but these natural sounds, they are just responses. That is the difference: the absence of enframing is that. I'm sure there can be a technology like that. A poem is a technology like that."[14]

As I think of that now I realize that no traffic scheme, mine or anyone's, not even the good hope of "a people-dependent technology", can make the difference if the goals, our personal goals, remain the same. If we are still in a hurry. A hurry that can propel us into a traffic jam even if we're forewarned of it....

The thought that must be somewhere in my mind as I think up and abandon scheme after scheme is surely a hope, not a command. The hope that, given the chance, we can let "the poetic" (that which does not follow from "the larger patterns" as Eddie calls them, or which disregards the "external references" as Annetta calls them) take over, the hope that we may have the courage to act as we feel, and love, and not as we seem propelled to. That's the question.

Can we "just respond?"

"I think the time of the car is over" said Annetta, when I showed her this, "don't YOU?"

The winds. The sighs.

But I'm not talking about the car. Or the bus. Or even the train. I'm talking about the system in reverse. I'm talking about people. About you and me. I'm talking about Mr Bassett.

And now Erwin I've come to the end of this story and my thoughts are running ahead to what could follow but there is no time for that. I have to post this off. But, if you, or anyone reading it, want to take it further I'm here, and once again ready to act, renewed by what I've learnt. I have the time, and the space, for some modest experiments. But not on my own.

I thank you, warmly, for provoking me to write, as I thank that page from Marcel Proust which got me going, led me to see what I might learn by looking back. I did not expect so much.

If you write something in reply I'd like it to be published here. No need to let me see it first.

best wishes

Chris.

John Chris Jones

My thanks to Edwin Schlossberg for permission to transcribe and to publish what he said. And for breathing!

1. Marcel Proust, *Remembrance of Things Past*, translated by C K Scott Moncrieff. London: Chatto & Windus, 1924, Vol 4, p228. (Elstir, the great painter, is telling the writer, yes, he was formerly the corrupt M. Biche.)

2. Erwin van Handenhoven, head of the systems and product design division at the Université de Technologie de Compiègne á Sévenans, asked me to write this contribution to E Van Handoven, The Non-agressive Car, Graduate Project PO, NHIBS, Antwerp, 1981.

3. J Christopher Jones, "Some Effects of Automation on Positions and Times of Work". Ergonomics Research Society Symposium, Bristol, April 1957. Unpublished.

4. Ibid., "Automation and Design 1–5", *Design* 103, 104, 106, 108, 110, July 1957 to February 1958.

5. Ibid., "A Credible Future for Urban Traffic", in *Proceedings of the First European Conference on Technological Forecasting*, Strathclyde, 1968. Edinburgh: Edinburgh University Press, 1969, pp369–388.

6. Ibid., "A Theory of Traffic Collisions", *Medicine, Science and the Law*, October 1962, pp489–499.

7. *The I Ching, or Book of Changes*, Richard Whilhelm translation, rendered into English by Cary F Baynes. London and Henley: Routledge & Kegan Paul, 1951, p13–14.

8. Internal report on car seat comfort, for Cox of Watford Ltd, Watford, 1962. Unpublished.

9. J Christopher Jones, *Design Methods*. Chichester & New York: John Wiley & Sons, 1970 and 1984. (Now published by David Fulton Publishers, London.) (See selections pp 350–355 and 371–374 for accounts of the car seat comfort research and pp 246–246 and 316–323 for accounts of traffic automation.)

10. Ibid., "Methods and Results of Seating Research", *Ergonomics*, Vol 12, No 2, 1969, pp171–181.

11. Ibid., "How My Thoughts About Design Methods Have Changed During The Years", *Design Methods and Theories*, Vol II, 1977, pp50–62, and in Spanner 17, Aloes Books: London, 1979.

12. Ibid., *Writings Remembered*. London: Jones Family Editions, 1976, (microfiche, available from the author).

13. Ibid., *Essays in Design*. Chichester and New York: John Wiley & Sons, 1981 (now published by David Fulton Publishers, London) (the first edition of this book).

14. John Chris Jones, *Technology Changes*. London: Princelet Editions, 1985, pp69–70. (Obtainable from Annetta Pedretti at 25 Princelet Street,

London E1 6QH.)

15. Giraldus Cambrensis, *A Journey Through Wales*, 1188. (Originally in Latin. Harmondsworth: Penguin Books, in English.)

16. John Chris Jones, *A Second Journey Through Wales*, 1979, with tape recordings. (Awaiting publication.)

17. Martin Heidegger, "The Question Concerning Technology", in *Martin Heidegger Basic Writings* (translated by David Farrell Krell). New York: Harper and Row, Publishers Inc., 1978.

Dear Chris,

Art & Automobile – the beauty of the car? – the beauty of the concept? I didn't expect so much either. Is it then that cars are that important for us or is it simply because of your rich experience in so many different fields? Anyhow, it left me thinking on various paragraphs. Here are some of the ideas.

In 1959, when I finished my first year of existence, you entered the competition to design "new roads for London". While you worked out the complex automised system of city traffic I probably tried to work out my first steps in the new world. I wonder if we had the same approach?

Like any system we both had an environment, an organisation (structure and interaction), and elements. I might have had a terrible job in dealing with the element (how to be a first-class walker) which would permit me, later on, to discover any environment. Organisation on the other hand, for instance how to cross a piazza, was none of my concern at the time.

I have the impression that the automatic traffic system, with that beautiful way of seeing automation, is mainly concerned with "organisation" and much less with "element" (the car). What if the sponsors of the competition had asked for "new cars to cope with the different road networks"?

This brings me to control and imposing one's ideas on others "for their own good". I still remember the spaghetti-meal in that small flat in Antwerp, about six years ago, when we discussed this question. I was convinced then, as I am now, that acting goes with thinking. And that, in order to act, one should be on the inside, not on the outside, of a system. But the whole point I think has to do with "imposing", or as I prefer to say, "making it happen".

If you propose a new system by its organisational characteristics rather than by its new elements you may indeed have to "impose" in order to make it happen. This is because built-up organisations ask for hierarchy, system control, system regulation and, very often, a change of habit for an important number of people. What's more, they are difficult to grasp and evaluate before they are applied in real situations. This may reject a lot of projects, especially if they are costly.

Driving a car means freedom of movement, exploration, choice. Extending human capacities. If this is the purpose why not have flexible elements (as we are) rather than rigid organisation? New car facilities don't need to be "imposed", a better network might be an automatic consequence. This is anyway what I tried to do in 1959 and ... as for the car, I have some ideas in mind.

In order to make it happen we need control. Control of the people? Control of the system? Control of the design process? I think the last one is in inverse ratio to the others. Only poorly designed things need to be looked after. They don't have enough built-in variation, they don't have enough storeroom to deal with a large number of situations. As you stated further on "sitting comfort comes of change, not static posture, no matter how well the seat fits the body". Can we generalise this as "systems comfort comes of change, not static organisation, no matter how well the system fits the person"?

The "soft-car" project, which was my first experience of car design, was done for O.N.S.E.R. (the present I.N.R.E.T.S. in Lyon, France, a national organisation for road safety) on a Citroen vehicle. As the study dealt mainly with pedestrian accidents the car problem was taken from somewhat different viewpoint. It had two aspects: the first one was how to prevent the car-pedestrian collision, the second how to diminish injuries if a collision occurs.

Some of the conclusions of the statistical and behavioural analysis for accident prevention were the following: Driving is a specific action, walking isn't. So pedestrians are not always aware of traffic rules – a false feeling of safety creates danger. A visibly dangerous situation creates caution. Pedestrians are better equipped for avoiding collisions than cars are, they have quicker reactions that are more direct and they have a higher acceleration. Many accidents are due to a wrong estimation of the vehicle speed by the pedestrian.

There were many more of them. Too many to go into detail. They showed that these predictions of the likely trajectories of moving objects you mentioned are of capital importance. Not only trajectory but also vehicle speed is necessary. (People are quite accurate in evaluating distance but far less accurate in evaluating speed. In order to decide whether to cross that road or not, you need them both, the distance of the arriving car and its speed.) The present cars tend to give more and more information to the driver but from the outside they are still mysterious objects. Paradoxically, "the non-aggressive car" (which was the title of the study)[1] ended up as a vehicle showing clearly its aggressive state (i.e. its speed) at a distance.

The second part was far more technical. Kinetics and dynamics of the pedestrian-car collision were analysed. Shape and structure of the "soft-car" were built up in order to diminish injuries both for children and adults.

You were right, Chris, the study was very well received. But only the second part gained interest. The part of the solution which one could hide

---

[1] See reference 2 on page xli

under the hood. The whole prevention concept was not their business although I still believe it. Prevention by well-designed elements rather than by traffic rules.

To the end of your letter, the roads unrolled for me. "The car should be no more than that" you wrote "a convenience only". Perhaps I'd prefer the convenience of shoes to that of roads.

Let's see where they'll take us both. On the road.

see you

Erwin

WE RETURN FROM ANGLE TO CENTER SUBSTANCE CHANGES

A complementarity arises where, in the act of distinction, a whole is severed. It is perceived as a complementarity where we perceive the whole severed by our distinction. Aspects distinguished are perceived as distinct where the act of drawing the distinction is itself passed over in silence. The distinction invoked between two aspects of a whole is brought into question where the act of distinguishing them is perceived.

Annetta Pedretti
The Cybernetics of Language

1
A THOUGHT REVOLVED

love, hate and architecture

or what is a method?

memories of a seminar in Bologna

This was written as an article for the architectural journal Zodiac, of Milan, in March 1973. The journal, which was edited by Maria Bottero, ceased before the article could be published.

When Maria Bottero asked for my opinions of "scientific" design methods as a way of "controlling the environment" my first thought was to refuse. My view of designing is deliberately unscientific and I hate the idea of controlling anything, even a hostile environment. Science implies sticking to what already exists and control implies lack of respect for something. Design implies respect for the new. However, Maria reminded me also of the happy times we both had at a seminar on design methods in Bologna* and I realised that it is human experience and not abstract theories that should decide what we do.

So, having agreed to write an article, I tried to find something to say that would include both experience and theory. What resulted is an imaginary conversation............The conversation is one of questions and answers. It is inspired by the notes I made while waiting for the translators to say what I had just said at the Bologna seminar. It is not, however, a true record of what was said, but a mixture of the thoughts, doubts and memories that I now have of the occasion.

My apologies to those who were present: they will realise how far this imagined conversation is from what actually happened.

*At the Institute of Architecture and Urban Planning in the Faculty of Engineering at the University of Bologna in 1971.

Q. What is the relationship between design methods and technology?

A. I don't feel that the relationship between methods and technology is the right question. Maybe its more helpful to regard methods not as things but as relationships, or as ways of enabling things to get into better relationship with each other. To me designing is a way of improving relations between objects and people. It is important that this relationship is two-way. Winston Churchill put it very well when he said "We shape our houses and our houses shape us". With the wrong methods one or both of these two life-shaping connections is missing. This two-way relationship should be one of complementarity such as exists between seasons, lovers, enemies, colours or between the observer and the observed (the uncertainty principle).

I guess that the big fault of industrial life is that relationships operate in only one direction but should operate in two. We now expect technical change to cause social change as a matter of course but attempts to make social change influence technology are still thought of as revolutionary. They should be normal. If they were, both "technology" and "society" should cease to be fixed objects or false gods. They would become ever changing elements of a new kind of living, something more like music or dancing and less like painting or sculpture.

Q. Is designing a process of mystifying or clarifying?

A. If a design method hides the real issues, it mystifies; if it reveals them, it clarifies. In planning a new university the methodologist, or analyst, could either accept or ignore the recent history of student protest. If accepted, the resulting plan might have, for instance, no separate departments and no administrative centre. If ignored, the plan would be conventional but it would be likely to provoke more protest later. In this case it might need extra buildings: for policemen.

Q. Is mystification inevitable if there is no theory, or frame of reference, within which to take design decisions?

A. To me theories are safe but temporary stepping stones across the dangerous waters of life, the unknown. But it is the unknown, not theories or principles, that are the source of the new. The whole point of transformation, the central part of the design process, is to change what already exists, and this includes both theories and practices. Each should influence the other. To make theory the master of practice is surely a form of repression! It is like being against one's children, one's ideas, one's unrealised potential. To make each responsive to the other is to create the conditions for love not hatred.

(At one point the seminar was forcibly stopped while the recording tape was changed. I objected to this as an example of letting the machine control the man, the part the whole. It seemed to me far better that some of the record was lost than that everybody's train of thought be broken for an ulterior technical purpose. This is an example of the very high sensitivity of human action to technology and of the very low sensitivity of technology to life.

How can this sensitivity be made to operate in two directions, particularly when the technology concerned is large-scale, as is a whole city?)

Q. Is there a conflict between designing, as a way of transforming life, and dialectical politics, as a way of acting historically against repression?

A. Within one's mind it is possible to see beyond both repressors and repressed to utopian transformations of life in which social conflicts are removed by the releasing of new life patterns. But to apply utopian thinking, to make it real, requires the political power to act against those who oppose the utopia. A designer would ask if there is any non-destructive means of changing the consciousness of everyone. McLuhan says there is. He believes that the existence of global electric networks, such as TV, irresistibly change everybody's consciousness by altering the mental processes by which we see the world. "What if he's right?"[+]

Q. Surely it is necessary to have some goals during the divergent stage of designing, when analysing the situation?

A. No. The purpose of divergence is to seek questions not answers. The effect of divergence is to deliberately create muddle and confusion in one's own mind, to upset one's own assumptions so that one can become more sensitive to existing reality and to new possibilities. There is no reason to fear chaos: it is our name for another form of order: that which we see as yet only in part. After exploring chaos one tries to "surface", to recover one's mental balance, to create a new picture of the problem, a transformation of the familiar and contradictory world in the light of the many different worlds it could become. But no transformation is possible if one keeps to fixed goals or aims. Very often it is mental certainty that turns out to be the underlying difficulty, the hidden control, the barrier to living.

Q. I liked today's discussion because there was conflict: we need conflict!

A. I did not like this conflict because too many speakers assumed that there are only two possibilities: logical agreement about theory or else a dialectic clash. Few seemed to believe that the deliberate searching for new syntheses by immersing and losing oneself in chaos is possible. But without this one is tied forever to the known and is incapable of dealing with what is uncertain, what is as yet beyond man. Historically we can see that "man" has always managed to reach what lies beyond. Woman too.

Q. What real difference is this plan* for a new university

*At this point we began to discuss plans for re-siting the the University of Bologna. +The title of Tom Wolfe's essay.

supposed to make to the lives of the people in it?

A. Apparently very little. To me it is hopeless even to discuss urban planning because it operates at too low a level to have any answer to this critical question. The new design methods are capable of being used at this higher level, that of life as it is lived, but nobody has yet tried to use them radically, in this way. What a challenge!

Q. What are the main constraints and variables in this planning situation? How stable or unstable is this view of what the constraints and variables are?

A. It seems, from the models and plans, that many things that will change during the life of the buildings (eg the existence of departments) have been built into the plan. In the accompanying book of the planners' thoughts and methods nobody has asked any fundamental questions about the activities of the people who will live in the new university. For instance how long will it be before education is carried out decentrally, using information media and practical experience of life, instead of centrally, using lecture rooms, libraries and laboratories?

Q. Why base a plan on traffic movements? Surely the activities which generate the traffic are more important.

A. Yes they are, but so far our new methods enable us to deal with traffic but not with the reasons for travelling. Is there a method of dealing with these too?

. . . .

References:

McLuhan, Marshall, Understanding Media, McGraw-Hill, New York, 1964.

Wolfe, Tom, 'What If He's Right?', in McLuhan Hot and Cool, edited by Stearn, Gerald Emmanuel, Dial Press, New York, 1967, (originally published as 'The New Life Out There', New York Herald Tribune, 1965).

4th August 1982:

I remember thinking what a pity it was that the planners were
thinking of moving half of the University of Bologna out of the
historic city centre into a plate-glass building in the hills.

Surely everyone would prefer to remain in the old city if that
were possible?

Perhaps with new technology it is.

Why not build an exact replica of every detail of Bologna I
on a site nearby
with exactly the same university buildings,
and all other buildings,
in which another set of people could continue the same style
of life:
Bologna II?

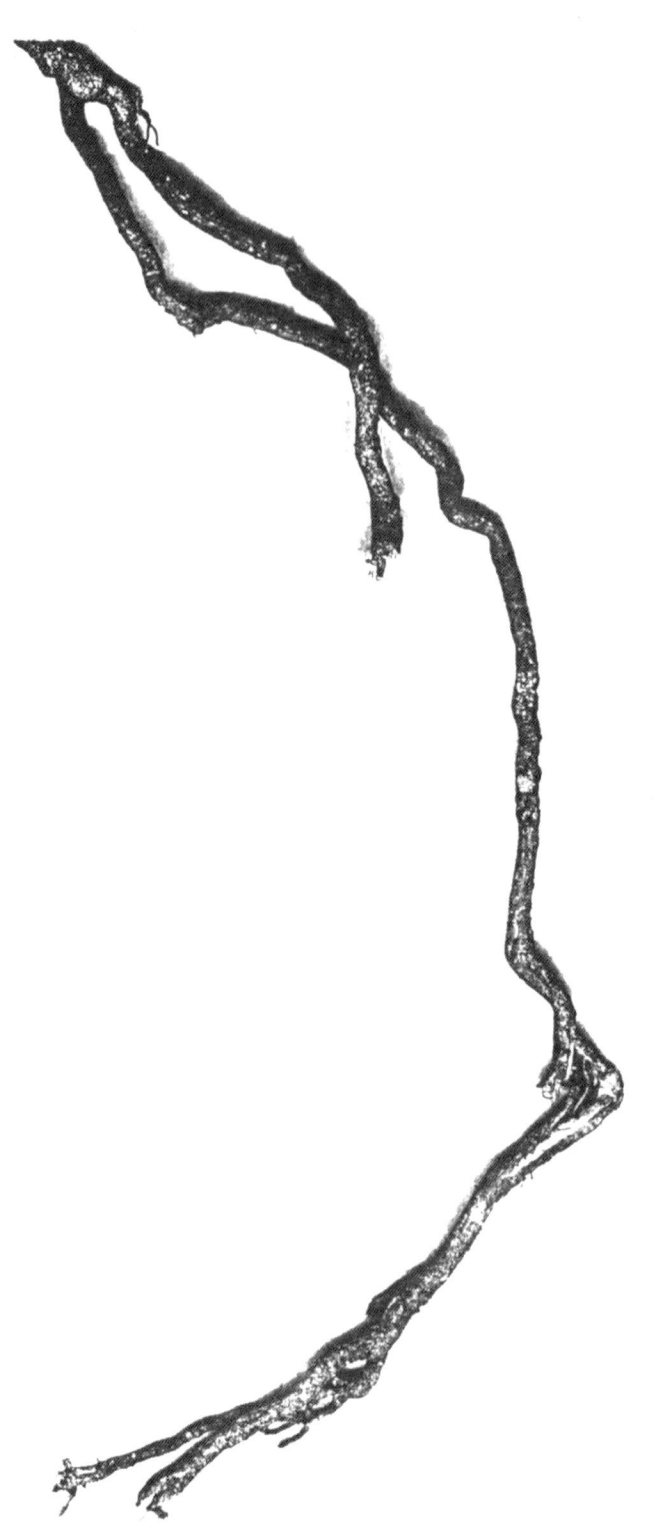

how my thoughts about
design methods have changed
during the years

This was written for Day Ding, in 1974, when he asked me to
lecture to the architects at Illinois Institute of Technology
at Urbana. He suggested the topic. The text has been left in
the original American typescript because retyping on this
typewriter would have changed the original line lengths and
hence the intention.

A paper written for the EDRA conference is described in the
essay: it appears later in this volume under the title Is
Designing A Response To The Whole Of Life?

The essay appeared first as an open letter to Day Ding in my
book Dear Architects published as a limited edition at the
College of Architecture at Virginia Polytechnic Institute and
State University in 1974. It was published in Design Methods
and Theories, volume 11, 1977, pp. 50-62, in Spanner 17, Aloes
Books, London, 1979, and in Spanish in Summarios, volume V, 28,
Buenos Aires, 1979.

HOW MY THOUGHTS ABOUT DESIGN METHODS HAVE CHANGED DURING THE YEARS

You don't know where you are
You don't know which way you're going

IN THE LATE FORTIES I BEGAN TRYING FOR WHAT I'D NOW CALL A HUMAN FUNCTIONALISM ie MAKING DESIGN THOUGHTS PUBLIC SO THAT THEY ARE NOT LIMITED TO THE EXPERIENCE OF THE DESIGNER AND CAN INCORPORATE SCIENTIFIC KNOWLEDGE OF HUMAN ABILITIES AND LIMITATIONS.

Surely that's one of the most human things in life
To be wrong
We all know that we have more affection for others when they're wrong
than when they're right
Sad, perhaps.
Some people called them systematic methods originally,
They've been mainly rational.

WHAT I BEGAN TO DO WAS TO RELATE DESIGN THINKING TO OBJECTIVE OR SCIENTIFIC FACTS ABOUT HUMAN PERFORMANCE.
WHAT IS NOW CALLED ERGONOMICS.
OR HUMAN ENGINEERING.

ALSO I WAS TRYING TO ANTICIPATE NOT IGNORE SIDE-EFFECTS.

This still has not been done, or applied at any large scale outside

the military fields.

But to apply this knowledge to life in general seemed to me

And still seems

An appropriate thing to do.

But it couldn't be done unless the design process

The thinking

The reasons

That led to the lines on the drawing board

Could be spoken about in clear language

Such as a scientist uses when he writes a paper about how people do

this, or how metals do that.

But the design process was illogical and all this knowledge was logical

So until you had a logical design process

You couldn't join the two together.

Could the car be adapted much more to the people inside it?

We looked in enormous detail at the process of eating

We discovered all the kinds of food and all the actions of eating

The result was nothing like the knives and forks we now use

Our designs looked much more like dental instruments

IN THE FIFTIES I WORKED IN THE ELECTRICAL INDUSTRY TRYING TO FIT DIALS, CONTROLS, SEATS, CONTROL ROOMS ETC TO THE HUMAN OPERATORS.

THERE WAS ALSO THE GROWING NEED TO DESIGN LARGER ENTITIES THAN PRODUCTS: COMPLETE SYSTEMS OF MACHINES, GROUPS OF BUILDINGS, URBAN CENTERS.

Everyone was coming to realize that all was not well with technology after all, it was creating problems as well as solving them.
All the equipment I'd ever handled seemed very badly designed in that none of it took account of side effects,
Road accidents for example.
I suppose the trip to the moon is the best example of a complete system which eventually worked after many failures and which used this kind of thinking

IN THE SIXTIES THE SITUATION CHANGED

THERE WERE MANY CONFERENCES ON DESIGN METHODS ENVIRONMENTAL SYSTEMS AND RELATED TOPICS.

I WROTE THE BOOK DESIGN METHODS,* A REVIEW OF THE LITERATURE, AND I BECAME A TEACHER OF DESIGN

AND I BECAME ACTIVE IN WHAT'S NOW CALLED FUTURES RESEARCH

They all wanted a complete recipe,

It appeals to the Latin mind, especially,

A lot of the design methods literature has been translated into Spanish and Italian, I'm sure its no accident that this is so.

There was one student who came to us from Argentia

"When" he said

"Chris, are we going to get the Grand Panoram?"

And this grand panoram didn't exist as far as I knew,

But he expected a complete ideology

Worked out & fully finished.

Many people wanted this and perhaps all students want it all the time

But I feel one should resist any such thing

If one's to continue living

Other than in the form of a

Intellectually speaking

Or actually speaking

I WAS SEEKING TO RELATE ALL THE DESIGN METHODS TO EACH OTHER,

AND TO EXPERIENCE.

I FOUND A GREAT SPLIT HAD DEVELOPED BETWEEN INTUITION AND RATIONALITY, REASON.

THERE WERE BLACK BOX METHODS LIKE SYNECTICS WHICH WORKED WELL BUT NOBODY KNEW WHY
AND GLASS BOX METHODS, LIKE DECISION THEORY, WHICH WERE LOGICALLY CLEAR BUT WHICH DIDN'T WORK.

What I could see was this...
What did I find out...?
We'll I found,...
In writing it...,...that book
A standard method of describing each method, so that they could be compared.
What's striking is that each method begins with a first stage that is extremely difficult to do
Which has no description of how to do it
Which is intuitive.

WHAT EMERGED
IN WRITING THE BOOK
WAS THAT TO USE DESIGN METHODS ONE NEEDS TO BE ABLE
TO IDENTIFY THE RIGHT VARIABLES
THE IMPORTANT ONES
AND TO ACCEPT INSTABILITY IN THE DESIGN PROBLEM ITSELF

ONE HAS TO TRANSFORM THE PROBLEM AND THE SOLUTION
ALL IN ONE MENTAL ACT OR PROCESS

Where is the essence of the subject?
For me the word in the index with the most sub-entries to it
Is "Instability of Design Problems"
Which has about ten entries
The whole problem becomes more unstable as you widen it
As you take more and more of life to be part of the problem you
don't get a more stable problem you get a less stable problem.
And this I think is not what the rationalists like.
I think that people who approach this subject because it seems
rational are those who like certainty in life.
If you wish for certainty you might as well leave this subject alone
Because design is to do with uncertainty
As far as I can see
But a lot of people who do wish for certainty do dabble in it
And I fear they're wrecking the subject
....
Especially transformation became evident...
How to get from divergent thought to convergent thought.

I WAS AT THE TIME DOING DESIGN RESEARCH INTO CAR SEAT COMFORT, OFFICE DESKS, SLIDE RULES USABLE BY SCHOOL CHILDREN, AND TRAFFIC AUTOMATION SYSTEMS

Incredible isn't it, the world is full of things, like slide rules, that college students with an IQ of 120 or more, can use, and the rest of the population, with a normal IQ, of 100, can't use.
Things like telephone handsets, which are used by the public, are extremely difficult things to design
Because you've got to design them so that a very large percentage of the whole population can use them.
A very interesting concept this
What percentage of the population can use your design.
You may say, if you're designing a building, that the whole lot can use it.
But I wonder.
The number of people who are too big or small to use it is quite high, millions.
Large numbers of old people, children and poor people don't use telephones
They've never got used to the difficulty.
They may use them for local calls but they can't possibly cope with complicated calls.
Even though its an extremely easy thing to use and there are operators waiting to help you.

IN THE SEVENTIES I REACTED AGAINST DESIGN METHODS.

I DISLIKE THE MACHINE LANGUAGE THE BEHAVIOURISM, THE CONTINUAL ATTEMPT TO FIX THE WHOLE OF LIFE INTO A LOGICAL FRAMEWORK.

ALSO THERE IS THE INFORMATION OVERLOAD WHICH SWAMPS THE USER OF DESIGN METHODS (IN THE ABSENCE OF COMPUTER AIDS THAT REALLY DO AID DESIGNING).

I REALIZE NOW THAT RATIONAL AND SCIENTIFIC KNOWLEDGE IS ESSENTIAL FOR DISCOVERING THE BODILY LIMITS AND ABILITIES WE ALL SHARE BUT THAT MENTAL PROCESS, THE MIND, IS DESTROYED IF IT IS ENCASED IN A FIXED FRAME OF REFERENCE.

My experience of design methods in the seventies has been of writing papers against the subject.

I received a letter asking me to write a paper for the EDRA conference and instructing me how to do it.

The writer of the letter outlined in ten pages what were the conditions applying to writers of papers for this conference

Use no more than five pages.

He'd adopted the whole language of behaviorism to describe to his captive authors exactly how they should do their papers.

And much as I like the man who wrote the letters, I like him very much really as a person, I still felt pretty annoyed at this sheaf of instructions he sent out

And I thought to myself "I wont give this paper, I'm damned if I'm going to...after all this time in this field to be told by him...he probably wasn't alive when I started in it...exactly how to write a paper."

And I felt how insulting really that we have all this mass of machine language instruction which we send to each other

In a bureaucratic manner

Throughout life.

Not only for arranging conferences.

....

At that time I suddenly got interested in chance processes

And I discovered the works of John Cage

All about how to use chance to compose music and to compose lectures

And he says in there

If you receive a nasty instruction

You could refuse it,

You could protest strongly to the person who sent you the instruction

Or you could do what he John Cage does which is, apparently,

To obey the instruction & then do more.

Its tedious & arduous but a nicer way of responding

So I braced myself a bit

I stomached all the instructions

In five pages exactly.

I composed the paper by chance

Its got characters in it who speak

Its got a character called EDRA

And its got Walt Whitman, who speaks another kind of American other than machine language

Its got Kant, who speaks machine language very much better than we designers do

Its got Jung who says that no method is any good unless the right person uses it

(which is an ancient Chinese view taken from The Secret of the Golden Flower)

And its also got some remarks by Graham Stevens

The man who left architecture as a student in the sixties to become one of the leading people in inflatables, or blow-ups.

Perhaps you saw him walking on water at the EDRA conference

In a blown up plastic bag.

I introduced Graham into the paper because his account of how he did it was so clear-cut.

He said

"We were fooling around with balloons & one day we got the idea of making them huge & filling them with water, all sorts of things, and that led to my life in inflatables."

Behaviorism, of the Skinner kind, had taken total command of the architectural part of design methods by this

and I still feel that's a mistake.

WHAT I'M DOING NOW IS EXPERIMENTING WITH CHANCE PROCESSES
(THIS PAPER IS COMPOSED OF A CHANCE MIX OF MY LECTURE
NOTES, IN CAPITALS, AND RANDOM SAMPLES FROM A TAPE
RECORDING OF THE LECTURE, in small letters).

I AM ALSO TRYING TO FIND WAYS OF INCREASING PERCEPTION,
AND OF REDUCING ACTION, IN DESIGN, SO THAT WHAT'S NEW
IS MORE SENSITIVE TO WHAT'S ALREADY THERE.

I'M REALISING THAT IF DESIGNING IS APPLIED TO LIFE, NOT
JUST TO PRODUCTS, SYSTEMS AND SOFTWARE, THERE HAS TO
BE MORE POLITICS (IN THE ATHENIAN SENSE) (TWO-WAY PROCESSES)
AND LESS PLANNING,
IF DESIGNING IS NOT TO BECOME TYRRANY.

I'D LIKE TO TRY OUT EXPERIMENTAL DESIGNS, WITH NO CLIENTS,
AIMED AT RESPONDING TO LIFE AS A WHOLE NOT JUST TO A
SECTION OF IT
AND,
TO COMPENSATE FOR THE EXCLUSIVELY VISUAL & SPATIAL
QUALITY OF DESIGNING AS IT WAS
I'M TRYING TO LEARN FROM THE TEMPORAL ARTS: POETRY,
FILM, MUSIC & THEATRE.

SOME CONCLUSIONS

What seems to have happened is this:
- an extension of the scale and influence of design processes, to take account of side-effects and of the integration of products into systems
- a search for greater precision & certainty in knowing what fits human bodies and abilities
- greater uncertainty and instability of design problems as they include more of life.
- psychological & social resistance to these effects, resulting in design methods being neglected by the professional designers but florishing as a rational but useless academic game.
- political resistance to the extension of planning, to the fixing of life in a rational mould
- data overload (as yet unhelped by computer aids) which prevents designers applying the vast existing knowledge which could otherwise permit a truly "human functionalism"

Generally design seems to be becoming a social art & to do this properly it seems we need to learn from experimental artists whose happenings & other events are making art a way of living.
Both art & design at last seem like meeting, across the Cartesian split of mind from body, to enable us to find a new genius for collaboration

not in the making of products & systems & bureaucracies but in the composing of contexts that include everyone, designers too.

To be a part.

To find how to make all we do & think relate to all we sense & know, (not merely to attend to fragments of ourselves & our situations.)

It was a question of where to put your feet.

It became a matter of choosing the dance

Now its becoming

No full stop

*Design Methods, John Wiley & Sons, New York & London, 1970.

now we are numerous

introduction to the Spanish edition of
Design Methods

The Spanish edition of Design Methods was published as Metodos de Diseno, translated by Maria Luisa Lopez Sarda, by Editorial Gustavo Gili, S.A., Barcelona, 1977. The third amplified edition, with additional material translated by Esteve Riambau i Sauri and bibliographic revision by Joaquim Romaguera Ramio, was published by Editorial Gustavo Gili S.A., Barcelona, 1982. Permission to reproduce this essay is gratefully acknowledged.

The reference to 'being numerous' on the last page was inspired by the verse:

> Obsessed, bewildered
>
> By the shipwreck
> Of the singular
>
> We have chosen the meaning
> Of being numerous.

from the long poem Of Being Numerous by George Oppen which appears in the book of that title published by New Directions Books, New York, 1968.

I have been asked to write an introduction to the Spanish edition of Design Methods so that readers in Spain, Portugal and Latin American countries will know what I now think of the subject and of its application to the problems of the present time.

My thoughts about the subject have not changed since, in the late forties, I found myself drawn to find ways in which it might be possible to make the man-made world of machines and industrial living better fitted to human life. At that time I imagined myself to be alone in this search because all the machines and ways of living with machines that I knew of seemed in some profound indefinable yet very real way to be inhuman; yet they are the main results of human effort through many centuries. Today, after a quarter century, an amazing quarter century, of efforts to humanize industrial life and methods, the problem remains unsolved; but its now much bigger.

During these years I found I was not alone in wanting to find ways of removing the obvious inhumanity from industrial work and planning; there have been many designers, thinkers, critics and activists who have tried in a variety of ways to change the methods and practices of the professions and to bring the public into the processes by which industrial life is formed. Some of these methods I described in the original introduction to this book and others have appeared since. But something has gone wrong. In ways that are clearer to me now than when I wrote it this wealth of new thinking seems not to have had the effects expected, at least by myself. Instead of being the means by which professional practices in design and other fields could be despecialized and made more sensitive to human needs the new methods have become convenient tools for larger and more rigid planning and have also become the means of making design into a barren academic subject removed from life, from the lives of those for whose benefit its supposed to exist, ourselves as consumers and users of industrial products. More and more we recognise ourselves not as users of industrial life but as non-persons, tools, objects that are used by the system. What has gone wrong?

It is tempting to blame the methods, to say that they are

inherently abstract, technocratic, inhuman, that they are a part of the inhumanity which persons such as myself say we were trying to remove from industrial products and the life that goes with them. It is equally tempting to blame the professions, the system, the status quo, to say that the new methods have never been properly used but have been resisted, that they have been limited to narrow applications which support specialization and prevent the questioning of the way of life. Certainly I would now agree that it was naive to have imagined that methods by themselves (and they are not selves, they are, as I found myself writing in chapter 5, "mere symbolic contrivances") that methods alone would remove the error of centuries of industrial evolution. But to imagine that it is possible to change the pattern of industrial life without, among other things, a collective language to replace and make public the up-to-now private and largely unvoiced thinking of professional designers and planners is surely naive too. One of the things I discovered while writing this review of the literature on design methods was, as is explained in chapter 6, that there is a big distinction between system-designing (which fits products to each other and to existing social organizations) and the wider process of what I then called socio-technical change (the fitting of products and systems to newly emerging forms of society). The section of this book that I most enjoyed writing, but which I'm sorry to say is the least used so it seems, was chapter 5, and particularly the last part of it in which the purpose of design methods is discussed. Re-reading that today I recall the sentence in which I attempted to condense this purpose as I see it: "methodology should not be a fixed track to a fixed destination but a conversation about everything that could be made to happen."

So to me now, as in the past, the purpose of seeking changes in methods not only in design but in all departments of life is to change the pattern of life as we make it, artificially and collectively, not to support the status quo and the inhumanities we inherit but to permit the composing of a form of life that is free of the errors of specialization and of alienation. To make a way of living that is beautiful, (can laws be beautiful, can work, can millions of people act together as trusted friends not

as distrusting manipulators of each other's lives?), to attempt
the best we can imagine and to use all intelligence to make it
real.

This aim, this purpose, this ideal, is not, I see now, implicit
in the methods, in the ink and paper in which they are composed.
Any aim that was would be a form of built-in control, another
inhumanity. The new methods can, like the alphabet and the
numerals, be used to say no or to say yes. But, like the alphabet, they permit communications that are otherwise impossible,
they increase the scale of human action and in doing this they
make ideals such as that I've just proposed more possible than
they were before. New methods cannot force us to do good, nothing
can, but they do change the context of designing. There is a
morality in widening the scope of life; what was before inevitable
becomes now a conscious choice. And once this widening, this
prior liberation, has occurred it is no longer realistic but
insulting to refuse the new ideals and purposes that now are possible. Industrial life HAS changed its nature in recent years
and thus includes the means of pursuing aims never tried before.
Of course the enlargement of what is possible includes the enlargement of what is bad as well as good, that is the risk,
unavoidable. A new responsibility for which the institutions
and professions and roles we inherit are surely unable by their
form and nature to respond.

Why then is there no sign of a new and larger beauty emerging
in the form of human life, why do we see nothing but growing
problems and greater inhumanities in the patterns of industrial
development throughout the world? And why, in design and planning,
are the new methods being used, if they're used at all, to make
life more uniform homogenous and alienating? The question feels
too difficult to answer but I'll try. Is it because we have
refused, so far, to see ourselves as real, as persons not as
ciphers, not as the objects which industrial living has forced
us to become? Is it that we have accepted as natural a bleak
vision of human nature, of man as the paid and helpless minder
of machines needing to do nothing but survive in ever growing
numbers? There are now several billion of us and soon more and

I for one rejoice in that. I cannot see that the presence of people is a problem if it is allowed that each of us is really human, whatever role it is the system has recently been forcing us to play. We ARE numerous:that is the challenge, the new excitement of life now as it never was before. It's time to change our aims, to see ourselves collectively as different, as able to respond to the new conditions of human life.

In writing these words I recall with pleasure the many Spanish speaking students, good friends, who have come to study design methods here in Britain, and particularly Arturo Montagu of Argentina who suggested that this introduction should be written.

                                                    J.C.J.
                                          London, 1976

beyond rationalism

an interview

with questions by Marina Waisman,
Arturo Montagu and Ricardo Blanco

Marina Waisman edits the architectural journal Summarios and teaches architectural history at the Catholic University at Cordoba.

Arturo Montagu is a design consultant and teaches design research at the Universities of La Plata and Belgrano.

Ricardo Blanco is an industrial designer and teaches industrial design at the University of La Plata.

The interview took place at the Summarios office in Buenos Aires in April 1979. A version of it was published in Spanish in Summarios number 28 in 1980. It is reproduced here with permission of Ediciones Summa S A, Buenos Aires.

The typing of this version was a little experiment in trying to find a form of writing that retains some of the liveliness of speaking-while-thinking and does not impose on it the order of grammatical texts. In all but a few lines I have retained as much of the informative pausing, hesitating, and revising-while-saying that I could perceive in the transcript. I was surprised to see how much more intelligent speech appears when one reproduces its accidents than when one edits it into grammatical form.

Marina Waisman began the interview by referring to the article How My Thoughts About Design Methods Have Changed During The Years. She said how surprised she was, and glad, to see so poem-like a piece of writing coming from one she had imagined to be concerned only with the rational approach to design.....

CJ: There was a phase in the sixties
when many architects had a mania for design methods
but
it wasn't everyone that had the mania
I think it was only the rational part of design methods
which became popular
and it only became popular
with the kind of person who is very keen on rationality.
In this paper which you pointed to
I think I say something about certainty.
The rational method
gives you the impression you can solve the design problem
with certainty
with mathematical certainty
and the kind of person who likes that
is not really a designer.
He is a person who should never have been in design.
It is not to do with certainty, design.
Design is creating the new.
The new is always uncertain
that's the whole idea
and you do need rationality
but you need it to allow you to have the courage
the courage to expand further.
Rationality is usable to help you go along the way
into more uncertainty.
But the rationalist's decision theory
for instance
creates a box of a million possibilities
and then
like a machine
you look at these possibilities.
But its not the idea of looking at each item in the box

the list of all possibilities.
The real creative thing is finding where the edge of the box comes
and then saying
OK
what's outside it?
You couldn't look outside until you had the box.
It expands your view.
But to spend your life in the box is sort of wrong
as you...

MW: That's the idea of the blackbox
where you put everything that you can't understand

CJ: No. That's not quite right.
The black box is a more creative idea
the glass box is the rationality
where you can see everything

MW: But (whatever?) this blackbox is
you put inside everything you don't know where...

CJ: I don't think you're quite right there
the black box idea is your own brain
its not something outside the brain
and its called black box in cybernetics
because nobody knows how the brain works.
You know
something goes in through the eyes and ears
and something comes out from the mouth
and its a mystery.
So its called black box because its like the magician's box
you see
and that's the meaning of black box
so that one accepts the idea that there is a mystery
in the brain
and if there wasn't we couldn't be creative.

MW: But if you put the blackbox in a certain

and very definite
moment of the process,
its not true...

CJ: No, you do it all the time.
Yes, all the time.
These formal methods
for doing brainstorming or synectics
etc
I think they are valuable.
They are blackbox methods.
Its important to use them
I use quite a lot of formal methods
with some discipline
all the time.
But I try to use them in a new way each time.
The individual methods are not the whole design process.
The whole design process is everything you do
and other people do
and within this you may use this method
and that method
and something else you thought of
and a person comes into the room
and they say something
and that becomes part of what you do
and everything is the process.
And the really good thing
I think
about this subject of design methods
is that you should be more conscious
of how you organise your own design process
and not just be confused by it.
You should leave perhaps one third of your time
you know
for argument's sake
a good proportion of the time
to say
"Are we using the right process?"
Now

I would say its no delight doing this
because it stops you
you know.
I know it looks as if its going well
but then you say
"Are we going in the right direction?"
"How are we doing it?"
Keep on asking "How?"

MW: So you think that one must be conscious of the process...
at least at certain moments
not all the time?

CJ: Well, very often,
in designing a building
for instance
a house, or a hospital, or something,
its going...
and you know from the beginning
its going to be pretty like
the usual hospital
and the usual house
so, then,
its silly to use elaborate methods
and all this stopping.
But sometimes you're designing something nobody has ever done.
You're trying to design
for instance
a system of modular coordination
that's very difficult
and no-one has done one right yet
I think.
You know
I think all this modular work
so far
has been mainly wrong
and lots of modular systems exist
in architecture
but people don't like using them.

You have 'moveable partitions' and nobody moves them.
All this kind of thing.
They stay there like concrete
you know.
And there are all sorts of difficulties
like that of trying to make a building with new forms of energy
solar energy
and things.
Nobody knows how to do it.
So
you cannot use an existing process
when you're in that kind of problem
with novelty
and a need for innovation.
Then you need to 'design the designing'
let's say
as well as design the output of the designing.
And this designing the designing
is really the whole thing.
'Designing designing'
that gives the feeling of it
its a rather poetic phrase
rather than mechanical
it sort of lifts you up a bit?

MW: But what about all the new enthusiasm for typologies?

CJ: What is 'typologies', now?

MW: The idea of having a precedent type
a building type
and from this working on all the new projects.

CJ: I'm not familiar with this.
A new enthusiasm for typologies?
It sounds to me like what they used to do in the old days.

MW: Yes, this is the reactionary-vanguardist type...

CJ: I think we're now in a terrible period of looking back.
I think the sixties were
psychologically, politically, and sociologically,
and everything else,
upsetting for everybody.
And even the revolutionaries now
are wearing suits
and pretending that they like the 1930's
or some earlier period.
And everything you see on television,
people are dressing in pre-war clothes,
this kind of thing.

MW: Yes, yesterday I saw in a restaurant
a lady exactly like William Morris's wife.
It was incredible.

CJ: I call this the back-to period
you know
and I think of it like the waves of the sea.
I was brought up by the sea-side.
I used to watch the waves coming across
and they hit the promenade,
the stone wall,
and the wave made a big splash.
And then another wave is reflected back from the wall
into the sea
the reaction wave
and that destroys the next wave that comes.
And the second wave behind that
is also destroyed by the reaction wave
and it doesn't reach the wall either.
But this reaction wave then dies.
The reaction wave doesn't have much life in it.
Then another wave comes from the sea
and that does reach the wall!
I think that now in the seventies
we're in the reaction wave
and some pessimists think that the sea will produce no more waves.

But I think there'll always be waves from the sea
and that there will be no more reaction waves
unless the waves reach the wall.
Its only as a result of the success of the sixties
that we have the reaction.
There would be no reaction
if the sixties wasn't quite successful
I think.

MW: Well, that's a very positive way of looking.
I was thinking that the seventies were the day after the party
a beautiful party
and the day after that
we are disenchanted
and so sad
and with headaches
and all this...

CJ: No, I think positive things have a life of their own.
Negative things live on the life they borrow from the positive.
Negative things
in the whole of the universe
don't generate life.
So you need never fear the negative
because it is death
it dies very rapidly
its made of death.

MW: That was Croce's idea also
of history
that the negative periods
were only to make better...

CJ: Yes, but we do need the pause.
It could be very very useful
this pause.
The sixties were very confused
very muddled

very hopeless in many ways.
I didn't like the sixties much
because I was thinking of these things in the fifties myself
in the beat period of Kerouac
and all that.
That's when I felt
I first felt
some life.
And I thought a lot of the new things
which grew up in the fifties
new kinds of thinking
which became popular in the sixties
but when they became popular
they were really rather destroyed
by the form of the popularity.
They were misunderstood.

And I think in this pause period now
its an excellent time to say
"Well those sixties ways were not the right way to do it
they were too crude
they were frightening everybody
and they were not at all effective.
They had nothing positive about them
they were often very negative too..."
And take this rational thing we're talking about
you see
the worst aspect of design methods
the over-rationalism
was the one which became popular.
The good aspect
which is to combine rationality and intuition
which is much more difficult
than to JUST be creative, or JUST be rational
but to combine the two
that can't be done in the rush of a revolution.
Its a slow progress
and we can do that now
nobody's going to stop us.

Its a nice and quiet time.
We ought to think properly about what we are doing.

MW: But we are suffering from this reaction wave
and all these people
that in architecture at least
are figuring like vanguardists
and are a reaction...

CJ: Yes, but if you turn your attention from the producer
to the consumer
you lose this difficulty.
The consumers are more concerned with actual living.
The users of houses
etc
We're all users
you know
most of the time.
I know we're specialists
and avant guardists
and every other -ists
but first of all we have to have breakfast
and we sleep
and we're like everybody else
and we do that in buildings
as users of buildings.
And so if you think of that
you soon forget that the -isms ever existed
you know
because they're always superficial
even the good ones
you know
they're never the whole thing.
And I much prefer ordinary life
to specialism.
you know
sometimes I have a dream...
its so annoying that most of the people you meet
they dont know about any of the new things

so you can't talk about them with them.
Its irritating if you're keen on new things.
But then I go to a place where there are
where there are people who ONLY think of new things
and there's something missing
the ordinary life isn't there
what they call the real world's gone.
And then I walk down the street
I see all sorts of people who've never heard of any ideas
and its much more stimulating to me
in a way
because that is the real thing happening
you know
So if we go to the ordinary life
which we all live
even avant guardists are ordinary people
we look at our own ordinary life
that's the true inspiration
I think
and that's always there.

MW: That would have to do with the new interest in history
for all the buildings
and all the towns
and for conservation.
It would be a part of this recognising the life of the communiity

CJ: That's the good thing about this reaction we're in now.
What happens is that people in art and design
are no longer interested in formalism
they're no longer interested in shape
really
pure form
and abstraction.
They can no longer see any beauty in abstract expressionism
and all those things.
But all the beauty hasn't gone
its just that no one is looking for it any more.

And what they want to see
is how this affects the life.
And the new art forms are all social art
performance art
various forms of social art
concept arts
they're all non-visual
or else they combine two or three senses.
Its very interesting in painting now
there really isn't any painting
there's kinds of art which you can listen to
and you have to move around yourself to see it
or do it.
So they become dance-and-music-and-vision altogether.
I don't actually think that the arts which are limited to one sense
like painting to the eye
music to the ear
have any future any more.
Really what people seem to want
is arts that take more than one sense.
And so architecture is becoming not just visual
but social, thermal, temporal, historical.
I'm sure I don't know much about architecture really
but there must be something which you know
which will tell you
that more than one sense in the body
more than the eye
is coming in.
And after all its ridiculous
if you think about it
to have an art of one sense when everyone has got many.
And how did it ever arise?......
So no wonder people are baffled by painting
you don't normally look without hearing.
You normally integrate the senses.
Watching television
you see
is a **very** good example
of an art which uses two senses

and its much more popular than radio
which has one sense.

Ricardo Blanco: You always speak of two moments
the rational moment
the creative moment
the creative pause
two stages
the methodological one and the creative one.
Wasn't it possible to think about a division
between designers who think about problems
and designers who think about solutions?

CJ: Well, I don't like these divisions.
I was explaining yesterday
actually
Ricardo
in that lecture
that although
when you write about it
you have to write about rationality on one page
creativity on another page
problems on one page
solutions on another page
that's because writing is linear
because you have to think about them separately
but you don't do them separately
you do them integratedly.
You see in this book here
(I was looking at my own book, Design Methods, the Spanish edition)
I've found a certain chapter
chapter 5
the title of this chapter is in english
The Disintegration of Design Methods
I don't know how to translate it
The disintegration of the design process
(Looking now as I type I see that the title is
The Design Process Disintegrated)
now

I used the word disintegration there after a lot of thought
that was to warn the reader
that what you're getting in this chapter
which is the most integrated chapter in the book
I'm calling it disintegration
because
as I was saying in our analysis of the design process
with designing designing
if we are going to re-design designing
which we have to do
there's no choice about this
we have to at first understand the design process
and the process of understanding does benefit
from breaking things into pieces
but only realising that they fit together again.
There's a lovely quotation from Coleridge
who is often known as a poet
but in fact was a splendid philosopher
and Coleridge says
that there is a difference between the crude type of philosopher
or thinker
and the subtle thinker
the crude thinker takes things to pieces
and they remain in pieces
the subtle thinker doesn't make breaks in things
he makes distinctions.
Now
a distinction is recognising parts of something
which is a whole
and the example which Coleridge takes is the word 'thought'...

...there is a distinction between the two meanings
of the word 'thought'
and these are two distinct processes.
There is what happens to the thought
when you write it down
and communicate it to somebody
and there's the process by which you arrive at the thought...

...thought and thinking.
And in the same way
design and designing
problem and solution
are like this.
Everything really
night and day
all of these things.
Life is full of these opposites
apparent opposites
which very often are complements.
Complementarities.
And we are really wasting our time if we're not going to recognise
that what seems like opposites
are often complementaries.
Don't do anything unless you are prepared to recognise that.

(here I've omitted a long section describing details of
chapter 5, and other sections of the book, leading into a
description of a typical method)

And then another thing about reading the individual method
is that they all start with steps
one, two, three, four, five.
If you start with the first step
say on page 96
step one...
well, I can't read it in Spanish yet,
never mind...
step one is always very hard to do.
Its a non-rational step.
For nearly all the methods
however rational
step one is a non-rational step
and has to be done with
not only intuition
but with experience.
That is

intuition which is informed with experience.
Intuition which is not informed by experience
is a very misleading thing
very often.
Intuition which is based on the right experience
is the only really good guide we have in life.
And this is why you say
"that man's a fool, I don't believe him".
You know his intuitions are not based on experience
they just pour out of him
but you know he hasn't lived it.
Someone who speaks much less
sometimes
is perhaps...
you might even not think of him as creative
but they are
because the few words they use are informed by a lot of experience
and as well as imagination.
And that's the integration.
But you can't do this integrating in a book
you can only do it in yourself.

MW: ...so that's why I am more keen on the historic kind of
introduction to methodology
than the rational one.
In the historical analysis
if you keep only dividing,
analysing,
you never understand anything.
You destroy the works you're trying to understand.
It is always necessary to...

CJ: There are times
though
when you do not feel very intuitive.
You cannot make yourself be intuitive, imaginative,
you have to wait
and then
when that happens

you should stop
and do other things.
But even if you're feeling very tired
you can do some useful analysis.
THERE'S a distinction
Ricardo.
I think you can separate them in time a bit
you can do some analytic work
you don't need to be in a very inspired frame of mind
always
for it.

RB: Sorry, I didn't follow the last phrase.

CJ: Perhaps you could translate for Ricardo?

(here follows translation from English into Spanish)

(Marina Waisman then translates Ricardo's next question into English:)

MW for RB: Very creative designers
when they approach the problem
they invent the problem.
They're so creative that they create the problem.

CJ: Well, I think Ricardo is quite right there.
You always have to invent the problem.
I don't think the prior existence of the problem is true.
I always hate the word 'human needs'.
I these guys who write 'human needs'
they imagine there's a dictionary up in the sky somewhere
where all the human needs
for all the future
are written down.
This is silly.
You're right that the needs exist
when the means of satisfying the needs exists.
There was no need for houses when people lived in caves.

And some man
some very inspired man
said "let's build a house"
and that was a great step.
And afterwards
when they got over the shock
some people preferred the house to the cave.
But there was no need for the house.
Life was perfectly allright in the caves.
Similarly with television.
There was no need for television.
And if you have colour television you can't do without colour
but before you had colour you'd see no reason for it.
Its three times as much money for hardly any improvement.
But when you're adapted to it...
so the need comes from being adapted.
That's all the need means
even the need to eat.
We know that people going in for fasting lose the need to eat
and they survive
for very long periods.
Even fundamental
seemingly fundamental things like that.
There are people in the world
who sleep for only quarter of an hour every night
and have lived this way for forty years
and they're perfectly ok
they've managed to live without sleeping.
And so you cannot find any fundamental human needs
that some freak hasn't done without.

Arturo Montagu: Le Corbusier,
when he speaks about the machine of living
is putting a concept which is extended to all the world
and is going to pressure also on the society
the modern society.
It is imortant to know the responsibility of the designer
how he interprets the situation.
When the designer develops the consumer's products

which is a different type of product
there is high motivation of the designer
to express himself through the product
which infact is his personal problem.

CJ: That's right.
You've completely got it.
That's his personal problem.

AM: Because we're always discussing in the faculty
this type of problem
because after a certain number of years
we come also to the problem of the students.
And its for us.
We are in both sides
the theoretical side and the practical side...
Its a key problem,
what he says.

(Ricardo Blanco speaks, in Spanish)

AM for RB: He says why the designer should feel guilty
about this expressiveness
about this need of expressing?

CJ: Well,
the functionalist aesthetic
of course
was an aesthetic of puritanism.
And it was a reaction against.
It arose in the Vienna Circle with Adolf Loos
and everything that comes from the Vienna Circle
the psychology that came from it
the philosophy that came from it
the music that came from it
the architectural theory that came from it
by all these great names

(I was thinking of Freud, Wittgenstein, Schoenberg, Loos)

they were all actually reacting against the wave
which couldn't or wouldn't go away
the wave of the Hapsburg Empire.
They were continuing imposed expressionism of the upper classes
on the buildings.
And they got rid of decoration and ornaments
as a cleansing.
They were all cleansers of a bad situation which had arisen.
and of course we no longer have to react against it.
That's over.
We don't like functionalism any more.
But that functionalism was never real functionalism
it was visual functionalism
it was formalism
masquerading as a function.
It wasn't really the function of the people in the building
or of the building.
It was the function of looking at it as if it was a function
and it was actually a visual style
and it was just as much self-expressive, in fact
as all the decoration of the older buildings.

I think what's nice now in architecture
are the very irrational buildings.
The ones I like are those which are amazingly functionless.
I, for instance, quite like the New York Five.
(line missing here)
they make it of wood and paint it to look like concrete
and
ok
it always was like that really.
They've been more truthful in fact
by admitting it was a decorative style.
And they take it to Palladian degrees
and,
you know,
make it more formal
and its only for rich men's houses
and it really hasn't much bearing on life

but there you are.
But the fact that fact that they are very spiritual is nice
and that's attractive.
We shouldn't remove spirituality in design
I think
in this whole business
because that's the inspiration of living.
But there are functional limits which really are negative
usefully negative.
They say there are certain forms of building
which are actually damaging to people.
And the functionalist theory
or the scientific analysis of building requirements
this tells you that if the pillars are thinner
and so on
the building will fall down and people will die.
That doesn't tell you how to do the building
it tells you how not to do the building
and that's negation.
The value of science is that its formalised negation
the method of science is not to prove things
but to work on the negative.
To disprove things.
That's why scientists are basically sceptical.
They work on
they're artists of the negative
we might say.
They use the negative to remove false ideas from the mind
and false assumptions.
We all make false assumptions
and only the scientists
at the end
have the courage really to test their assumptions
and they usually find they're wrong
they're happy to be wrong.
A scientist is a man who's happy to be wrong.
When he's wrong he discovers something.
And the rest of us haven't learnt this

particularly in design.
We have to manufacture a kind of certainty
in order to proceed
and a confidence
and so we are very unscientific.

But the really useful function theory
I think
doesn't come from avant guarde movements
it comes from the kind of design called ergonomics
which investigates the human being.
Ergonomics won't tell you what makes people happy
what makes people feel sublime.
But it can tell you what will give people headaches
and eyestrain
and backaches
and all those things.
But these are to do with the body.
The mind
ergonomics is a very bad guide for.
The kind of ergonomics that has got into design theory
is this wretched behaviourism
Skinner, and pidgeons, and all this stuff,
and this kind of behaviourism
is trying to apply physiological thinking to the mind
where its out of place.
And its great for the body.
So behaviourism is fine if you want to discover how people act
in a bodily way.
But these behaviourist models
afterwards made into a computer program now
to model the behaviour of people in a city or an urban area
I think are very dangerous
because they try to model what people's wishes and desires are
and what's on their mind
and this has to remain open.
If you plan this
then life is gone.
And they should limit themselves

these computer men and behaviourists
to the bodily thing.
But they don't have the modesty to do that...

(a confusing section of the transcript is omitted here)

MW: Really that's what you said
about the need for an intuition based on experience
and knowledge.
So there's a need for very much knowledge beforehand
and then you can free yourself...

(another confusing section)

CJ: Yes, that of course.
You see, there's a difficulty there
I think
and its this:
that when the building, the motor car, or whatever it is
is going to be fairly similar to the last one
and they nearly all are, actually...
...where that's the case
then you can get experience from the older ones
which are relevant.
But the typical modern problem is one like I said
with solar energy or something like that
which is quite a new concept
which there's no experience of.
Now
with that
you cannot find anybody who has the informed intuition.
Therefore you have to generate artificial experience.
I always say that the scientific part of the new design methods
is designing designing
is designing a quick education for yourself
as a designer.
The designer has to design an educational programme for himself
every time he designs
so that he learns rapidly enough to become experienced

and he makes his final decisions when he knows
that he is using experienced intuition.
He makes his initial guesses
which should be very wild
knowing that he is going to throw them away.
And the traditional designing method
in all fields
doesn't really allow for this.
Traditional design method
in architecture engineering and other fields
really starts with the chief architect or the chief engineer
in only a week or so
making all the major decisions
and this is very destructive
practically hopeless for what we are talking about.
Those decisions have to be taken in the last week of the process
not the first
and all the rest of the time should be spent with many people
not just the chief designer
or team
trying to educate themselves very quickly
and trying to lose their...
you see
experience you bring to a new problem
is experience of all the problems
is very misleading
you're happy with it
you're confident in it..
but it doesn't relate to this problem.
So you have to go through the process of unlearning.
And the most useful effect of the irrational methods in this book
is that they're very rigid
and I like that rigidity
because that rigidity forces you to unlearn.
You won't unlearn without a stick
you know
or a carrot or something
you know.
You need formalism to help you unlearn.

AM: All the need for alternative technologies
or alternative architecture
comes from a very good understanding of the bad ways
that architecture and technology have leaned to
so this kind of negative experience is necessary.
If not
you wouldn't think about the wind
or the water
or the sun.
So its the suffering of modern technology
the modern architecture...

CJ: Its very interesting
you see
that the curtain wall was a creative idea once.
It sounds quite a poetic word
'curtain wall'.
A curtain wall
you know
what a beautiful concept.
And now the curtain wall is the symbol
of all that's dreadful
in homogenous plastic architecture.
But what I was really thinking about the curtain wall
is this:
there's almost no curtain wall that doesn't leak
there's almost no curtain wall that doesn't have wind problems
and actually
though thousands of them have been made
there's very few cases where they've really solved problems
which in the brick wall
and the ordinary window
were solved centuries ago
because although we thought we knew how to solve them
we still can't really do it with the new materials.
Amazingly difficult.
Such a simple thing.

MW: Now you put in the air conditioners

but you don't think about the sun
and the glare
the terrible glare
and its very usual in Argentina
sometimes in my town
in Cordoba
which is very hot
and very sunny
its terribly brilliant
the sun
and you put a wonderful curtain wall
and then you can't live inside
it's impossible
you must wear sun-glasses inside.

AM: If not
you cannot work.

MW: You feel invaded
by all this glare...

CJ: Well, of course
this really comes from a religious point.
All the people in the 1930's were sun worshippers
they were disguised religiouses
they all claimed to be very irreligious
but they all worshipped sunlight.
The tower block was the idea that one should get sunlight
and the curtain wall was nature coming into the house.
What nobody said was "why do you have a house?".
Now
you have a house because
for most of the human things
which animals don't do
like reading
and writing in particular...
Have you ever tried to read and write on the beach?
It's terrible.
I mean the glare is impossible.

You cannot read anything
and the slightest bit of wind blows the papers around.
Those two simple things.
There's nothing flat enough to put things on
they roll off
and they get sand in them.
You just can't do what we're doing now on the beach
you know.
We'd have given up a long time ago
and gone for a swim perhaps.
It would have been better!
But
if you want to do these modern things
you have to have non-natural surroundings.
Whether we're wise in this I don't know.
We may be very unwise in the long run.

MW: I think man is now a cultural animal
lives in a cultural surrounding
and needs this cultural surrounding to...

CJ: Mind you
the new concept in design is sufficiently broad
to ask even big questions like
"Should we carry on writing?"
"And reading?"
"And locking ourselves up in boxes?"
"With or without our windows?"
you know.
And previously there was no way
in the architectural profession
or the engineering profession
for handling a question as big as that.
Now
I like to think that these new methods
which some people call a fringe movement in design
and I always say that this fringe movement is a bad name
given to new things by the old
the old people say its a fringe

its not a fringe
its the new centre!
The new thing makes the old into a fringe.

(some confused words here in the transcript)

...and this central new idea
of widening the design process
means that you don't use the process for the same things as
you use the old process for
you don't actually use these new methods for designing buildings.
There's very little in that book about designing buildings
its mainly about designing intangible things...

(a section about the appropriateness of formal design methods
to the designing of computer systems and software)

...design an educational system
a traffic system.
A traffic system has hardware in it
it has streets and buildings and cars and things
but the essence of it is the movement
which is somewhat intangible.
You're designing movement.

MW: So, the aims of design are conditioning the process of design.

CJ: The new process has new aims
it doesn't have the same aims
so its no good saying it has failed
as a means of designing buildings.
It wasn't meant for that.
It was meant to do what buildings won't do.
Buildings won't design the movement.

MW: But
for some time
we will still live and work in buildings.

CJ: We will always perhaps have buildings
but preferably buildings which are compatible
with a much more beautiful form of movement in life.
The movement we have in the city generally is ugly
it really is ugly
and it has never been considered as a subject for design
but now its very irteresting that in the fine arts
they've been onto that for some time now.
They are trying to find ways
if you like
of making the movement of life beautiful.
That's what performance art is
that's what concept art is
its beauty of thought
or beauty of doing things.
They're starting off in rather seemingly ugly ways
because they're iconoclasts
but nevertheless what they're trying to do
in this least understood form of art
which is now appearing
is to look at life itself
at the movement if you like...

MW: Its very difficult
I think
to understand and to transmit
that you're designing non-tangible things.

CJ: Yes.
People say to me
you know
O, he has never designed anything.
I feel annoyed
because actually I've designed a traffic system
and a lot of intangibles.

MW: A traffic system is at least something that you can understand.

CJ: And designing the design process

is the most subtle of things...

(a section on the obstacles to a general recognition that it
is right to pay attention to the design of intangibles)

AM: I would like to make some remarks
about what Chris Jones feels
when I took him
not around Buenos Aires
but in our daily trip to La Plata.
What he was saying
is that when we were just moving through the Avienda Calchaqui
which for an architectural eye
or for our architectural feeling
is such a kind of chaos
with all the houses without any plan
all the houses different heights
the colours the form the morphology
he told me something which struck me.
He told me that "I am learning a lot about this country
when through this avenue
because I am seeing how the people feel
how the people live
how the people are doing things without professionals".
Then
and he was very happy that I was taking
this type of route
I said "Its the only route to La Plata"
although I was very frightened I must admit...
He was very frightened by the traffic (very fast & irregular)
and then he told me
please, if you can go slowly with the car
just because he wanted to look
not only because he was frightened.
He likes to look at these particular architectural things.
But then
when we entered the new route to La Plata
which they call Camino Centenario
which for us is a big improvement

this new way
with lighting at night and four ways
he said "Its not Argentina for me
because I saw the same route in Japan, America,
I prefer the Avienda Calchiqui".
This was my remark
according that all the movement of Chris Jones now is
he's against the
what he called the "world of plastic"
which is surrounding Europe and part of the United States
and his recommendation to us is
that we
as professors and designers
should try to avoid this type of situation
not to convert Argentina into a world of plastic.

CJ: I like the word 'homogenized'
because it identifies what's going wrong.
We produce the homogenized world
homogenized architecture
homogenized milk
and really we don't seem able to stop this.
I spent a year in Virginia Tech.
and there was a large department of architecture
which was itself in a rather homogenized building...
...they had many students
and they were all producing these little models.
I was curious about the models.
They were very elaborate
balsa wood
other kinds of material
plastic models really of the new buildings
and their forms were extemely irregular.
By now irregularity of form has become
in that architecture school
a new formalism.
It wasn't straight simple shapes
everybody had the most interesting complicated ground plan
and everything was curved

there was really nothing at right angles to anything any more
and you might think that that wasn't homogenized
and that the buildings which would come out of it
would not be.
But nevertheless
when you saw the models in a row
when you see the designs which have come out of them
it still has exactly the same feeling in the mind
of "we're in a homogenized world".
I'm sure that the architectural profession know this
and is very puzzled by their own situation
and can't see their way out.
I can't either.
Its a really baffling thing
but geometrical variety doesn't seem to get you out of it.

MW: No,
because you choose geometrical variety
instead of geometrical rationality
but its the same thing.

CJ: I think the surrealistic buildings
which are beginning to appear in the USA
I don't know if they are appearing here
with, for instance
a part of the wall broken away deliberately
and bricks tumbling down
you know the ones I mean
I can't remember the names of these architects...

MW: Yes, SITE. S.I.T.E., its one of the groups doing this.

CJ: That's right
with this sort of Salvador Dali approach
almost
to architecture.
That breaks out of it (homogeneity)
in a very strange way
because that is rather arresting

you know
it takes your attention
and very strongly
perhaps too strongly.
But I like that too because it is at least a beginning
of getting away from that kind of homogeneity.

MW: Yes, I think that this kind of vernacular architecture
and the respect for the local...can give some way of...

CJ: That book Architecture Without Architects
is very interesting visually.
Its a pity that the words in it don't somehow explain more.
Because nobody's understood more I suppose
and you can't ask the people
because they're not that kind of person.

AM: It could be very interesting to show Chris
something of our vernacular architecture...
Of which I suppose you are a specialist...

MW: We have some slides but I don't have them here.

CJ: When I go to Rosario is there something I can see?

MW: Rosario is a very new town
its a nineteenth century town.
Our town is a more colonial town.

CJ: Really I should go up in the hills
should I?
A long distance......

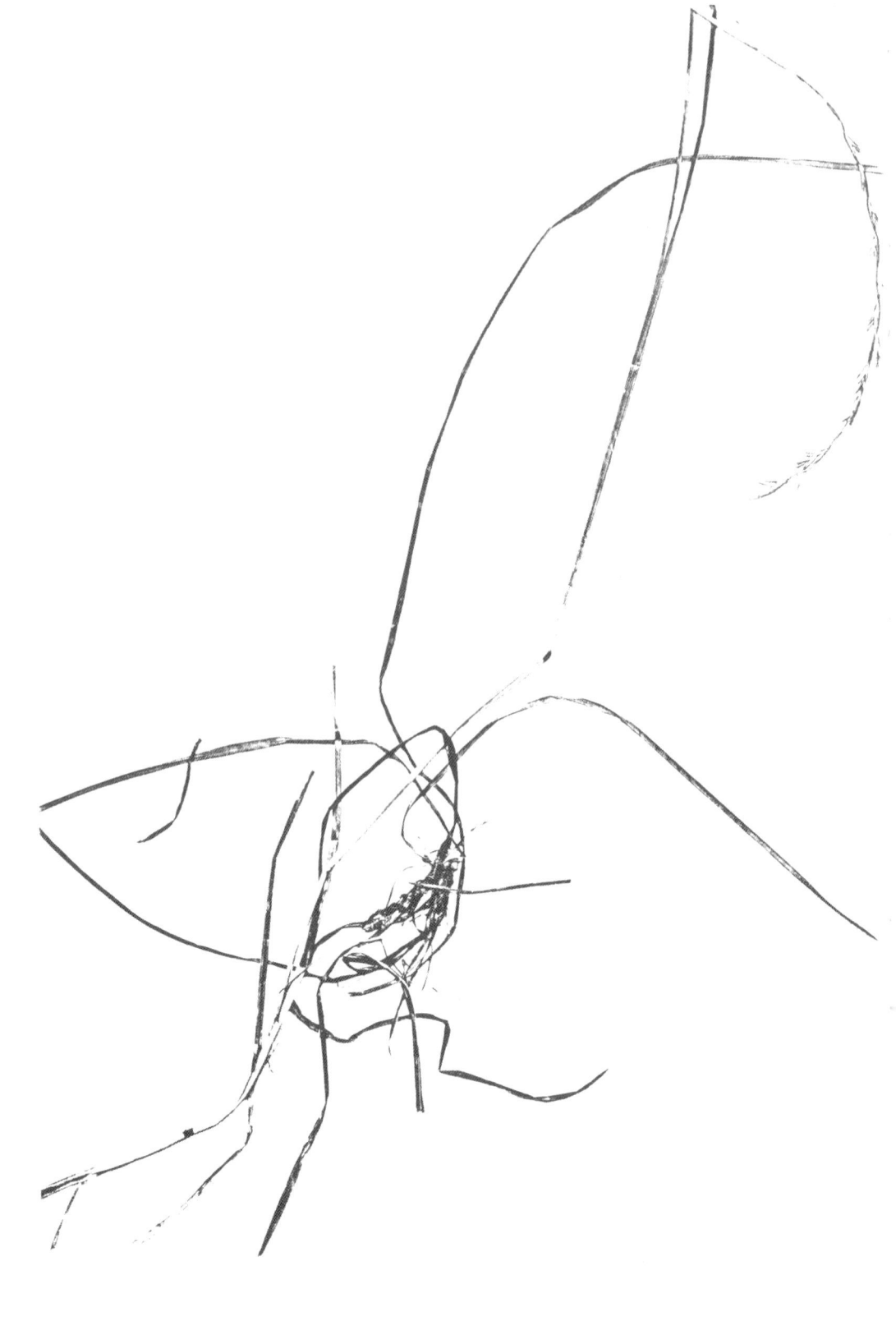

principles in design

Sydney Gregory, the editor of Design Studies, invited several
people to react to ten principles proposed by W. H. Mayall in his
book Principles in Design, published by the Design Council,
London, 1979. This review of the principles first appeared in
Design Studies Volume 1, number 3, January 1980, pages 182-3,
published by Butterworth Scientific Limited, PO Box 63, Westbury
House, Bury Street, Guildford, Surrey, GU2 5BH. I am grateful
for permission to reproduce it here together with quotations from
W. H. Mayall's book (with the permission of The Design Council).

Here are my reactions to the ten principles of design
formulated by W.H.Mayall. These are my first thoughts on
reading the principles alone.....without reference to what
Mr Mayall has to say about them in his book.

1. THE PRINCIPLE OF TOTALITY
   All design requirements are always interrelated and must
   always be treated as such throughout a design task.

Yes and no. The degree to which any pair of requirements
are related, which can vary from negligibly to critically,
depends upon which of many possible designs is chosen, eg
if one decides to provide a digital watch then the
requirements 'indicate the hour' and 'indicate the date' are
likely to be strongly interconnected : not so if one
decides to provide a dial watch and a calendar.

2. THE PRINCIPLE OF TIME
   The features and characteristics of all products change
   as time passes.

Yes, but again one has to know the degree to which these change
before one knows whether it is going to affect one's design
decisions. A more useful principle would be one which helped
one to discover this, eg to ask the question 'to what extent
do the assumptions and decisions made in the proposed design
remain true for the expected life of the product?'.

3. THE PRINCIPLE OF VALUE
   The characteristics of all products have different relative values depending upon the different circumstances
   and times in which they may be used.

Yes. The values differ also, I believe, according to which
of the possible alternative designs one decides upon, our
wishes being much conditioned by the availibility, or not,
of any means of satisfying them, eg the value of tv was to
most of us nil until we got used to it, equally the value of
colour tv was nowhere near 'three times the price' until we
got used to that.

4. THE PRINCIPLE OF RESOURCES

The design, manufacture and life of all products and systems depend upon the materials, tools and skills upon which we can call.

But the materials, manufacturing processes, and the skills of making, and of using, are all highly variable, and, I believe, almost unpredictable. So, if we begin our design trying to fit only the existing resources, we will miss most of the opportunity for making something new and be led into a too conservative result?

5. THE PRINCIPLE OF SYNTHESIS

All features of a product must combine to satisfy all the characteristics we expect it to posess with an acceptable relative importance for as long as we wish, bearing in mind the resources available to make and use it.

This sounds like the writer straining to make a single sentence embody a mass of conflicting requirements while providing a single criterion to indicate success. To attempt this is, I believe, to push language further than it will go. I dont think there is a rational way to indicate that a design, or any other composition, is 'right'. Measurement, and reason, can each go part of the way, but, when it comes to assessing the whole, each person is obliged, implicitly, to express his or her view of life, his or her self, and these are beyond what can be stated rationally. To attempt certainty, with respect to the whole, is, I think, to take away the opportunity to be oneself, or to act unpredictably, as a person, not as a thing. I feel sure that one of the reasons why the designed world has recently become to be experienced as inhuman and over-homogenized is that we have tried to seek this kind of rational certainty where only what used to be called 'the heart' can speak. The place for science and reason, in design, is a large one, but it is not in usurping the imagination. It is in extending its range and sensitivity.

6. THE PRINCIPLE OF ITERATION
   Design requires processes of evaluation that begin with
   the first intentions to explore the need for a product
   or system. These processes continue throughout all subsequent design and development stages to the user himself,
   whose reactions will often cause the iterative process to
   continue with a new product or system.

Iterating, which I prefer to call repeating, or 'going back
to square one', is of course a common experience for designers.
It is to avoid the cost and delay of this that we have tried,
in recent years, to find more certain design methods (as well
as for the more positive aim of making things better in themselves, more usable, beautiful, and less harmful to bystanders,
more fitting to life as a whole). I believe that to be driven
back to square one is a confession of failure, something to
do as seldom as possible, an indication that one's design methods
are inadequate to the situation. Adequate methods will, I
believe, enable one to learn, in a pre-design phase, much of
what one may repeatedly fail to learn if one plunges ahead
without them. The right way to design a design process is to
recognise that one is trying to give oneself the experiences,
early in designing, which will teach all those unexpected things
that one often learns about the product, and its context, only
when it is too late.

7. THE PRINCPLE OF CHANGE
   Design is a process of change, an activity undertaken not
   only to meet changing circumstances, but also to bring
   about changes to those circumstances by the nature of the
   product it creates.

I like this principle, it is one which has been absent from
much of what has been thought and written about design: the
realizing that the problem and the solution are interdependant.
New possibilities change our picture of the world and change
our ideas of what we need. It is for this reason that I am
critical of the attempt, in some of Mr Mayall's other principles

as well as in much recent design methodology, to stabilise
requirements by ascribing to them values on a rational or
numerical scale. To allow, in designing, for the interrelation
of requirements and possibilities is to admit to life, to
what makes things worth doing for their own sake, to all that
is beyond the reach of calculation. Without this, design
is a form of social control, a perpetuation of ourselves as
we were, not an exploration of how we may become.

8. THE PRINCIPLE OF RELATIONSHIPS
   Design work cannot be undertaken effectively without
   establishing working relationships with all those activities
   concerned with the conception, manufacture and marketing
   of products and, importantly, with the prospective user,
   together with all the services he may call upon to assist
   his judgement and protect his interests.

I like this principle too, but I don't think it goes far
enough. What I understand it to mean is that designing is
no longer a solo activity but, increasingly, the concern of
many experts, users, pressure groups, and others, all of
whom are more strongly affected by the results of designing
now that what we make is more powerful, of a larger scale,
and more highly interconnected, than it was. What this
calls for is, I think, more than 'establishing working
relationships with all those activities concerned'. It
requires collaboration, on an increasingly equal basis, and
a sharing of the responsibilities, which designers, so far,
keep to themselves. 'But only a single mind can create'
we might say to ourselves, 'not everyone, and certainly no
committee, can exercise design skill'. Yes and no. The kinds
of design skill which are presently taught and practiced by
the design professions are adapted to the assumption that
one mind is adequate to designing in the new situation of
increasing interconnectedness in which we find ourselves, but
it is not adequate. And the kinds of design skill which
are called for in using the newer design methods, which the
professions as yet do not seem to take seriously, are suited

to collaboration, to the sharing of responsibilities between
users and experts, and to designing imaginatively in a
collective process, as was the case in craft evolution.

9. THE PRINCIPLE OF COMPETENCE
    Design competence is the ability to create a synthesis
    of features that achieves all desired characteristics
    in terms of their required life and relative value,
    using available or specified materials, tools and skills,
    and to transmit effective information about this synthesis
    to those who will turn it into products or systems.

Here again is something that I am beginning to recognise
throughout these principles : the attempt to pack, into
single sentences, the increasingly wide-ranging criteria by
which the increasingly over-loaded centre, the designer,
is to measure his success in meeting increasingly wide-
ranging requirements that his work has to satisfy. At what
point do we recognise that centralized designing ceases to
be effective and becomes an obstacle, and not the means, to
'good design'. Surely there is such a point. I believe we
have already passed beyond it and that it is time to rethink
designing, design education, and the need for design professions,
in relation to the growing dissatisfaction with technology,
design, planning, and their effects. The new competence which
the situation now requires is, I believe, not that of deciding
the shape of a product or system but the shape of a new
context or process in which everyone, not just designers or
experts, is enabled to see what is needed of him or her if
the form of industrial life is to get better, for everyone,
and not worse. To arrive at this is not to continue to design
but to do something at a different scale from that, the scale
of the whole problem, the scale of decentral action, thought,
imagination.

10. THE PRINCIPLE OF SERVICE
Design must satisfy everybody, and not just those for whom its products are directly intended.

I dont think that this is any longer an ideal, a voluntary extra, something to be done only when one can afford it. It has already become a necessity that new products are assessed, discussed, researched, and tried out in unharmful ways, before they are launched to ensure that they do not cause more harm than good. But the present way of attempting this, through centrally organised design, market research, technology assessment, drug testing, planning, operations research, etc, has not only got beyond what a single design profession can do, it is failing to correct the increasingly obvious fault of industrial life : that it is becoming impersonal, homogenized, an inhuman system that does not seem, in the way it has been set up, to recognise us all as persons. What's to be done? Far more, I think, than to present overloaded professionals with exhortations to act by better principles. To do that is, I'm sorry to say, to make things worse, for it diverts energy and good will to a scale of action that cannot work when it could be applied to one that will. The best service, the bravest, is to stop designing, in the ways we do now, and to try for something better. To raise our individual thoughts to the scale of our collective actions. And to give ourselves the space to act accordingly.

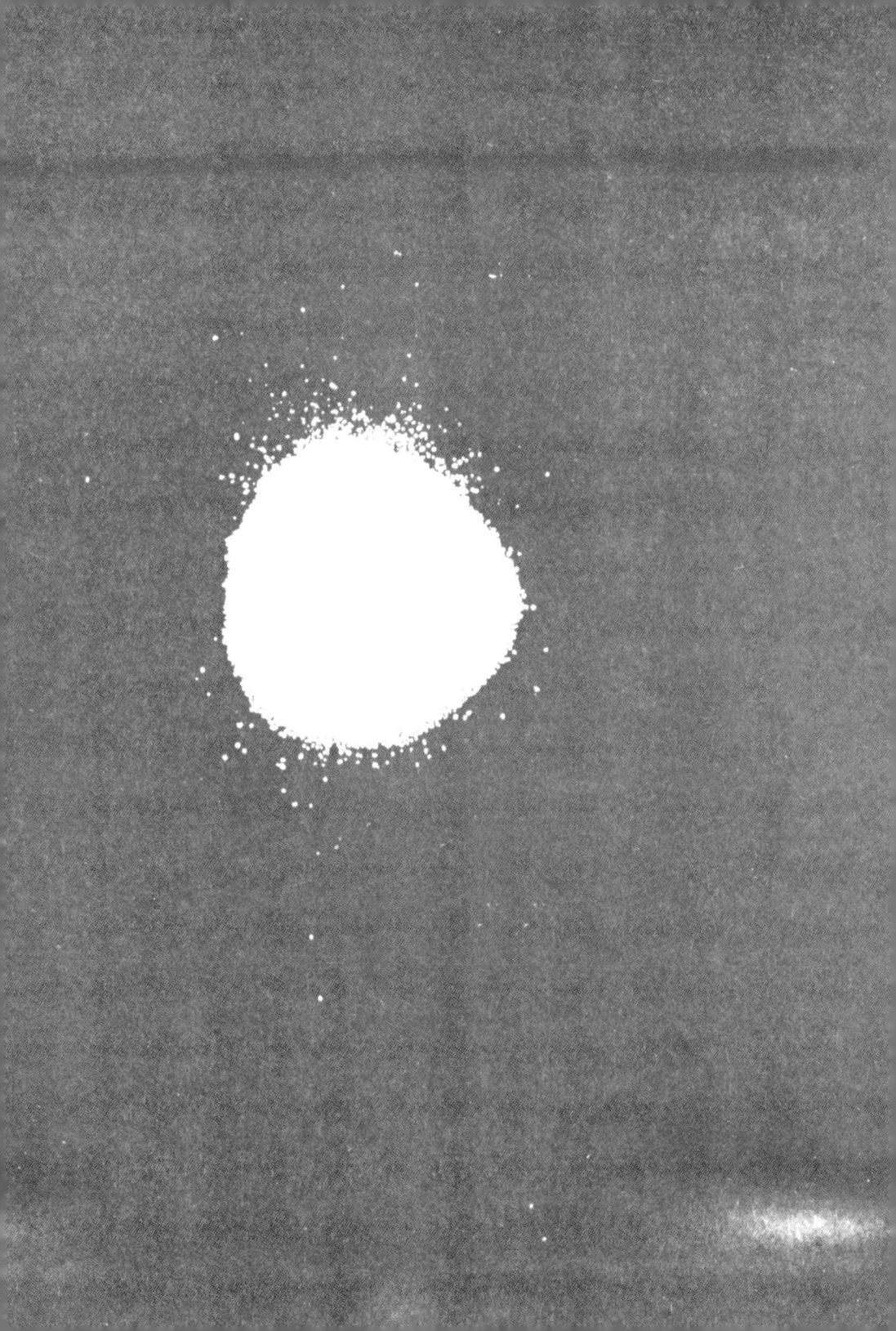

largon It they itsnowifatjohns geth
      rubcit path

for onedofybleachedthey night?

                                    John Cage
                                    Empty Words

2
THE WORLD WITHOUT IMAGINATION

St Ives by chance

I was invited to contribute to the lecture series 'Description: Invention: Reality' organised by Ranulph Glanville and Annetta Pedretti at the Architectural Association, London, in 1979-80. The lectures appeared in a special issue of aaq, the Architectural Association Quarterly, volume 12 number 4, 1980, edited by Dennis Sharp in consultation with Ranulph Glanville. The essay is reproduced with the permission of the Architectural Association Quarterly.

Ranulph told me that his lecture series had a connecting idea: that things designed, and perceived, are influenced, perhaps more than we think, by the perceptions, the ways of seeing, of ourselves as designers and perceivers. Those are not his words: they are the words that are close to my memory of what he said and may well be quite far from those he used, memory being so largely the inventing of details which support our present feelings about some past event which we have forgotten in its details and which we may not have paid much attention to at the time. (That, as I understand it, is the gist of the analysis of memory in Frederick Bartlett's book Remembering, published in the early thirties and still, perhaps, one of the truest writings about memory?)

Looking in my slide collection for something in the spirit of this idea I chose some slides made in 1972 when I was on a family holiday in St. Ives. I was tired of the beach, and of being limited to the things that a holidaymaker is expected to do. And I'd been reading one of John Cage's books (A Year From Monday) and beginning my attachment to his ideas, which has lasted ever since. I noticed that, in one of his writings, he says that the invention of the camera, the Kodak box camera that anyone can use, was just the kind of step he likes: a move that shifts the 'artistic' role, and 'skill', from the specialist to the amateur, the ordinary person. I wondered how John Cage would himself use a camera, and, as I knew of no example of him doing so, I decided to guess what he might do with it. I asked my daughter Sarah to lend me her Instamatic for the afternoon and set out to try to photograph St. Ives in the manner of John Cage, as near as I could manage, knowing him only through his books.

I looked first at the picture post-cards of St. Ives and immediately realised now very close _to_ these views, carefully chosen for being 'typical' or 'picturesque', are ALL the holiday photos we take, by the million. (How odd that certain

views of the earth, and of ourselves, are photographed so
repeatedly, each summer, with such pleasure yet with so little
'originality'.) I decided that what John Cage would do, with
an Instamatic, was to remove intentionality from the choosing
of the views to be photographed. Instead, I guessed, he'd
leave the decisions as to where and when to point the camera
to chance. Not just to a careless and thoughtless pointing of
the camera but to a carefully designed 'chance process' as he
calls it, as he does when he has to determine the sounds to
be played in a piece of music. A chance process in which
personal preferences, the wish of himself as composer, as
photographer, to control the result, has been systematically
thwarted. He would, nevertheless accept the results, whatever
they may be, beautiful or ugly according to accepted canons,
as something to be liked, something to be learnt from, a fresh
view of what constitutes 'music', 'art', or 'reality'. A
different view of St. Ives. Not the one we remember, or invent,
when we think of the place.

The technique of doing something by chance (which I was learning
from the paragraphs, before each of his published writings,
describing exactly how it was composed) requires a carefully
chosen <u>system</u> of numbers, letters, or the like, with which
to denote all the possibilities one is leaving 'open to chance'.
It also requires a <u>source</u> of specific numbers, letters, or
whatever one is using, that are completely uninfluenced by any
bias, so that the results are picked out of the whole range of
possibilities in a completely random way. Random selection,
speaking mathematically, is that in which each choice is
uninfluenced by any other. In a row of random numbers eg
71788296143450210388294463963695600116348894088456366422626365
each number has an equal chance of being any of the numbers
0 to 9 regardless of what comes before or after it. That is
why there are quite a number of repeats, when the numbers are
chosen without bias, whereas, in a row of numbers chosen to
fit one's IDEA of 'randomness' there may well be no repeats.
To eliminate all repeats is to impose pattern, idea.

My 'system of numbers' with which to denote all the possibilities

for photographing 'St. Ives' was a tourist map of the town. As
I was interested in seeing what chance photography would produce
in place of the 'typical' views in picture postcards and
holiday snaps I decided to restrict it to the most picturesque
part of the town: the neck of land connecting to 'the Island'
upon which are most of the fishermans cottages and which forms
the background to the harbour. My 'system' consisted of 10000
points on this part of the map at the intersections of a
100 by 100 grid. As soon as I saw the shape of this grid I
had visions of chance points landing on the beach or in the
sea, or inside someone's house. Wherever there was a chance-
selected point I'd be obliged to go, and take a photograph,
however difficult, embarassing, or 'untypical of photography'
it might be. And however much it might be 'not like me' to
do a thing like that. The St. Ives pictures were, I think,
my first chance process. Since then I have experienced many.
I've learnt, in all this, that this aspect of being driven, by
one's 'promise' to accept the results whatever they may be, is
perhaps the greatest fascination, though it can at times leave
one very exposed. It is the reality, the actual experience,
of being driven outside of 'oneself', one's idea of what one
likes, or dislikes, of 'who one is'. It is the process of being
exposed to parts of life that are inaccessible to one unless
one's preferences are given up. It is being put in touch with
aspects of life that are beyond the range of one's habits and
one's skills.

How to pick, from all the points on my imaginary grid, the ten
I planned to take? As I had no table of random numbers with me
I looked around for something in the environment itself which
permitted the selecting of ten points randomly from the ten
thousand. I found it in the church close to the lifeboat house:
a list of the dates of the various clergymen who had been in
office there since Elizabethan times. I copied out the last
two figures of each date and found there were enough numbers
to select five of my ten points. So I used the same set in
reverse order to select the other five, a slight departure
from true randomness which today I'd avoid. I realised that
the ten points, alone, did not suffice to determine what to

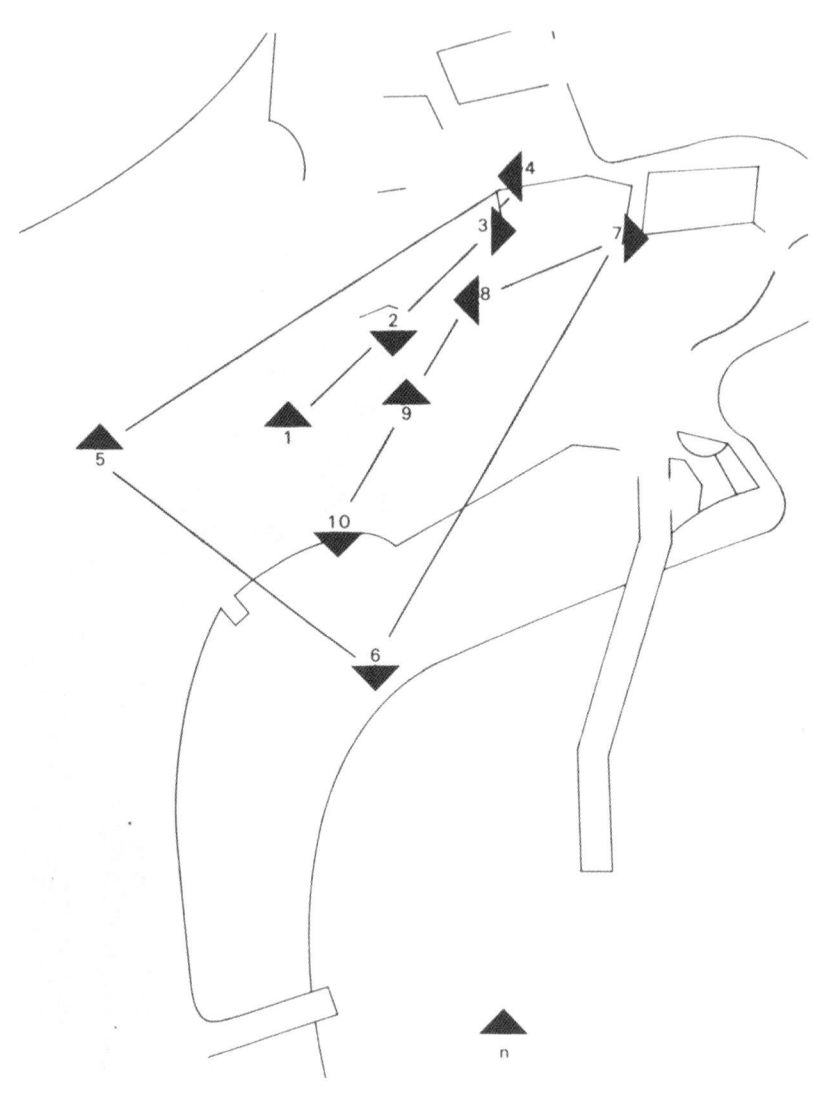

A map of St Ives, showing camera positions and the direction from which each photograph was taken

photograph. I'd need some way of randomizing not only the location of the camera but its direction too. As time was getting short I did this very crudely by allocating the compass directions (I assumed North was at the top of the map) in the sequence NSEWNSEWNS to each of the ten photos.

photo 0
Taken before the chance photos to show the area of St. Ives where they were to be taken, and as an example of a 'typical' holiday view.

photo 1
For this and the other chance photos I was obliged to be
seen photographing obviously 'odd' views and experienced, for
the first time, the slight embarrassment of so doing. This
turf accountant's shop, which does not correspond to my notion
of such a place, or to my notion of 'St. Ives', is perhaps the one
that reveals most of that mass of experience we ignore, or cannot
assimilate consciously for want of any 'idea' or 'stereotype'
capable of including it.

photo 2
The first of several photos in which I had to stand ignoring
'prettier' views behind me to take what looked like ridiculously
close-up shots of seemingly dull walls etc.

photo 3
The chopping of the windows, and the slightly provocative arrangement of rectangular areas in this photo, would suggest to me now that it was done deliberately like this, to hold attention, if I did not know it was done adhering to the chance process as closely as possible.

photo 4
While taking this one I was beginning to feel the experiment was a mistake. I'd have preferred the envisaged adventure of having to knock on a door to say that I was obliged to take a photo of, say, the inside of a house, because the chance process had led me to that spot. (That accident did not occur.) To take this photo, for which I had to stand alongside someone's house and direct the camera <u>along</u> a wall instead of <u>at</u> it, felt like something too trivial to be tolerated. Its amazingly difficult, for me at least, to do something that is so bereft of any purpose that is self-evident, or easily explainable to bystanders. Although the camera did not show it, some of the photos were taken with other holiday-makers at my elbow: for others, like this one, there was nobody in sight and I was almost tresspassing.

photo 5
I'd looked at this signboard several times before as it was near to where we were staying. It is something of an intended 'sight' in itself: a 'recognisable point of interest' such as a guide might point out.

photo 6
For this photo the chance process put a point on the water in the harbour. I should have obeyed it and swam out with the camera, or hired a boat. As I was short of time, by this (the points being quite far apart and the whole process taking longer than I'd expected), I compromised by directing the camera at the chosen point from the nearest spot on the quay. This seems to have resulted in what is very close to a 'composed' holiday snap. I'm always impressed by the way in which, given a thing to photograph, it is so very difficult to stop oneself conforming to some preconceived notion of composition (eg eighteenth century landscapes or Dutch interior paintings) every time one aligns the viewfinder. The VIEW finder! A view, it seems, is not what's there, what one's eye is capable of looking at and noting, but a MEMORY of what others have done in composing what they saw?

photo 7
Perhaps the oddest photo in itself - half a car and a bit of a house. Who would ever take such a picture? Some years later my sister saw these slides and recognised this house as the one her family had rented when they went to stay at St. Ives. After many such seemingly spooky coincidences, arising from chance processes, I have begun to be surprised not at their occurrence but if, by chance, they do not occur. It seems to me now that such unexpected connections exist between many of the features of life we thought to be unconnected. Our everyday perceptions are so narrowed by immediate purpose and intention as to hide from us most of the connectiveness of life. Deliberate chance processes break out of this a little by obliging us to pay attention to what we are normally incapable of noticing. Is that it?

photo 8
Another close-up of a wall which, had I not known its origin,
I'd say was the work of an artist-photographer intent on
drawing attention by deliberate disregard of a recent convention
in how to 'compose a picture'.

photo 9
Again, though not a tourist's view of things, the chance process seems to have led to the kind of composition reminiscent of what some artists might well contrive.

photo 10
This last chance photograph is missing. The accident of losing it gives us the opportunity of looking at something I did not expect at all while taking the photographs: an image of St Ives that leaves everything to the imagination; or else an image of the frame, or idea, of 'a photograph' free of content.

Looking now at these photographs, eight years later, I doubt if they are at all what John Cage would have done. For one thing they embody only a part, the most managable but least adventurous part, of his notion of chance composing. They are an example of what I'd now call 'systematic' chance processes: those in which there is a limited set of possibilities out of which a few are selected randomly. The more adventurous kind of chance is what John Cage calls 'indeterminacy': the giving-up of all idea of what may result, as in his musical piece 4' 33" (four minutes and thirty-three seconds in which the performer makes no sounds from the musical instrument and in which whatever sounds occur spontaneously in the hearing

of the audience comprise the music). But, even if John Cage
had himself decided to take photographs of St Ives, or if
anyone else but me had done so, trying to see the effect of
chance, the results might have been very different. They
would be different because, at the scale of 'the initial
decisions' (in my case: which part of St Ives to photograph,
how many to take, when to do it, how to organise the chance
process) there are still many many personal preferences to
be expressed, inevitably. But what matters, I think, is not
that the process, at its general level, remains intentional after
all, but that, at the scale of what are normally taken to be
the main decisions, intention is given up. Given that, there
appears enough of an opening for life, as we fail to predict
and to remember it, to enliven what we do.

For those who attended my talk, which included other things
besides this, here is a small quotation from John Cage's
Lecture on Nothing, which I recited. It is chosen by chance
using numbers taken from the dates of the St. Ives clergymen:

> It is not irritating to be where one is. It is only
> irritating to think one would like to be somewhere
> else.

References: The Lecture on Nothing appears in John Cage's
book Silence (Wesleyan University Press, Middletown,
Connecticut, 1961; Marion Boyars, London, 1971). A Year from
Monday is from the same publishers, 1967 & 1968 respectively.

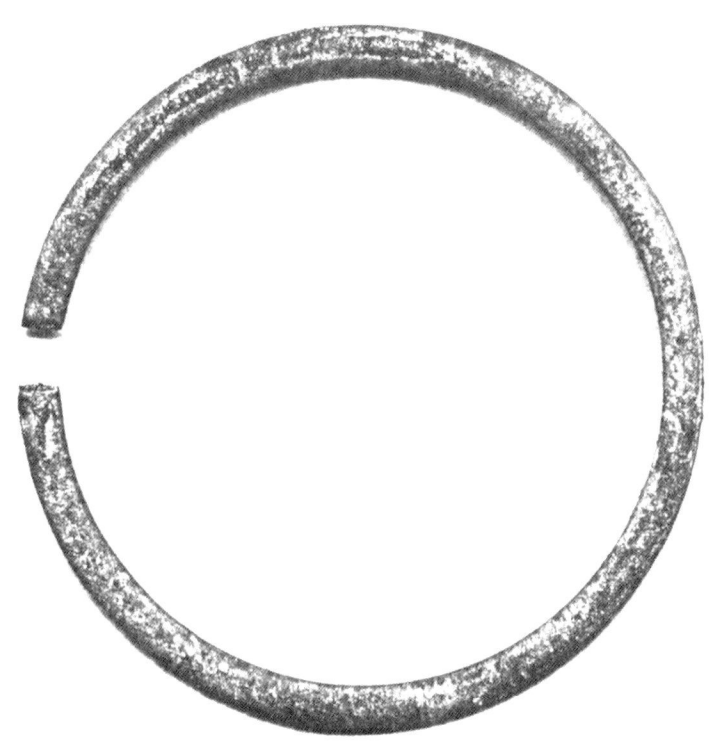

composing by chance

In 1978 Chris Crickmay invited me to describe and demonstrate
chance processes in art and design to the people attending
an open workshop at the Whitechapel Gallery in London. I put
the essence of what I had to say on the poster which could
also be used as a work sheet. To show that chance composing
is not incompatible with traditional ideas of order I set out
the poster symmetrically and left the sequence of statements
and the selection of stencils and typewriter face to be determined by random number. I wanted to demonstrate that the
use of chance is not a hapazard action but is in its own way
precise.

SUNDAY AFTERNOON

once you've decided the composing process stick to
it, accept what comes

COMPOSING

HINTS FOR EASY COMPOSING
BEGIN WITH YOUR FEELINGS AND STRONG CONVICTIONS A-
BOUT WHAT YOU ARE COMPOSING / CHOOSE SOME SOURCES
TEXTS PLACES PEOPLE ETC RELEVANT TO THESE FEELINGS
THEN USE CHANCE PROCESSES

not just music : anything

poems plays novels journeys days lives pages films
radio-programs meals walks holidays philosophies g
ames concerts laws welfare medicare last rites any
thing that has to be organised before one can expe
rience it

BY CHANCE

```
35494 25220 91424 94750 70750 97663 18316 16741
50617 01404 78331 76908 68195 18714 28695 56066
21108 23021 31950 37840 33674 81877 92490 34588
```

WITH CHRIS JONES

This process, or something like it, occurred in the composing of several of the essays and is described within some of them. Other chance processes, perhaps closer to that described on the previous page, are outlined here.

Choosing the quotations before each section:
First I chose authors from whom I'd learnt something during the time when the essays were written and related one author to each section. Then I took one or more books by each and used random numbers* to select a page and a line (and also a book where there was more than one). Lastly I chose a few lines of text in which the line occurred to make evident the thought of which the line is a part. For two of the quotations these chance-selected lines seemed to lose significance out of context so I searched for similar pieces of text which could stand independently. The opening quotation is from an author from whom I'd learnt before the essays were written and was selected in the same way. The titles of the sections were selected similarly, as described on page vi. Quotations, titles and photos were positioned by chance.

Choosing the illustrations before and after each essay:
The photographs are from colour slides I made during the time when the essays were being written and the xerox pictures are from objects found at chance-locations in Zurich and London. At first I tried to consciously choose one photograph to match each essay-title and one xerox picture to match each of the essays for which there was an empty page left at the end. However I found myself getting more and more dissatisfied with these choices, perhaps because I was drawn into over-interpreting the titles and the essays. There seemed to be too much of the essays, and of myself, in what I was doing, and too little of the world. Eventually took a slightly different selection of photographs and xerox pictures, in about equal numbers, excluding those that had been chosen for a particular essay but might not fit others, and used random numbers to determine where each was to go. Although nervous of this producing juxtapositions which might worsen rather than improve the book I found that I liked the chance-positioning better. It seems fresher, less heavy. I did however change an essay title to avoid a juxtaposition that I did not like. The ruled paper on page 242 was included because I originally ex-

pected it to accompany the essay "some reflections on chance" with its references to determinism and because I wanted to include somewhere in the book the pure beauty of such designs. The letter shapes on page 190 were drawn by Joel Fisher from the accidental shapes found in the minute hairs in rag paper and were originally selected to illustrate this essay. I found the illustration by fixing a point in my room using random numbers for the directions x,y, and z and taking the nearest object to that point which could be xeroxed. The T-shirt on page 218 was found in the same way as were other objects that I did not use. Most of the other xeroxed objects were found by picking what I saw at pre-specified places (fountains in Zurich) or pre-specified times (on journeys in London). I decided to include the frames of the colour transparencies when I noticed how they drew my attention and how they kept the photographs from too close an association with particular essays. The photographs of windows and window poems at the start and end of the book were chosen deliberately when I noticed how well they related to the last paragraph of the preface. The opening photograph is from a colour slide chosen because it was made before the essays were written.

This account, written after the event, makes it seems simpler than it was. It took me weeks. The most difficult bit was choosing, and rejecting, various sources of words and pictures until some were found which in some indefineable way felt right and likely to lead to happy accidents. Trying to imagine the results, perhaps the main skill in conscious designing, undermines the confidence, in life, that is the basis of design-by-chance. These examples are of course rather limited and circumscribed, hardly 'pure design'. I've yet to see an example of real indeterminacy in visual design, equivalent to John Cage's 'silent' piece of music. It's difficult, very, to think how and where to begin such an attempt. Perhaps the spatial world is not as free as the temporal? Or is that a false distinction?... This wasn't meant to be an essay. Just a note.

* One source is A Million Random Digits with 100,000 Normal Deviates, The Rand Corporation, The Free Press, Publishers, Glencoe, Illinois, 1965. "This book is the classic as far as random numbers go." S.P.

some reflections on chance

an exchange of letters with David Miller

August 10, '78.

Dear Chris,

Have just come across some reflections on <u>chance</u> in the composer Iannis Xenakis' book <u>Formalized Music</u> (pp. 204-5, 206), which I find interesting; wd. be interested to see a response from you if you have time & interest. Here are the passages:

"We know... that if an element of chance enters a deterministic construction all is undone. This is why religions and philosophies everywhere have always driven chance back to the limits of the universe. And what they utilized of chance in divination practices was absolutely not considered as such but as a mysterious web of signs, sent by the divinities (who were often contradictory but who knew well what they <u>wanted</u>), and which could be read by elect soothsayers. This web of signs can take many forms — the Chinese system of I-ching, auguries predicting the future from the flight of birds and the entrails of sacrificed animals, even telling fortunes from tea leaves. This inability to admit pure chance has even persisted in modern probability theory, which has succeeded in incorporating it into some deterministic logical laws, so that <u>pure chance and pure determinism</u> are only two facets of one entity...."

"... Epicurus, who <u>admits</u> the necessity of <u>birth</u> at an <u>undetermined moment</u>, in exact contradiction to all thought, even modern, remains an isolated case [<u>footnote</u>: Except perhaps for Heisenberg.], for the aleatory and truly stochastic event, is the result of an accepted ignorance, as H. Poincaré has perfectly defined it." (What Xenakis seems to be pushing for here is the acceptance of uncertainty; & of indeterminism <u>along with</u> determinism.)

Anyway — if the above suggests anything to you, I'd be interested to hear yr. comments./Hope all is well.

love,
<u>David</u>.

```
David Miller was born in Australia and lives in London.  His
poem The Story was an inspiration for the essay Opus One,
Number Two.  The correspondence is reproduced with his permission.
```

August 10, '78.

Dear Chris,

Have just come across some reflections on <u>chance</u> in the composer Iannis Xenakis' book <u>Formalized Music</u>*(pp. 204-5, 206), which I find interesting; wd. be interested to see a response from you if you have time & interest. Here are the passages:

"We know... that if an element of chance enters a deterministic construction all is undone. This is why religions and philosophies everywhere have always driven chance back to the limits of the universe. And what they utilized of chance in divination practices was absolutely not considered as such but as a mysterious web of signs, sent by the divinities (who were often contradictory but who knew well what they wanted), and which could be read by elect soothsayers. This web of signs can take many forms -- the Chinese system of I-Ching**auguries predicting the future from the flight of birds and the entrails of sacrificed animals, even telling fortunes from tea leaves. This inability to admit pure chance has even persisted in modern probability theory, which has succeeded in incorporating it into some deterministic logical laws, so that <u>pure chance</u> and <u>pure determinism</u> are only two facets of one entity..."

"...Epicurus, <u>who admits the necessity of birth at an undetermined moment</u>, in exact contradiction to all thought, even modern, remains an isolated case (<u>footnote</u>: Except perhaps for Heisenberg.); for the aleatory, and truly stochastic event, is the result of an accepted ignorance, as H. Poincaré has perfectly defined it." (What Xenakis seems to be pumping for here is the acceptance of uncertainty; & of indeterminism <u>along with</u> determinism.)

Anyway -- if the above suggests anything to you, I'd be interested to hear yr. comments. /Hope all is well.

            love
            <u>David</u>.

*Iannis Xenakis, Formalized Music, Indiana University Press, 1971.
**I Ching or Book of Changes, especially the Wilhelm/Baynes translation published by Routledge & Kegan Paul, London, 1968.

12 August 78

dear David

Nice to get one of your profound questioning letters again. I once
started to read a thick book by Xenakis but put it down when I
ran into what I felt was the rationality-first assumption that is,
I believe, the recurrent symptom of whatever is skew-iff about
this culture we are socially in but, I trust, in our beings,
each much wider-than. There are no regular words in my repetoire
for trying to say how I think it is, only for saying how its
taught to be. So I keep getting drawn into hyphens, and to
words like wider that do not come very close to embodying what
I'm trying to think?

But perhaps I was wrong about Xenakis. I hope so, as his life
sounds good. I dont know his music.

Chance. As you may guess I have a lot of thoughts and notes
stored away (I'd intended to write a book on chance processes)
so I welcome this opportunity to think these thoughts again, and
perhaps to get a little further towards the clarity I dont think
I've managed to reach.

The quotation from Xenakis:
Firstly I cannot imagine how anyone can seriously _want_ or
intend to make 'a deterministic construction' : the idea of
trying to do this fills me with uncomprehension, what possible
satisfaction could there be in doing that? I imagine that it
would generate in oneself that dislike of what one is doing when
one catches oneself making a doodle of some utterly predictable
pattern, or when, lying ill, one gets maddened by the repeats in
the wallpaper? The next sentence 'This is why religions and
philosophies everywhere have always driven chance back to the
limits of the universe' suggests to me a totally different
process than that of making a deterministic construction. To try
to make an explanation of the universe, to try to explain experience, is surely different from composing a new piece of experience. I feel it would take many pages to sort out a mass of

logical muddle that is implicit in making this comparison......

I feel that in both composing and in philosophising the charm and attraction of the apparent completeness comes of the presence of that which lies outside the construct : the presence of oneself, one's mind, the composer or philosopher too, and the inexplicable complexity of life? The completeness is an agreeable contrast to that but surely not the elimination of that, of the possibility of life outside the construction?

But I seem to be quibbling at the inconsistencies coming not so much from Xenakis's thoughts but from the vocabulary he is obliged to use because we so lack words for saying this kind of thought in a way that rings true.

I like what he says about oracles and the mysterious meanings and intentions of the gods, or of fate, or of 'chance' imagined as being a god or fate, and note immediately that Ed*, in his book The Philosophers' Game, makes the writers of the I Ching propose that this oracle shall be so constructed that it is seen to be pure chance, and not an external fate, so that the person consulting it is enabled to see that the decision lies entirely with him or her. The oracle providing only a changed viewpoint that the person could not have got unaided and which allows a chance of seeing one's own bias, or narrowness. Perhaps, if Ed's right about this, the I Ching is a means of getting immediately the more balanced view of what one is doing that can otherwise be got only by waiting a long time, eg when one puts a piece of writing away for a year or so and later is able to see it quite differently?

Although, in using the I Ching, I've often had what seem, at first, to be magical coincidences, I've realised with much experience of the book and of using chance in composition, and in living, that what it does is to enable one to be aware of a mass of connections, between all we experience, that is hidden by our intentions. Its not that the oracle is uniquely the cause or

* Edwin Schlossberg & John Brockman, The Philosopher's Game, Elm Tree Books/Hamish Hamilton, London, 1978.

trigger of what one then sees is happening : it is I'd say the means of losing the engrossment in one's purposes and thoughts that hides what is happening, makes one unable to look.

There is I'm told a new school of mathematicians that denies the logical laws of statistics to which Xenakis refers. The most incredible of these laws, to me, is the one saying that, no matter how many heads you toss in a row, the chance of getting yet another head is still fifty-fifty. The law is obviously true for imagined coin-tossing, in which a pure Platonic kind of chance is assumed to be possible (ie one in which there can be no physical connection whatever between one toss and the next), but for any actual tossing, or other random-generating process, how can one be absolutely sure that the connection between two events is zero? Obviously one cannot. It is interesting that random number tables are recognised by mathematicians to be what they call pseudo-random because the process by which they are calculated, though intentionally very complex, is not completely impossible to describe. The tables of random numbers are close to being unpredictable, ie such that there is no connection between numbers, so you cannot tell what the next will be by studying the previous ones. To get the feel of what mathematical randomness is like try writing out twenty numbers, single-figure numbers from 0 to 9, in a row, before comparing what you have done with the row I will copy onto the next page from a random number table.

What Xenakis says about the laws of chance being deterministic seems to me to be wrong : the law I quoted above surely does posit pure chance?

I did not know that Epicurus had made that so fascinating statement about the moment of birth being undetermined but I like it very much. The replies that astrologers give to the criticism that birth is surely the moment of conception, not separation from the mother, seem very weak, especially when you realise that their trade would be difficult or impossible if they had to accept the moment of conception. I've always felt that the image of time as a thing, or as a line along which we move, is

inadequate, misleading, and feel its likely that esp etc is mysterious only if one holds to our probably grossly wrong view of time, or even the word itself, which seems to confuse rather than clarify.

Of course I agree completely with Xenakis when he calls, as you say he does, for acceptance of uncertainty along with determinism. That is the whole point, I'd say, the religious belief in the bounded nature of what we know and in the coherence, but not the determinism, of what we do not.

Here is the string of random numbers:
22985951665490461995.
The repeats surprise many people as does the absence from a short string like this of some of the numbers, in this case 3 and 7 are absent.

There is a big difference, which John Cage acknowledges, and makes much of, between the results of a deliberately chosen chance process (which all fall unpredictably WITHIN a chosen range of possibilities) and the results of choosing to make something that is indeterminate, as is his piece 4' 33", a duration (four minutes, thirty three seconds) in which any sounds that occur are accepted as music. In the second case there is a genuine giving-up of control of what is to happen but in the first there is only the widening of its range, keeping still to pre-set limits. Cage's dislike of recordings (he seems not to count a replay of a performance as music at all), and much of what he writes, suggest that the true use of chance is outside the range of "chance processes which are meant to be obeyed exactly". In some or all of his compositions he does I think include dis-obedience of the self-imposed law of chance.

I could go on & on but I don't feel that I'm writing what we have not discussed before, or getting close enough to the heart of the matter, so I'll stop now.
All is a lot weller than it was.

                              love
                                  Chris

Here are some words chosen randomly, using random numbers to find
the page and the entry on the page, from the Shorter Oxford
Dictionary which contains about 75,000 entries:

respectively
olio   (stewpot or medley)
acceptable
ypsiloform   (y shaped)
jural   (relating to law or to rights & oblig-
                             ations)
predestinate   (to fix beforehand, or God doing so)
take   (to carry)
tent   (probe or dressing for a wound)
butt   (object of ridicule)
torment   (to agitate, shake or stir)

(LATER: I see now that the words & meanings chosen <u>could</u> be read
as magically relevant to our topic.)
I've tried to indicate the particular meaning chosen by random
process when there are several, or when the word is obselete or
unfamiliar to me. All that is weak about using chance processes,
the lack of any presence of mind, is evident in this example, as
is the release from being in the hands of one person. I'll try
now to make a chance process that is not like that : one in which
the initial decision about where to choose the words <u>from</u> is a
felt and intended communication.*

I look at the books on my desk here seeking something I much like
and notice a book of Lorca's plays, in which are two announcements
to the audience that I love and which I asked to have read in
Spanish at points in my lecture in Argentina** to remind us of the
fantastic, so absent from the functionalist conception of design.
Here are ten words at random from the announcement read in

---

* Actually, I remember now why I chose the Oxford Dictionary.
I'd been listening to a poet reading poems a bit like Lax's,
for 7 hours, & wished that his words had been less his choice
& more the whole range of English words, : the experience for
a listener would be that much more free, inspiring, releasive,
strong, etc?

** See the essay "....in the dimension of Time."

Rosario:

audience
everywhere
becomes
dramatic
Silence!
fighting, fighting,
you
off
curtain

The repeated word, and the exclamation, occur in the text at the points chosen randomly and are included in the list as an improvised disobedience of the self-imposed rule (of taking only one word at a time).
Not very happy with this as a sample of the text I try another kind of sampling, this time copying most of the line from which each word came:

To the audience.
Everywhere walks and breathes the poetic creature
becomes visible reality
to set the dramatic example
Silence!
she is ever fighting, fighting,
You come in from the street.
He takes off his tall silk hat and it becomes illuminated
Grey curtain.

I find, as always, during the tiny drama of seeing what comes next (which makes chance processes more interesting to operate than to see the results of) that I lose all ability to react to the words as a reader of the text I am composing. Even now, minutes later, it has a not-from-me quality that is nice, and a quality of nobody, me included, having been in on its composition, and so not yet having understood it, or 'read' it in the sense of letting it form what meanings it can in my mind. The writer becomes a reader, no more informed than any other. That,

I think, is very nice. Also the fact that anyone can do it, provided they have some sensitivity to the making of the initial decision of what to sample, what text or repetoire of items, and of what constitutes a unit of sampling. Obviously, in this not-so-hot example of mine, the letters and syllables, and even whole words, (which can include say a lot of the's a's of's etc) will not embody much of the reason why the text was chosen, so one has to decide the size of unit after a little trial and error, if sampling the text (to see what it is <u>like</u>) is one's intention.

I suppose using chance processes is no different in principle than for instance deciding to use the sonnet form. What it does is to enable one to operate one's intuitions at a larger scale than ususal, to compose using a far larger range of sources than is in one's memory, in detail, and is outside the capacity of one's word-producing-and-choosing process-skill to do itself. BUT, I find repeatedly, that after some hours/days/months of persistent and seemingly dumb-headed attempts at composing thus, one's intuitive process of word-and-thought-making-and-choosing is much improved, more catholic, and one has learnt not to censor one's words etc and to accept as relevant much that one could not use before. eg my later plays, like Arch & 35 wishes*,were done with a using of almost any (no, not ANY, but with a more inclusive acceptance) remark or event going on in the room as I typed, whereas Superman came entirely from randomly chosen pages of texts in mechanical obedience to process such as I've used here for the dictionary and for the Lorca list of single words. Enough? That anyone can write a single word : that's the real marvel.

---

*35 wishes appears later as an essay. Arch, and Superman Has Had His Day, have appeared in the poetry/performance journal Interstate published in Austin,Texas, issues nos 6-7 & 12.

August 15, '78

Dear Chris,

I _think_ what Xenakis means is that if chance follows laws, predetermined patterns, which can be codified by means of divination tables (e.g. _I Ching_) then what is being named by "chance" is only another version of cause & effect. _Chance_ which is caught up in a network of relations is _meaningful_ in the sense of being given _human meaning_.

The answer to this is perhaps that the meaning is that _provided_ by chance & when we accept it, it means our boundaries of meaningfulness have been in fact _extended_. I believe this is another way of putting the same thing you mean by: "It...enable(s) one to operate one's intuitions at a larger scale than usual..."

What Xenakis may be leaving out of the picture, in regard to _I Ching_ & related sources, is the whole question of _interpretation:_ one must be open to meaning & one must also select. Interpretation -- not only being _able_ to interpret but _having to of necessity_ -- belies determinism. The value of such things as _I Ching_ may be that they can provide one with an opening onto a horizon -- but in this sense chance would perhaps be a method rather than a law?

love
David.

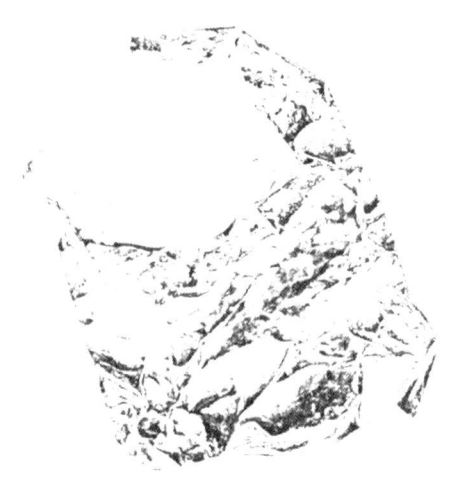

designing designing

Les Belady asked me to speak at a conference on the design
of computer software in 1978. The paper was originally
published under the title 'Designing as a Creative Activity'
in Infotech State of the Art Report; Structured Software
Development (edited by Peter Wallis) by Infotech, Maidenhead,
Berkshire, 1979. It also appeared under the present title in
Design Studies, volume 1 number 1, July 1979, pages 31-35.

This version is photocopied directly from the original typescript because I was attempting to communicate the process
of composing it and this is more evident there than in any
edited copy. Like some of the other essays appearing here it
was written by a process of typing 'camera-ready' pages directly out of mind, with some notes but no previous draft.
The process was carefully plannned but the content not. I
have found that this is not as difficult as it sounds (it's
certainly quicker) and it greatly alters what one writes as
well as how. It is more like speaking in that each word or
phrase inspires the next and what has been said cannot be
recalled once it has been uttered. I permit myself the use
of liquid paper eraser or even to start a page again, but
once a page has left the typewriter it cannot be changed.
It's published. Once it's typed it's published.

This essay was my first with 'prepared pages' in which sub-
titles, quotations, and the lengths of paragraphs are decided
(partly by choice, partly by chance process) before starting
to type. In this way the 'page one problem', or 'how to begin?', a recurrent difficulty when writing for strangers,
is avoided. All one has to do is to invent text to connect
the titles and quotations fixed in advance, trusting in the
process.

OUTLINE OF THE PAPER

The evolution of hardware (craft processes)

Conscious design of hardware (design by drawing)

The designing of intangibles (system desiging, software designing etc)

Design thinking (rational and intuitive)

Designing the design process (designing designing)

Design process control (five criteria)

Design process reviews (changing one's mind as one learns)

Divergent design processes (exploring the situation)

Transformational design processes (perception of problem/solution interdependancy)

Convergent design processes (limits, alternatives, evaluations etc)

The essential point of my paper is that to invent something new, and to bring it into being, is to change not only one's surroundings but to change oneself and the way one perceives, to change reality a little perhaps?
Thus the design process is one of devising and experiencing a process of rapid learning about something that does not yet exist by exploring the interdependancies of problem and solution, the new and the old.

A question : is it necessary, or even possible, to understand complelety the complexities of product and of its operation when one is designing?

DESIGNING AS A CREATIVE ACTIVITY

Some years ago I wrote a book about designing : it was meant to be my goodbye present to the subject, which I then proposed to retire from after twenty years or so. I thought I had been in it long enough and I was beginning to feel that it was not such a creative or liberating activity as I had once fancied it to be. In fact I was beginning to see design not so much as a process of creation as a process of control, a way of fixing things, in the drawing office, that would be much better left to the decision of those whose lives were being conditioned by the shape and form of man-made-things. But, having written the book, there was no escape: I am continually being drawn back, from the activities to which I tried to move, to give talks like this one to audiences who apparently like to hear about the subject from one who has been in it yet not entirely of it, part enthusiast, part skeptic.

However I did escape from designing for long enough to learn something from the other arts, the time arts like film, poetry, music and theatre, to which I became attracted. In particular I learnt a lot from the composer John Cage and began to copy his methods of composing by chance, giving up deliberate control of the result. Another lesson learnt from him is that, if you want to preach, the best way is by example. Everything John Cage does is, as far as I can see, an example of what he recommends. So, now that I am asked to write this summary of some of the main aspects of 'how to design', I am reluctant to do so unless I can make the paper itself an example of the methods I am to describe. How to do that?

Looking for a clue as to how to begin, how to initiate a pleasant flow of thought and words (pleasant for both of us, reader and writer, I trust?) I examine closely the very clear instructions

provided by Infotech for speakers at the conference. The first
instruction, which had to be completed three weeks before sending
the paper, is to provide a short list of major topics,"10-12
subject headings". I provided ten. Another instruction calls
for a written paper of minimum length 3000 words. I calculate
that this would take about ten pages of typing so I immediately
decide to accept these two instructions as determinants of both
the length and the form of the paper : I take out ten blank
sheets intending to write exactly one page on each of the ten
topics. At this point I am in much doubt of the feasibility,
or even the wisdom, of taking such arbitrary decisions, but
I persist, trying to adopt the attitude of 'trusting the process',
the intuition, which tells me that this will turn out alright
even though at this moment I have no evidence that it wont be
a flop.

Next I realise that, though often in the past very attuned to
the subject, and full of words ready to come out, today my mind
is not on it at all. I am still thinking of some quite different
matters that have this week demanded attention and I cant see
any way of getting my thoughts about design back into the
forefront of my mind without a lot of tiresome re-reading and
note-making. And there is not time for that : the paper has to
be posted tomorrow. So I decide that I need a quickly-accessible
source of variety on each of the ten topics, something to get
me going immediately, something to react to. The most accessible
source I have is the book I wrote and my favourite way of consulting a book is by chance process, using random numbers to decide
the page and the sentences to read. I have often found that
an amazingly small number of sentences, picked in this unbiassed
way, and studied carefully, gives much of what one can learn by
reading the whole text. This paper, I decide, will include one
sentence from each of the chapters to which my ten titles refer.
And each section of it will consist of whatever that quotation
brings to mind, now that I am thinking about the designing of
computer software.

Looking now at the first quotation, which is about the evolution
of the complex and beautiful shapes of farm waggons by craftsmen

who knew exactly what to do, in detail, but seldom knew why,
I am reminded of what might, by now, be called the collective
folk-art of writing computer programs, an art in which many
collaborate in an evolving work that is seldom seen and understood as a whole by any individual. To make my process of
composing this paper as much like that as possible, I decide
to pick all the quotations, randomly, before starting to
write, and to type each quotation at a randomly chosen point
on its page before writing anything else. Now all I have to
do is to think of words that will fit my thoughts exactly into
the spaces before and after each quotation. This seemingly
irrational decision feels to me as if its going to add some
difficulty, but also a little excitement, to the process of
writing, as I tailor my words to fit the spaces decided in
advance. Certainly this design of the composing-process will
get me over the writer's perennial difficulty of 'how to get
going' while being only too aware of the many objections that
readers might have to any thought that comes to one's mind, and
being equally aware that any false move may upset the structure
of the paper as a whole and drive one back to square one (a
familiar enough place to all designers, as well as writers).
With my arbitrary design of the form of the paper to adapt
myself to I will have little time or need for these worries.

Not having anything else to say before turning to the first
new page and subtitle I decide to pick at random an illustration
from my book to fill up the rest of this page:

Fig 1

THE EVOLUTION OF HARDWARE (craft processes)

I was asked, in this paper, to describe "how, in general, you do it" ('it' being design) : how one creates THE NEW. And also to say how one evaluates alternatives, how one formulates requirements for a system without pre-judging how to do it, etc. Before attempting to answer these modern questions, which assume that the designing of man-made things is a wholly conscious process in the mind of one person, the chief designer, it is helpful, I think, to look at the works of the past, many of which, though of complex and coherent form, were not 'designed' at all but were evolved over generations by slight modifications made by craftsmen responding to the trials and errors of practical necessity in a social and physical situation that, by modern standards, remained stable for centuries. It is also helpful to think about the evolution of natural forms, a process that is even slower, is probably more complex than anything we do in design, and is even less a conscious process. And we, with our ability to evolve and design things, tangible and intangible, are, apparently, one of the results of this evolution. Its hard to believe.

My knowledge of craft evolution comes largely from the writings of George Sturt, one of the few people to have practiced an ancient craft and afterwards to have put his experience into writing. Normally craftsmen are, perhaps of necessity, people of few words, and often illiterate. He describes how, in making a farm wagon, he relied on knowledge 'which was set out in no book':

> I knew that the hind-wheels had to be five feet two inches
> high and the fore-wheels four feet two; the the "sides"
> must be cut from the best four-inch heart of oak, and so on.

Yet the results of this 'mystery' as he calls it, this body of knowledge 'residing in the folk collectively' is a precision, in relating one part to another, and in relating the whole to the slightest differences in needs and preferences of particular customers, that now seems lost forever. Cybernetically, we might say, there is hidden intelligence in seemingly blind evolution. And a subtle flexibility.

THE EVOLUTION OF HARDWARE (craft processes)

I knew that the hind-wheels had to be five feet two inches
high and the fore-wheels four feet two; the the "sides"
must be cut from the best four-inch heart of oak, and so on.

(a "prepared page" as it was before the text was written)

CONSCIOUS DESIGN OF HARDWARE (design by drawing)

It seems that, traditionally, craftsmen used no sketches or scale drawings. In fact the pictures which George Sturt drew for his book are pathetic examples of inability to draw and envisage in two dimensions, apart from the object itself. But 'design-by-drawing' evolved, out of craftsmanship, perhaps by putting together, on one sheet of paper, the curves and templates used for recording cross-sections, and the like, which could not be retained sufficiently exactly in memory alone. Once discovered, this putting-together onto one sheet, into one data structure as we'd call it, permitted many new developments which were outside the scope of the dispersed intelligence of craft evolution. For instance it allowed a jump in scale:

> Initially this advantage of drawing-before-making made possible the planning of things that were <u>too big for a single craftsman</u> to make on his own, eg large ships and buildings.

This advantage, together with others, equally great, comes of giving up the craftsman's flexibility, his freedom to adjust each part to fit the next and to fit the unique requirements of each customer. Craftsmen are replaced by operatives obeying, without knowing why exactly, the precise dimensions and tolerances of a scale drawing, so that designers, a new class, are enabled to organise the works of several operatives so that they will fit together even though manufactured by people working at different times in different places. Thus it becomes possible to switch from piecemeal evolution, at the scale of the part of a design which itself is largely stable, to the conscious changing of the design as a whole, using a symbolic geometric model, the drawing, to permit experiment that is not possible when changes are limited to the product itself. What strikes me most, about this new freedom to design instead of just evolve, is that it is obtained at such high cost, the loss of the ability to adjust the shape of things to reflect what makes life really human. There arises a profound conflict between the geometric uniformity of what the designers <u>have</u> understood and the barbaric ignorance of everything non-visual that the scale drawing <u>fails to represent</u>.

THE DESIGNING OF INTANGIBLES (system designing, software designing, etc)

The traffic problem (congestion, parking, accidents, etc) is typical of the seemingly insoluble problems arising today when the growth of designed products (eg vehicles, roads, carparks, traffic signals), each designed in isolation by specialists, creates enormous difficulties outside the range of what designers and the drawing process can respond to. So now there exist a number of new design methods that are intended to operate at the scale of these problems, the scale of system, the scale of the invisible and intangible patterns of experience and use.

> Unfortunately the information necessary to assess the feasibility of a new system proposal is scattered among many brains and many publications and some of it may have to be discovered by new research.

That reason is one of several that explain why these new methods of designing at the scale of system are not yet very successful. To solve the problems created by the specialization of the craft process, its fragmentation into a growing number of professions each highly specialized, requires more than a change in methods of thinking and of modelling. It reqires an ability we do not yet have : the ability to communicate fully and quickly across the barriers that separate professions and which isolate their thinking from the experience of users. Perhaps it requires the disbanding of our tradition of separating planning from using, and a return to much less specialized, and more integrated, forms of responsibility and work. Certainly it needs some really fresh thinking about how to use computers and communication media. Our efforts so far to organise life at the scale of the system seem to rely not on rethinking the aims and purposes and modes of operation of activities like transport, education, medical treatment, housing, telecommunications, etc. All we have done so far is to homogenize : to force life to fit increasingly standardized systems that are simple to design but insensitive to how it feels to use them. And our excuse, as professionals, as non-persons, is 'I only work here'. It is clear to me that no big change is possible till we change ourselves and our ideas.

DESIGN THINKING (rational and intuitive)

There is plenty of evidence, apart from what I have to say about the inadequacy of our design methods and the over-specialized way we work as professionals, that we inherit a poor way of thinking about reality, a picture of the world, of life, that fails to reflect the connections between things, and in particular the connections between aspects of life which we habitually divide into seeming opposites : art & science, theory & practice, work & leisure, fact & opinion, etc. We have a split view of life, a view that may well have been necessary to the solving of physical problems, mechanically, but which has now become the main obstacle to solving the problems created by mechanization. In designing, this difficulty appears as the separation of the rational from the intuitive, the practical from the creative. But the briefest study of how the most successful artists, engineers, scientists, etc work and think suggests that they have one thing in common : they have found ways of avoiding this split, of combining reason <u>with</u> imagination, of being both creative <u>and</u> practical, of knowing when its rational to be irrational and when its rational work by experience. To reconcile what seem to be opposites, to resolve contradictions, is the essence of design. And to do this one has to rely on one's nervous system, one's uncontrollable inspiration, one's mind-body.

> The technique can be regarded as one of removing the social inhibitions that each person normally applies to his output during a conversation: it is a deliberate return to the illogical and 'ego-centric' talk of children that has been recorded and explained by Piaget (1959) and others.

That is a description of brainstorming, one of the new techniques for deliberate, rational, stimulation of the irrational, the seemingly crazy, the source of insight and originality. It is the rationale for using the irrational. Equally, a description of what is happening in a seemingly rational technique, like classification, shows that it depends upon intuition, upon making decisions with an inner confidence that cannot be justified by reason.

DESIGNING THE DESIGN PROCESS (designing designing)

The new design methods (brainstorming, system engineering, operational research, and many others) are not easy to use. They very easily become uncontrollable and confusing so that the designers get swamped in a mass of information, and a rigidity of procedure, that prevents common sense, intuition, and one's own abilty to think, from remaining in control. This is because they are presented as what they are not : panaceas, complete substitutes for thinking for oneself, for being responsible for what one is doing. The missing element is what I call 'designing designing' : the conscious direction of part of one's activity and energy, while designing, into the meta-process of designing the process of design. At any point one should be aware of 'what you are doing' and 'why'.

> A great advantage of the formal statement of a possible strategy is that everyone who is expected to put it into effect is able to contribute to the choice of methods and can see clearly how his own actions contribute to the whole.

The design process, or strategy, can be expressed as a program or sequence of proposed techniques, each likely to generate the answer to a question and enabling the next question to be posed. Thus the design process is the designer's way of discovering what he knows, and what he does not know, about this new thing that he has promised to invent, and to integrate into the world as it is. When the designer is a group of people, unused to each other and to the problem, as is so often the case today, the conscious attempt to continually design, and redesign, the design process is an excellent way of seeking the kind of understanding of what is afoot, and willingness to do it, that is so easily lost in working in a design team. The essential step is to recognise that nobody, least of all the chief designer, has,at the start,the knowledge to say how the design will turn out,or even what the problem really is - how it will seem when, eventually, everyone's intuitions become informed by the experience of having designed it. At he start one's intuition is likely to be wrong, informed by what IS,but not by what is to be conjoured into existence.

DESIGN PROCESS CONTROL (five criteria)

One of the most obvious ways of trying to improve one's designing is to identify, and take steps to avoid, the causes of design failure, the reasons why such a high proportion of new products do not succeed (its said to be 4 out of 5). There is quite a lot written by experienced designers about how and why design blunders occur and how to avoid them, eg:

> The actions expected of the design team members must be those of which they are capable, in which they have confidence, and which they are motivated to carry out.

From such very obvious-seeming, but apparently easily-overlooked, statements, by those who have learnt the hard way, I have compiled a list of five most-common causes of failure and expressed these as the following criteria to be applied when asking oneself 'is my design process adequate?' :

1. Identify the critical decisions (those which, if wrong, mean certain failure, eg choice of objectives), and review these at intervals using the best available advice.

2. Relate the cost (of design and research effort) to the penalties for not doing it, trying always to identify the questions it is supposed to be answering.

3. Match the design activities to the abilities, motivations, and confidence of those expected to carry them out.

4. Before seeking the answer to any question assess the reliability and relevance of the sources one intends to consult.

5. Always explore the interdependancy of the product and its environment, ie assess the sensitivity of the supposed definition of the problem to change when seen in the light of novel solutions.

A more detailed description of these criteria appears on pages 57 & 58 of my book Design Methods.

DESIGN PROCESS REVIEWS (changing one's mind as one learns)

One of the simplest ways to organise one's design thinking and documentation is to keep three sets of papers for three categories of thoughts and data : set 1 being for information about the problem and attempts to analyse and understand it, set 2 being for tentative solutions (which should always be developed and noted at the moment of their occurence and never inhibited in favour of more rational work; they can also be usefully categorised as immediate improvisations, new designs which fit the status quo, and more fundamental solutions which call for considerable reorganization), set 3 being for spontaneous thoughts, feelings, doubts, hunches, etc which may well conflict with what is in sets 1 & 2 and which will be useful in periodic reviews of one's strategy, telling one how one's mind and morale is reacting to the procedure one has decided to follow. If one externalizes all these kinds of thinking, instead of just experiencing them, one has the beginnings of the meta-process with which to control one's designing so that it does not get out of touch with reality (reality, in design, being as much one's suppositions, imaginations, and feelings as it is one's picture of the so-called 'real world'). Design process reviews should be occasions when the contents of these three accumulating results of what one has been doing are studied, compared, pondered, slept-on, etc. In reviewing, and changing, one's design process one tries to keep it sensitive, human.

> The new terminologies and procedures of designing and planning lose both their realism and their validity as soon as they cease to reflect the personal issues which matter most to the people who take decisions or are affected by them.

This means that, at any point, no matter how much has been invested in what has been done so far, one retains the readiness to abandon anything that feels wrong, absurd, misguided, etc, and to switch, at all costs, to what seems sensible and right in the light of what one has just learnt.

DIVERGENT DESIGN PROCESSES (exploring the situation)

Divergence is polite word, borrowed from mathematics, for the
process of letting oneself become deliberately confused, uncertain, unworried, uninhibited, etc, in one's thinking about
what the problem really is and what kinds of solution are
relevant to it. As one is, in fact, more likely to be over-
sure, anxious, inhibited, narrow-minded etc in one's initial
assumptions about how to tackle the problem it is useful to
accept the discipline of some of the newer design methods
which are intended to help the designer to break out of
pre-conceptions and thus to be able to see the problem, and
its possible solutions, in a fresh light. There are methods
such as brainstroming and synectics, which help one to change
and widen one's point of view, and methods like observing
users (ergonomics) and rapid searching of literature which
get one out of the desk-bound mentality into some direct
contact with the people and situations one is supposed to be
trying to assist. Its obvious, once you think about it, that
no new thing, no originality or creativeness, is going to
emerge if one sticks rigidly to an orderly design process in
which one never gets in a mess, never loses touch with one's
pre-conceptions, never lets go of THE KNOWN. The first practical step, to this end, is to set aside the objectives, as given
by the sponsor, and to treat them as tentative guesses which
are likely to be revised once the design situation has been
explored. Equally, one sets aside one's own ideas of what is
relevant and what is not. Creativity is not so much having
good ideas as being willing to attempt what is unfamiliar,
being willing to change one's mind.

> It may be useful to think of divergent search as being
> a testing for stability, or instability, in everything
> connected with the problem; an attempt to discover what,
> in the hierarchy of community values, systems, products,
> and components (and also in the minds of those who will
> take critical decisions) is susceptible to change and
> what are to be regarded as fixed points of reference.

Without this divergence, this rough-and-tumble, designing is
merely an ingenious perpetuation of the status quo, the self.

TRANSFORMATIONAL DESIGN PROCESSES (perception of problem-solution interdependancy)

Many design situations do not call for a change in how one perceives the problem, or in the kind of solution that is seen as appropriate. They resemble the situation of the wagon maker, the craftsman, sensitively assisting in a vast collaborative process in which the creativity resides outside the conscious reach of any one designer, and which calls for a selfless dedication. That attitude has been, perhaps, the real strength of engineering, as it has been the strength of Chinese art, Noh theatre, etc. Ego-free, modest, and extraordinarily effective in the long run. But now, in the new situation of partial breakdown of technology itself, brought about by the unquestioned expansion of all feasible technologies regardless of how harmfully they interact, we seem to require a drastic change in how designing is done. To be creative now is not to perpetuate technology but to find new directions, to find ways of acknowledging, in the development of the new, the interconnectedness, the coherence, of life. Particularly, is this so, in the designing of new means of communications, and of computing. Transformational designing is the process of finding new points of reference, while discarding the old, and out of this, an induced doubt, a new skepticism, making a new picture of reality.

> Out of all this comes the general character, or pattern, of what is being designed, a pattern that is perceived as appropriate but cannot be proved to be right.

This is the new, and enlarged version of the 'flash of insight', the eureka-feeling, that comes of finding a new way to perceive the design situation as a whole, a perception in which the conflicts, and apparent opposites, of an 'insoluble' problem are resolved by finding a new kind of solution in which those contradictions do not even arise. One cannot force one's mind to hit upon such insights to order. But what one can do is to plunge boldly, and intelligently, into the previous state of divergent search, confident that, if one tolerates its uncertainties, one's nervous system will do the rest.

CONVERGENT DESIGN PROCESSES (limits, alternatives, evaluations etc)

>One is the conventional <u>out-in</u> strategy, such as an architect may employ when proceeding from the external shape of a building to the arrangement of rooms within it.

That is a description of the customary design strategy in professions like architecture and engineering where, until recently, it has been both possible and desireable to rely, for the general pattern, the organising idea, upon the experienced judgement of one person, the chief designer. But now, when the thing to be designed is often outside the experience of anyone, particularly in its effects and interactions with other things, man-made and natural, the <u>out-in</u> method is a recipie for failure, for perpetuating what is wrong. in the situation as a whole. The strategy for converging on the general form of the design is more likely to be right if it begins with the details, the mass of seemingly conflicting and irreconcilable requirements, and, out of this confusion, seeks a new order. There are, in the repetoire of new methods, several which are very helpful in the data-handling problems of juggling with far more alternative sub-solutions than can be held in memory, and these, as one would expect, make use of computer programs.(eg AIDA, and morphological analysis). However, it is likely that this <u>in-out</u> procedure, if relied upon as an automatic pathway to originality, will turn out to be as unhelpful as was the earlier reliance upon the back-of-the-envelope-sketch, the design tool of the over-confident chief. I suspect that the best designers, in the past as now, have always used a personal mixture of these two approaches, contradictory as they seem, and somehow found ways of getting the advantages of each: speed, clarity, combined with detailed realism.

Now, having come to the end of my ten pages of text to be composed to fit titles and quotations pre-arranged upon the page, I am wondering which of these strategies, and of the others mentioned, I have managed to demonstrate in the writing?

SOURCES

The first quotation, about wagon making, comes from George Sturt's book The Wheelright's Shop; Cambridge University Press; London, 1923, which is a marvellous little book and has remained in print since it was first published.

The other quotations are from my book Design Methods and are the copyright of the publishers John Wiley & Sons; London, New York; 1970. The specific methods, such as brainstorming, synectics, AIDA, etc, mentioned in the paper, are descibed in some detail in this book, which is a review of the newer design methods and an introduction to the principles of design.

The photograph of a farm wagon is from the collection of the Museum of English Rural Life at the University of Reading. It is a South Midlands Spindle-sided wagon from Hailey, Oxfordshire, built in 1838.

(The book by Jean Piaget, which was not given in the original paper, is The Language and Thought of the Child, published by Routledge and Kegan Paul, London, 1959.)

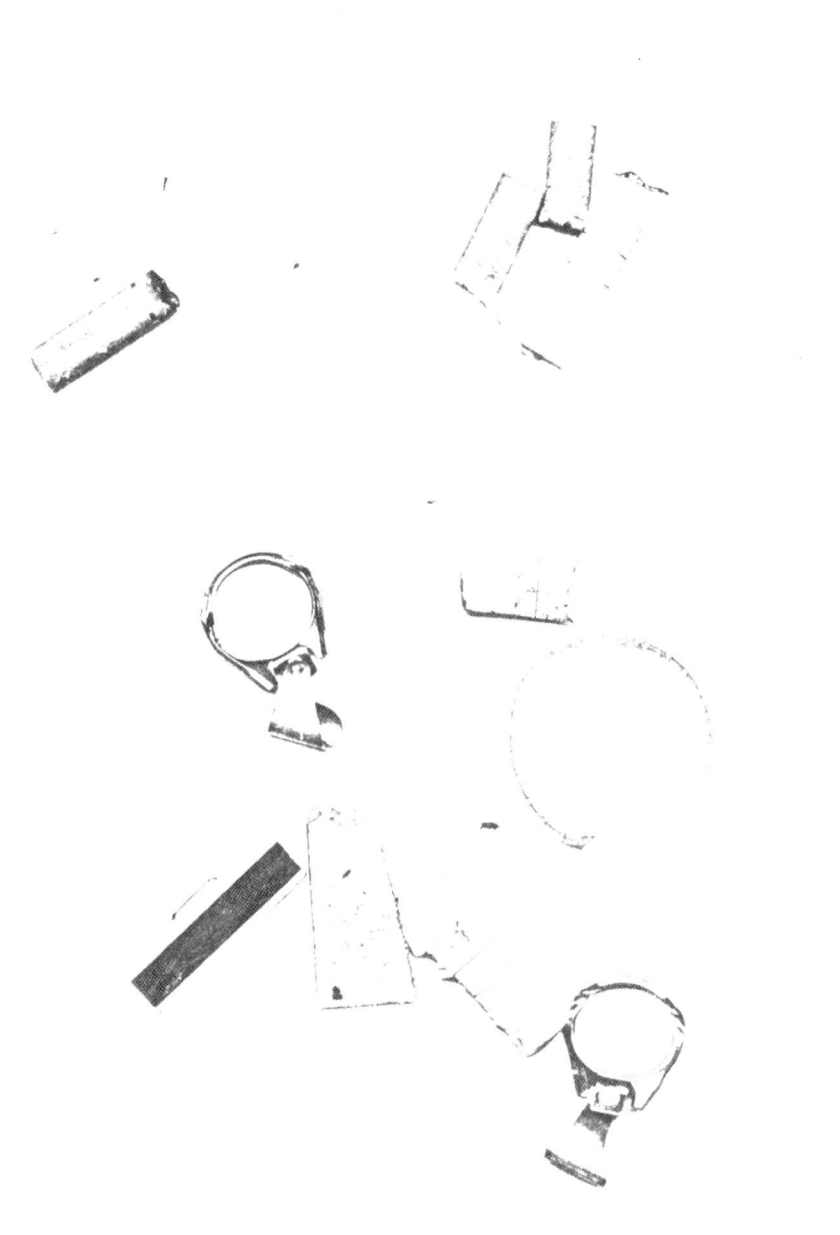

It seems clear that if I wrote to you about something I would not be writing to you but for you and therefore creating an object rather than trying to realize a context where ideas could be experienced. Also, I would be engaging in the peculiar emotional role of asking you to read something not as a direct communication, but as a finished piece, of which you could only be a passive observer. I am not interested in passivity at all and so the process of composing for me is an active process to relate through the context of these words how I think and therefore how I am thinking. The context and the content are interacting and making me as present as I can be without the alienating posture of describing an objective reality - whatever that might be.

                                            Edwin Schlossberg
                                            For My Father

3
IT MUST GIVE PLEASURE

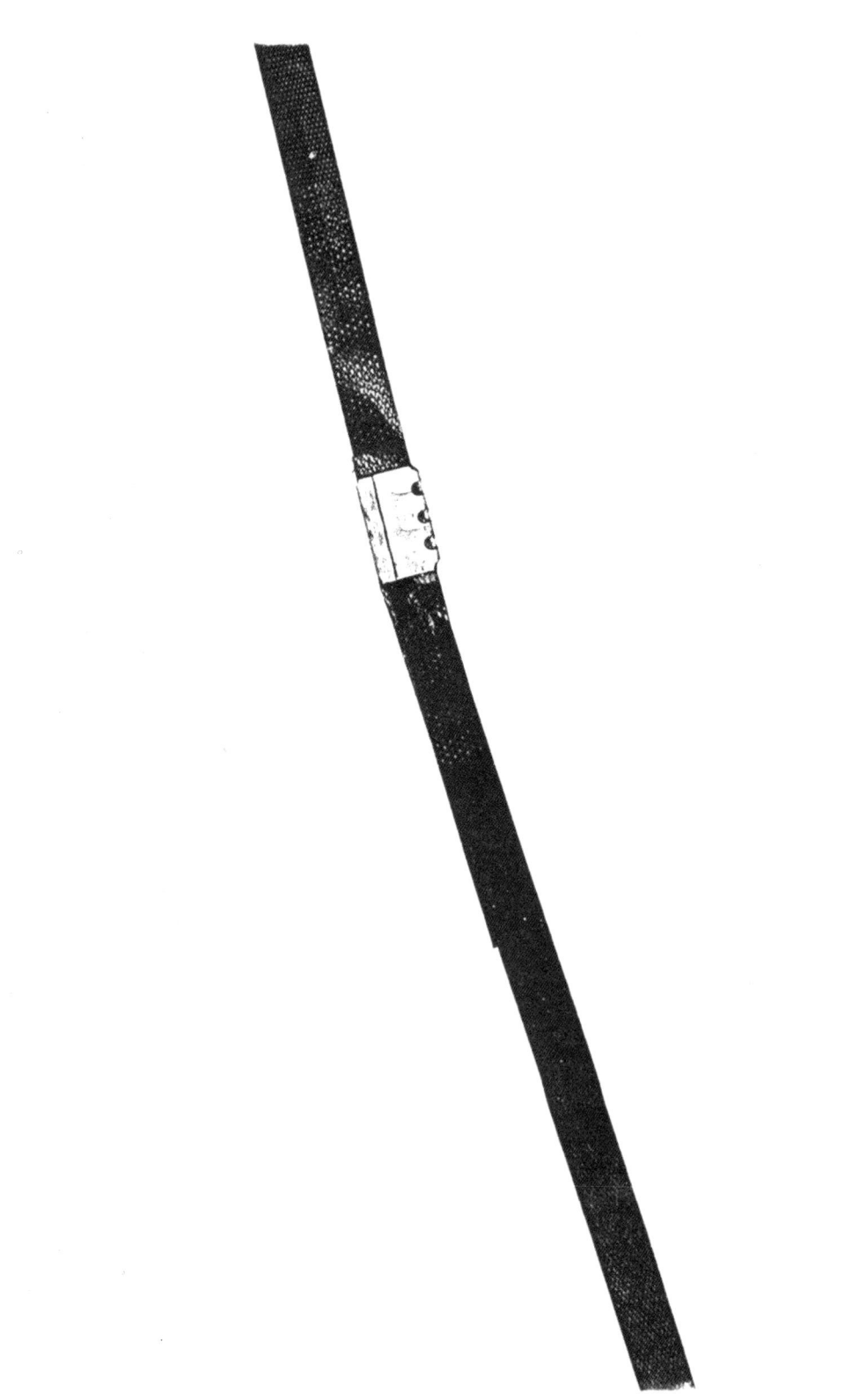

opus one, number two

In 1978 Tony Ward, one of the organisers of the Portsmouth conference on design methods of 1968, invited the speakers to re-assemble for another conference, ten years later. He asked us to speak of our (probably changed) views of the subject and of its relation to 'the real world'. The conference did not take place but some papers were written and published in Design Studies. This paper appeared in Design Studies volume 1 number 6 in October 1980 pages 373-7. I am grateful to Butterworth Scientific Ltd (formerly IPC Science and Technology Press Ltd) PO Box 63, Westbury House, Bury Street, Guildford, Surrey GU2 5BH, for permission to reproduce it here.

The paragraphs at the start of Part 1 and Part 2 were written after the paper had been completed.

Part 1 The architecture of the Open University

My attempts, while thinking-at-the-typewriter, with the help
of various authors, to understand why design methods seem to
have failed, why industrial life seems to have failed, become
rigid, homogenized, inhuman. What's missing?
. . . .

Since 1968 I have found myself leaving most of what, up till
then, I had been doing. I left design methods, feeling that it
had become a rigid and inhuman activity, and I left academic
life, at the Open University, feeling that that too had become
rigid and inhuman. And now there are many critics of design
methods, as applied to architecture, who imply that the rigidity
came from the misconceptions of those, like myself, who foisted
mechanical ways of thinking onto the architectural profession,
which thus lost some of its freedom. The methods did not fit
the mind.

I do not want to continue this dispute. It would surely be
better to seek (in thinking about what we have experienced these
last ten years) not blame for what has gone wrong but some
responsibility for putting things right.

I chose this title 'The architecture of the Open University' not
because I have a lot to say against the way it is organized
(which I have) but because the title makes it evident that we
are now living on the other side of a revolution in industrial
life: the...

Just as I am thinking how to complete that sentence I am amazed
and delighted to hear, on the radio, something of a kind I've
never heard before:

> at a break in a concert a most un-announcer-like voice,
> presumably a member of the orchestra, sitting some way from
> the mike, says 'we will play the finale – opus one number
> two'

I am amazed because I can't recall any occasion when I've

noticed a broadcasting authority giving up, and thus making
visible, its normally hidden exclusion of anyone but those
with officially approved voices, and officially approved words,
from making any announcements. This control, absolute as it
usually is, is, if you think of it, the way in which all broadcasting organizations put limits to the public space which they
control. I'm delighted to have heard this tiny breakdown in
that homogeneity not only because it is an accidental blow for
freedom but because it immediately opened to the imagination an
utterly different, and far more human, kind of broadcasting that,
in the 50 or so years since the invention of radio, we have hardly
ever been allowed to experience. A radio in which the authority
is gone and we rely in the studio, as we do in conversation and
in most other occasions for talking and communicating, on impro-
vization and not on planning.

That little interruption, from whoever spoke those not-quite-
official words, has almost said what I was about to say about
the recent revolution in industrial life. The change from products to processes, from hardware to software, from architecture =
buildings to architecture = the way life is organized. The
Open University's buildings are a small and irrelevant part of
what it offers to students whereas the teaching programmes, and
the papers and broadcasts by which they are transmitted, together
with the odd corners of houses and technical colleges where the
learning takes place, are what the university consists of. The
change from university-as-place to university-as-procedure
(which can occur in almost any place) is the revolution I am
talking about.

The revolution-within-that-revolution, which has never happened,
but which is hinted at in that half-unofficial announcement, is,
to me, what is missing from design methods, from software designing, from architecture, from industrial life : humanity.
Industrial life, considered as a set of organised procedures,
excludes, at almost every point what broadcasting authorities
exclude from announcements : the freedom to act as a person and
not as a THING. Things, which are not expected to think for
themselves, being the model for professional behaviour. For

doing what you are paid to do. But to be a person is surely to BE. We have somehow accepted, as normal, as "in the public interest", that industrial life is to be organised to eliminate all opportunities to be.

But I promised not to argue, to get angry, and here I am beginning to do that..........Is there any way to put things right?

It is now some hours since I put that question but no answer comes.

The question is too difficult.

So I begin to consult some of the voices to which I have been listening, during the years. Perhaps an answer may come, unexpectedly, from another mind, if I sit here a little longer, waiting. And typing out some words from an armful of books taken from my shelves. Some of the books that have taught me to look outside that world of methods; which once seemed larger than it does today.

---
    you & I, we, already exist
    in this work. it has no doors.
    we already exist in it.

    without too great a fuss
    we have taken posession
    of the restaurants & cabaret of West Europe
    & we sing, eat & drink to your health.

Perhaps that one voice, David Miller's, is enough.

Enough to let us realise that to talk and think of the world as something apart from ourselves is nonsense. We cannot be outside.

Though, I guess, our roles can limit us to small segments of the world. So that it seems, as Tony Ward put it in his letter inviting papers for this conference, that what's "actually done" is "out there, in the world". But we are in the world. We are the world. All of us. What is this paradox, this near-certainty that we are not alive to being alive?

A few days ago I read something (in the draft of a thesis on design methods & architecture) which allowed me to recover much of my old enthusiasm for the subject:

> the isolate is an abstract fiction: to understand reality is to see and understand things in their connectedness and in their interpenetration, one to the other.

The thesis is by W H Nichols. What I suddenly recaptured was the conviction that, whatever may have become of design methods in recent years, the original intentions of those of us who tried to improve design processes, ten or more years ago, was to respond to the connectedness of everything. To cease splitting life into fragments, particularly when it is people and the experience of life that is being fragmented. I realised that the intention of the new methods, (mine anyway, and I think its true of many others) was to overcome the limitations of professional procedures in all the design professions. Their inability to respond to life itself, which was becoming the object of design, as the extent of what is man-made grew and grew. To make what Thomas Khun has called a paradigm-shift, in the nature of designing. To change the objectives, the criteria, the procedures. To abandon specialisation, which pre-supposes that products, buildings & the like can be adequately designed by separate groups of professionals, in isolation, leaving the connections between designed things and what exists to take care of itself.

I think now, when I reconsider this notion, that what has happened is this:

Interconnectedness was accepted as a fact.

Design processes have somehow been adapted to permit the integrated design of building-complexes, shopping precincts, hypermarkets, multi-storey hospitals, urban motorways etc

But the paradigm-change was resisted. We still have specialised design professions, and we still have the old idea that what is being designed is "objects". The designers persist in acting as if they themselves are objects and the people whose lives are being shaped by this objective process are being treated as objects. Without minds of their own.

We have yet to face up to the changes needed in everyone's roles, self-images, procedures, and ways of life, if the interconnectedness for which we design is to include the most difficult part of the problem:

what makes us people, and not objects, is that we <u>are</u> the interconnections.............as objects we interconnect to a large degree, but as minds we interconnect far more than that.

So, if, as we have done, we design for interconnection only at the object level (limiting ourselves to what can be calculated and neglecting what can only be imagined, and felt, but not measured), we are bound to create a way of life which is experienced as inhuman. Homogenized architecture : homogenized milk.

we will play the finale - opus one, number two

At last. at last, this piece of writing begins to feel good. Begins to be a nice process. I'm beginning to enjoy doing it. Reading it? That's another matter. Unpredictable.

What can we learn from architecture? The old architecture. Buildings, places............places to be. As described by P'ei Ti, writing a thousand years ago, in China:

> In front of the balcony,
>   as the expanse of water
>   fills with ripples,
> The solitary moon
>   goes wandering without pause.
> From the depth of the valley
>   the cries of the monkeys rise;
> Borne by the wind
>   they reach me in my room.

The building itself is barely mentioned. Yet its presence is felt. What is described, recreated, is the experience. Of being there, and of what else is there. The state of mind. Consisting of all these things. This, this so delicate awareness, is closer, I suppose, to "life", to what I'm now calling the new architecture, the architecture of being, of being here, of making the connections, for oneself. ?

When we design the interconnectedness what becomes of this?

The architecture of the open university, of industrial life. The architecture of process. Of life as process. As process designed.

> at this point:
> viola music.

I'm still quoting from David Miller's poem. The Story.

> to question the term "unit" is to
> question the term "totality"
> & I question it.
> no one knows what is meant by
>   "perception".

---

opus one, number two

the new architecture

the architecture of all that's made

we speak for ourselves

as the architects

of how we live

when can we begin? all of us

That was not meant to be a poem. It was meant to be a list.
A list of some of the nicer thoughts to be extracted from what
has appeared so far, in this piece. From what has come to mind.

Briefly, what seems to have happened, is this:
The new methods, which once seemed as if they could, and would,
be used to make designing more sensitive to the ways in which
life's now lived, have instead been used, if they have been used
at all, to make it less so. In widening the field of what is
designed we have retained the control that a craftsman exercises
over his work, the artist of his medium. Forgetting that the
medium has changed its nature. That, in a widened designing,
we begin to be the medium ourselves. And we dont need to be
made, to be designed. We already ARE. How then, in widening
design, are we to share control, to share the role of architect?
I know very well that that question can be said to be in the
realm of politics, not architecture. Of course its impossible
to fit into the conventional notion of what architectue IS.
The old conception has to go. Beautiful as it was, in front
of the balcony. The paradigm has changed. And what we see
so far is very ugly.

......true beauty is forced far off, and retires to distant places.

> we already exist in this work.
> it is not context. there is no containment.
>
> a wilderness.
> a house.
> a City.
> in the work our faces (& the faces of our friends)
> assume a reckless humour,
> I
> love them, the glass
> floods with light.

A light used to flood, in the fifties, when we thought about
design-as-process, about all designing as one process, a collective work. The same light flooded, in the thirties, and before, when they talked of function, function as liberation from
self-expression, from arbitrary imposed forms, from tyrrany,
the tyrrany of the old, kept alive, as imposed forms, long after
the life those forms reflected, and imposed, was over. It
was a light. Where is the light now?

we will play the finale
though its not a finale
more like a new start
opus one, number two
the architecture of the open university
the architecture of
              of

It hasn't happened yet. And yet its surely here, already,
in its essentials, in ourselves, and in what we have made, in
the accidents, the implications, of what has been done, to extend life. Just as all the words to be written are present,
potentially, in the making of pens, paper, presses, computers,
and the like. So many houses, implicit in the brick. These
words. These people.

What's absent is ourselves. Hiding in our roles. Here we are.

Not many of us are members of the Open University. Not many of us are architects, or engineers, or politicians, or announcers,

Why not? Why are we excluded, from being? The open university could have been for everyone. Perhaps it still can. Like the phone.

It needs a discipline, obviously. A discipline of process. An architecture, of being. A way to share control. Here we are. We've got the wrong disciplines. (These staccato sentences: they were written very slowly. Is that a hint?) We need a little recklessness.

How to put things right?

Part 2   Opus one, number two

More thinking-at-the-typewriter in which I realise that, in
attempting to change the processes of design, in trying to
increase the scale, the scope, of the man-made, we failed
to change the aim, the goal. Design-as-process, design at
the scale of being, does not have a goal. Its non-instrumental.
Its a question of living, not of planning life-not-yet-lived.
Design without a product. The idea seems nonsense if applied
to designing by professionals. But, seen as part of an
historic shift from product-thinking to process-thinking,
isn't it what we overlooked? Designing disappears : becomes
a way of using, an enlivening of how we live. There is no
outcome. Its a question of being, without stop
. . . .

OPUS ONE, NUMBER TWO

the architecture of process
the architecture of what is happening
the architecture of being

A time for relearning.
Ten years later we realise that, as makers of methods, we have
got lost.
The situation created by what we did, and by the reactions to it,
does not allow us to proceed. We are obliged to pause, to rethink, to discover what went wrong. The obstacles that now
confront us give us the opportunity to relearn, to develop, to
grow. To give up whatever it was that led us astray. Let us
use the opportunity, this conference, to do that. What we did
before is finished. We cannot repeat, we have to change. We
are in a muddle. Let's begin with ourselves in trying to sort
it out. Where did we go wrong?

My guess:
We sought to be open minded, to make design processes that would
be more sensitive to life than were the professional practices

of the time. But the result was rigidity: a fixing of aims and
methods to produce designs that everyone now feels to be insensitive to human needs. Another result was that design methods
became more theoretical and many of those drawn to the subject
turned it into the academic study of methods (methodology)
instead of trying to design things better. The language used to
describe designing, and to describe the aims and purposes of
things designed, became more and more abstract. The words lost
touch with how it feels to be a designer and how it feels to
inhabit the systems being designed. Abstract language can often
be a release from the status quo. It was a release in the
beginnings of functionalism, and in the beginnings of design
methods. But it can so easily become fixed, in which case it
turns, overnight, into a tyrrany.
That, I think, is what went wrong. We did not see that what we
proposed was good only as long as it remained a process, and
that it would become bad the moment we allowed it to become a
product. A thing.
And why did the new methods become fixed? Become objects?
My guess, and its only a guess.....

no, I shouldn't say 'only'......the word implies that guessing
is a poor substitute, for 'proof', or for 'logical certainty'
or some such objective statement......but objective statements
are, in the discussion of designing, a delusion, perhaps the
very delusion that set us on the wrong tack?.....they are
'things'...

my guess, my feeling, my impression, my thought about this, is
that, though we saw the need to change the processes of designing we did not see the need to change its aims. We retained the
concept of 'product' as the outcome of designing. We did not
see that we were accepting only a part of the challenge which
we took up : the challenge to transform the idea of progress,
which presumes a specific goal, into the idea of process, which
does not. This transformation is I now realise, a main event
of the twentieth century, though it may have started earlier.
A change which is happening in many areas of life, not only in
design. I'll pause, for a moment, in this most difficult bit

of thinking for me, to name a few examples of the change from
progress to process in other fields of life, before discussing
our blindness over this question of goals.

I've been reading the books of Martin Heidegger, whose way of
doing philosophy can be seen as a change from progress to
process. What he does is to refuse to be drawn into making any
fixed conclusions, concepts, or theories, which are the accepted
aims of Western philosophy. Instead he writes and teaches a mode
of what he calls 'meditative thinking' that is not intended
to reach conclusions but to keep the process of thinking alive.
While this kind of philosophy is happening, while the thinker
is thinking, then its happening. As soon as he reaches a conclusion its over, dead. The aim does not disappear but it
changes its nature. For what Heidegger calls 'calculative thinking', thinking-as-a-means-to-an-end, the aim is external to the
process. The use of thinking to establish truth, certainty; to
control something. But for 'meditative thinking', or what I am
calling process-philosophy, the aim is internal : to maintain
the process. Because, says Heidegger, only while we are
giving our minds to whatever it is that provokes our thoughts
are we being truly human. Calculative thinking being something
that diminishes us, to a degree. His books are full of warnings
that if, through the technologizing of life, calculative thinking
becomes the universal mode of thinking, then the most valuable
part of human life will have gone. That which makes us human.
He does not say that technology and calculative thinking should
be ended but that they must not become the whole of life. He
accepts that, in their way, they are realities, parts of ourselves, something we cannot discard but something we should be
free to accept or refuse according to the occasion.

I've also been drawn to the works of Samuel Taylor Coleridge
who seems, in the early nineteenth century, to foreshadow this
change in the mode of doing philosophy. He repeatedly points
to two meanings of the word 'thought'. It can mean the conclusion, or image, or whatever, that comes to mind. It can
also mean the process of arriving at a conclusion. These two,
he keeps saying, are indivisible : you cannot have one without

the other, just as you cannot have a cake without cooking (though
I suppose you can have cooking without cake). His ideas are full
of instances of awareness of this relationship between process
and its result. The idea of complementarity, as we'd say.

Is there a more practical example than these, of the change from
progress to process? What about 'production' itself : the process industries, like chemicals or electricity, or perhaps the
construction industry, where the processes are not so obvious?
It IS obvious that, in all these cases, there is a continual
changing of the nature of the production methods : from making
things a few at a time to making them in larger batches or by
continuous flow production. The products and their 'consumption
patterns' are changing in the same way : from individual artifacts made 'to last' to disposable goods and service-processes
the purpose of which gets harder to explain to unwilling
consumers except as a means of creating jobs so that they can
earn enough to buy the products and keep the production system
going. That is perhaps an unfair description but it does point
to a shift of some kind in the relation of means to ends. I'm
surprised to see how close is this apparent loss of purpose in
industrial production to the 'purposeful purposelessness' which
John Cage attempts in his music and which he sees in zen. I
remember wondering, at a conference of designers who were
trying to come to terms with 'artificial obselescence', (about
which they felt guilty) if the throwaway culture IS bad. It's
uncannily similar to natural cycles of growth and decay, spring
and autumn, birth and death. Our joy and sadness. Consider the
lilies. Not only zen, and christianity, but all the religions,
seem to have taken up this point as central. They all seem to
recommend a giving-up of intentionality, purpose......a giving
of oneself. One of the nicest statements I've seen of this is
by Rabindranath Tagore, speaking, in his 'song offering'
Gitanjali, of the ideas of Indian religion:

> Children have their play on the seashore of worlds. They
> know not how to swim, they know not how to cast nets.
> Pearl divers dive for pearls, merchants sail in their
> ships, while children gather pebbles and scatter them
> again. They seek not for hidden treasures, they know not
> how to cast nets.

I'm getting the feeling that this bit of learning that I'm trying to do is going to reveal that there is nothing to learn. That we know it already : what was wrong with our methods, or with how we used them, or failed to. That what we were trying to achieve, to impose, would happen of its own accord, if only we stopped trying to make it happen? But I cannot make that jump. I have to procede, with the process, the process of thinking through the idea of design-without-product, design as process-in-itself.

I once heard the Italian architect Sergio Los talking of the using and inhabiting of a building as a process, a physical process, differing only in scale from the physical process of constructing the building. In both processes materials and people move about over the site changing the positions and forms of what is there. So, in this view, building is a form of living and living is a form of building. That's one way of realising that there are no products, no fixities, only continuous flux. And that designing, making, and using are all processes that are added to, and interact with, the natural processes of the places where these activities occur.

But to return, as I promised, from these examples to my guess that the new methods became rigid, though they were not intended to, because we, the method-makers, did not realise that we were recommending only a part, and not the whole, of the historic shift from the idea of progress to the idea of process. What we failed to see, or, if we saw it, what we failed to act on, was that, though progress has a purpose external to itself, process does not.

When you go to process, you lose the goal, you lose the aim.

I'm beginning to see it now.......THERE ARE TWO KINDS OF PURPOSES ....the purpose of having a result, something which exists after the process has stopped, and does not exist until it has stopped......and there is the purpose of carrying on, of keeping the process going, just as one may breathe so as to continue breathing?.......the purpose is to carry on.

In the old idea, the purpose was to STOP, to reach the PROMISED LAND, the end of progress......that's it, I think I've grasped it.

So the fault in method-making was that we made methods as 'products' and handed them on to the designers expecting them to use them, as 'tools', as means to an end. Which became a logical trap, turning the idea of process into its opposite? And many designers rejected these tools, which was fortunate, perhaps.

We didn't realise that the design-as-process outcome is the design process....... for everyone.......not for designers... ....we didn't liberate ourselves from being designers..... designers of predicted outcomes......we didn't drop the role.....

.....we didn't realise that the people inhabiting the world-designed, if we changed to process-design, have to be designers, every one of them.....

SUDDENLY MY THINKING SPEEDED UP.....SHOT AHEAD OF TYPING....AHEAD OF BEING BAFFLED, STUCK....SUDDENLY I CAN SEE AGAIN.......I'LL try to give the feeling of it in these scraps off the tape I made when I felt I could not continue the slow, slow, thinking-and-typing which I've been doing up to now......

         .....they have to be all designers, all designing, all process, all continuing, never stopping, blah blah blah.....this is IT!
this is it I'm SURE!....this is, this is, is......terribly roughly .....this the EDGE, to get over, the phase difference, or something, the paradigm change, callitwhatyouwill, change of phase,.....

.....here we are.....designing, now, DOESN'T HAVE AN OUTCOME..... we were too embarassed to go on with that thought.....we should have stuck with it.....

.....design has an outcome, a continuation,......the outcome is that it continues....and the professionals have to stop being there AT ALL, in THAT role.....they have to just be people, like everybody else.....

So it was our talking about design from the point of view of the professional that made it impossible to GET ON......that led to that uneasy feeling that the whole business was going wrong.......

.......talking about design processes in the way we really BEGAN (with the Indian Village*,and all those other fine thoughts, and they WERE fine, far finer than what's been thought since) from the point of view of trying to respond to the interconnectedness of everything,....if we'd stuck WITH that......(and now we can still DO that, I think).....if we stick with that idea, if we HOLD it......the process should go right...?

Chris Alexander, where are you? *

Time for music. The violas. The finale even. No. Not music. None of that rushing on and on. Its a question of being. Of being here.

REFERENCES & NOTES

* ALEXANDER. Christopher Alexander's book Notes on the Synthesis of Form, (Harvard University Press, Cambridge, Mass, 1964) & his Indian Village design, were a recurrent topic at the Portsmouth Conference, though he was not present in person.

BROADBENT & WARD. The Portsmouth Conference was organised by Geoffrey Broadbent and Anthony Ward who also edited the proceedings as Design Methods in Architecture (Lund Humphries, London, 1969).

CAGE. I cannot find the several places in his writings where John Cage refers to 'purposeful purposelessness' but the idea permeates most of what he has written about music and life eg in his first book Silence (Wesleyan University Press, Middletown, Conn., 1961).

COLERIDGE. Samuel Taylor Coleridge's ideas are not easy to find and understand and many commentators do not seem to have grasped the point to which I refer, which I found most readily in Owen Barfield's book What Coleridge Thought (Oxford University Press, London, 1971). This book is an attempt to reconstruct, from his scattered writings, the main ideas of the great book of philosophy which Coleridge promised but did not write.

HEIDEGGER. All his writings embody his way of making philosophy a process of thinking rather than its conclusions. Particularly relevant to design and technology are the essays What Calls for Thinking? and The Question Concerning Technology in Martin Heidegger, Basic Writings, edited by David Farrell Krell (Routledge & Kegan Paul, London, 1978).

MILLER. The quotations between horizontal lines (which appear as integral parts of the poem) are from David Miller's poem The Story (Arc Publications, 3&4 Oldroyd, Todmorden, Lancs, Britain, 1976). In case of difficulty finding this, or other, of his writings (they exist only in small press editions and are often out of print) write to David Miller, 36 Colville Terrace, London W11.

NICHOLS. W H E Nichols in his as yet uncompleted thesis on Design Methods, at the Dept of Design, North East London Polytechnic.

P'EI TI. The verse quoted is from The Pavilion of the Lake, a section of the Poems of the River Wang by Wang Wei and P'ei Ti which appears, translated by C J Cohen and Michael Bullock, in Anthology of Chinese Literature, from Early Times to the Fourteenth Century, edited by Cyril Birch (Grove Press, New York, 1965).

TAGORE. The quotation is from Gitanjali (Song Offerings) by Rabindranath Tagore (originally published in the poet's own translation from Bengali by Macmillan & Co, London, 1913, and republished extensively).

Looking now at this list of largely poetic quotations, which enabled me to feel that I was coming close to what is missing from design as we've known it so far, I am reminded that the question 'what is it for?' is irrelevant to poetry, as it is to a tree, or to life itself. Since completing this article I have been using the names pure design, and contextual design, to describe this notion of design without purpose, other than that of fitting what is, which includes both physical nature and the minds/bodies of all who are involved in the activity and what it brings into being.

I am reminded also that, for poetry as for life, the role of objective critic, of outsider, is a dead one, destructive of what is being created : a new experience. In this new conception of design, which seems slowly to be appearing here and there, there is no outside; we are all players. 'We will play the finale, opus one, number two'......

---

you & I, we, already exist
in this work. it has no doors.
we already exist in it.

"...in the dimension of Time."

This was written for the architecture-and-environment journal Espacios CEPA, published in Argentina by Ruben Pesci. Ruben asked for exactly 17 pages to fit a space in a forthcoming issue (that was the length of another essay which I had promised him but which had to be withdrawn as I'd forgotten it was already promised to Marina Waisman's journal Summarios). As there was very little time left to write it in, and as I had no topic in mind, I used again the method of composing 'camera ready' on 'prepared pages' bearing quotations chosen and positioned by chance, letting the quotations decide what I was to write. It was one of the essays that I most enjoyed writing, free of anxiety and full of surprises. If I remember rightly, the title was not decided until somewhere near the end of writing it. But it was quite difficult to write: all that diversity and not knowing where it led.

After sending the essay off to Argentina I was disappointed to find that it was not going to be published after all as the journal was re-organised, and is now called Ambiente. However, on a later visit to Argentina I met Ruben and he promised to print it eventually in the new journal, together with an interview. An edited and typset version of the english text first appeared in Design Studies, volume 1, number 3, in January 1980. I am grateful to Butterworth Scientific Ltd (PO Box 63, Westbury House, Bury Street, Guildford, Surrey, GU2 5BH) for permission to reproduce it here.

This text is reproduced from the original typescript.

Looking for a way to begin this article I came across the last
paragraph of Marcel Proust's Remembrance of Things Past in
which he realises that each of us exists, outside the dimension
of space, as an immense (perhaps grotesque) being,"plunged
into the years",consisting, at any moment, of the effects and
memories of all that we have experienced in our lives. What
becomes of design if we try to make it operate in time as well
as in space? And if we accept that each person is a lifetime?

> Bruce asked me to advise him about a chair he was
> designing. I realized in talking with him that its
> probably a mistake to impose one's ideas upon a product,
> an object. Better to use one's design ability to design
> a process by which the object can be shaped by the users
> and by the whole situation.

That quotation, like the others which I have already chosen
for this article, was picked by a chance process from the
books and papers about me as I write here, in London, and,
like the other quotations, has been pre-typed on the page
at a position which has also been picked by chance. Thus,
in composing the article, I am faced with a task that is
in some ways similar to that of a designer who has decided
to make his design process, and the resulting design, sensitive
not only to his present ideas but to his past, and to the
past activities and lives of others. A deliberate attempt
to compose something not so much by conscious intention
and control, but by letting what already exists arouse the
ideas that are being given form and substance here.

In the case of Bruce's chair I was appalled, as always[*], by
the high degree to which his designs and sketches imposed,
upon the wood and other materials he intended to use, a
conception of 'what is a chair' and 'what is sitting' that
owed much to all the designs seen in glossy magazines and
very little to the exact nature of materials, of production
processes, and of the very varied ways in which people
actually sit. Nearly every design one sees, it seems to me,

* not only by this design, but by most designs

is so strong a reflection of our ignorance of the lives of those for whom its intended and of the designer's assumption that his thinking is adequate to what he is doing to the world. Poor world. What are we doing to it?

But, as soon as I catch myself typing that deadly word 'it', I realise that the world is not an it, is not a thing, detached from ourselves. It is ourselves. The world is not just the earth and sea and sky and plants and animals and houses and roads and cities and cars and farms etc. It is also our lives, our experiences and memories, our minds. When we say 'the world', and when we call it an 'it', we are making a false distinction between the things we perceive and the processes of perception and recognition by which we learn to see and act. It is obvious, as soon as one stops to think about it, that an abstract word like 'world' is not the name of an object. It is the name of a great mass of shared experience out of which we infer the existence of the planet earth and of all the things upon it. For everyday living it is of course necessary and appropriate to use this verbal convention as if it were a fact, but when we are designing, when we are trying make a change, or an improvement to what we call world, it is surely right and necessary to understand what it is we are really doing, and not base our decisions on words that we know to contain a false picture of reality. Designing, as I see it now, is, or could be, the process of unlearning what we know of what exists, of what we call the 'status quo', to the point where we are able to lose our pre-conceptions sufficiently to understand the life, and lives, for which we design,   and where we are aware of the ways in which new things, added to the world, can change the way we see it. Visiting a foreign country, or returning after many years to a place one knew, one feels immediately the surprise of a person whose ideas have ceased to fit reality.

> Any probing of perception seems to quickly undo so many assumptions. And to dispose immediately of the mind-body split. I'm amazed that so far perception theory seems not to have dented both physics and philosophy,

making nonsense of the humanist position. There is no
human. There is no life. Let alone "other planets".
These are words. Are words these?. What is. This
degree of uncertainty, that's good, surely, and real.
No need to fear the universe. Or to DEPEND on words.
Deepend. The words are real words. Absolutely! But
really nothing else. Yet we do communicate, we think we
do. The sender usually. But communication's probably
in fact the other way round, an opening of oneself to
others to perceive more than we think? Here too? What
will others see through this that's hidden from me now?

I wrote that in 1976, while composing a book of memories of
what I'd been writing and thinking over twenty-five years:
writings remembered. Why is it that so much of what has been
learnt of reality, and of how we perceive it, how we ARE
what we perceive, has so far had little or no effect upon
how we organise life? Why are we ignoring the main discoveries of our time, in art and science (eg relativity,
the uncertainty principle, the findings of Cezanne) in our
attempts to understand and solve the massive problems of
the twentieth century, problems arising from our own interventions in the world of nature and of mind? When I ask such
a question I can feel myself getting angry, impatient at the
seemingly too-slow evolution of the processes of planning and
design to cope with the situation brought about by these very
processes. But then I ask myself if I am right. Ideas, however right they may be, can be realised only at the pace of
life and experience of those to whom they refer. And through
the seemingly imperfect understandings of each of us, our
minds, our ways of organising experience, being so amazingly
different from one person to the next. Perhaps its a wonder
that things go as well as they do? These are new thoughts
for me. In the past I've felt a moral duty to try to apply,
or even to impose, what I conceive as being the right way
of doing things. But now, after some years outside the worlds
of practice and designing, and while interesting myself in
what I call the time arts (music, film, theatre, poetry etc)

,and in oriental thinking, I am beginning to be more willing
to accept the pace of evolution and not to try to force it.
I can see, very readily, from my experience with design methods,
that, when one attempts to introduce a new idea of how something
should be done, that its either ignored, as design methods were
in the fifties, or, worse than that, its misunderstood and
applied in a way that contradicts the original reasons for
seeking a new method. In the case of design methods my
intention was to find ways to make the design process more
sensitive to life but what happened was the imposition of
methods that were of a larger scale than those we had before
but which are less sensitive. Rationality, originally seen
as the means to open up the intuition to aspects of life
outside the designer's experience, became, almost overnight,
a toolkit of rigid methods that obliged designers and planners
to act like machines, deaf to every human cry and incapable
of laughter. That's what made me leave designing, for a
while at least. And, once I'd left it, I found that the
first person from whom I tried to learn, in the world of
music, John Cage, was engaged in a vast essay on world
improvement, which he titled "Diary: How To Improve The
World (You Will Only Make Matters Worse)". The Cagean method
of composing not only music but life itself was, I learnt, to
give up intention, to seek unpredictable results. Indeterminacy.
In place of control. Accepting what we did not choose.

> I think that the systems approach is inherently ambiguous,
> it isn't entirely objective,
> that it does involve a drastic shift
> from mechanical thinking,
> with fixed aims,
> and one-track processes,
> like railway lines from A to B.
> Systems thinking, quite obviously,
> is a way of looking at all the things that are
> connected with each other,
> and everything is in the end,
> ......but certainly looking at the
> more obvious connections between things.

This, as those writing about it often say,
is mainly an attitude, a state of mind.
......If you have the systems attitude
you will immediately feel the sense
of trying out complex systems, (eg transport, education, etc)
several at a time,
to discover their interactions.
In an experimental city......
If you are not normally a systems-thinking person,
you wont feel this as an instantly acceptable idea.
It will be a puzzling idea,
you'll think 'how expensive' 'what's the point?'.

Interviewer:
This idea of the systems approach
is very different from what is sometimes called
the systems approach,
that's things like systems engineering,
and operations research....

Yes, that's the number-crunching,
input-output analysis approach,
where you do look at the interactions,
but only within systems that are pre-specified,
....like designing a chemical plant
where only the choice of existing components,
and the pattern of the pipes,
is the main decision.

That's taken from a tape-recorded interview in which I was being asked, by Robin Roy, to explain some ideas about experimental cities and to justify my confidence (in 1972) in the systems approach. I am amazed now, in listening to it for the first time since the interview, that I was at the time unaware that the popular use of this term refers to a rigid kind of system approach that is practically the opposite of what I had in mind and what I'd learnt from such pioneers of the idea as Norbert Weiner, West Churchman, and others. Somehow the inspiring aspect of seeing-the-world as an interacting system was replaced, as soon as the idea reached practical application, by the deadening notion of representing the whole of life by a rational block-diagram which is limited to those aspects of life that are capable of measurement and of calculation. Which, of course, (though we did not see it at the time) excludes much, or all, of what makes life worth living. That which is incalculabe. That which cannot be put into words, unless they are used poetically, with real feeling........I remember some words of Fredrico Garcia Lorca which Cristina Caffaro read at my lecture in Rosario to remind us of this. They are from the prologue to his comedy The Shoemaker's Prodigious Wife:

> THE AUTHOR: Worthy spectators.......The poet does not ask benevolence, but attention, since long ago he leapt that barbed fence of fear that authors have of the theatre. Because of this absurd fear, and because the theatre on many occasions is run for financial reasons, poetry retires fron the stage in search of other surroundings where people will not be shocked at the fact that a tree, for example, should become a puff of smoke, or that three fishes through their love for a hand should be changed into three million fishes to feed the hunger of a multitude. The author has preferred to set the dramatic example in the live rhythm of an ordinary little shoemaker's wife. Everywhere walks and breathes the poetic creature that the author has dressed as a shoemaker's wife with the air of a refrain or a simple ballad, and the audience should not be surprised if she appears violent or takes bitter attitudes because she is ever fighting, fighting with the reality which encircles her and with fantasy when it becomes visible reality.
>
>   (Shouts of THE SHOEMAKER'S WIFE are heard: I want to come out!)
>
> I'm hurrying! Don't be so impatient to come out; You're not going to wear a dress with a long train and matchless plumes; but a torn dress; do you hear? The dress of the shoemaker's wife.

(Voice of THE SHOEMAKER'S WIFE is heard: I want to come out!)

Silence!

(The curtain is drawn and the darkened stage appears.)
Every day in the cities it dawns like this, and the audience forgets its half-world of dreams to go to market just as you enter your house, prodigious little shoemaker's wife.

(The light is increasing.)
Let's start! You come in from the street.

(Voices and arguing are heard. To the audience.)
Good evening.

(He takes off his tall silk hat and it becomes illuminated with a green light from within. The AUTHOR tips it over and a gush of water falls from it. The AUTHOR looks at the audience a bit embarrassedly, and retires backward, with great irony.)

I beg your pardon. (Exit.)

That quotation's an exception: it was not chosen in advance, by chance, but deliberately, now. It reminds me of a perfect evening when chance processes had seemingly magical harmony with the life of Rosario. Discussing silence, as the most extreme example of uncomposed music, I paused, for a full minute, before continuing to speak. Almost as soon as I stopped talking the clock struck eight. And later, when I demonstrated John Cage's piece of music, which consists of four minutes thirty-three seconds of silence, a bat flew in at one window and out at another. And there was the lecture in Buenos Aires when I went into the street to get cool before beginning, only to get drenched by a bucket of water thrown from an upper window! The more I abandon cautious planning in favour of chance, and of acting on slight impulses, the more I wonder at what I have been missing.

......if we do go in for experimental cities,
of a kind which does not consist of
one lot of people pushing something onto another lot,
but genuineopenness   collectiveopenness to the future,

a conversation about the things which could be made to happen,
if it becomes a kind of physical conversation about the future,
through people trying things out,
and the political difficulties of doing that
are solved somehow or other,
goodness knows how,
with new kinds of political institutions,
new kinds of legal systems,
more dynamic than those we have,
......if all that comes about, then,
I would expect it to be important
not to start with a collection of experimental cities
which the people now living think are right,
and fit their expectations.
We should expect quite unpromising things,
or even threatening things,
to turn out to be different when we try them.
And quite promising things,
like most of the utopias,
suggested by Plato, and by many other people since,
for which the recipies read well,
but for which, in retrospect,
there is always a hidden fault......

......for argument's sake we might start with half
of the experimental cities of that type,
which <u>look</u> promising,
and half that definitely don't,
and just wait and see what happens.
Unless there's some genuine doubt
its no good investing such effort anyway,
......unless we are really open-minded
as to whether its good or bad,
what's the point of experimenting?

More words from the interview. Robin Roy was questioning me

about an article that I wrote for Design in 1966. It was my
first against designing and it was popular with the young
doubters-of-the-system of the nineteen-sixties. I remember
now that the article was itself a transcription of a radio
talk: here it is now being transcribed once again from tape
to writing. In the original article, and perhaps in the
radio talk too (I've forgotten what I said), I was criticising
existing methods of design, those used by the professions,
as being "conservative, persuasive, and rigid" and I was
suggesting that instead of fixed professional planning
processes we should try a more public way of designing, with
much more doubt and openness. My suggestion was the test-city,
as I called it, in which many new ways of life could be tried
out before everyone is committed to any one of them by large-
scale irreversible investment such as created the new towns
around London. I was thinking of something much less permanent
and more flexible: a site, resembling an airfield, in which,
using all sorts of improvisations and simulations of new types
of buildings, communications, transports, educations, productions,
agricultures, etc, a completely new way of living would be
tried out, probably by volunteers or perhaps by paid adventurers.
The design principle was to test the most unexpected and
unpredictable aspects of new systems : the interactions
between them. And more important than that, to discover the
extent to which, through experience and adaptation, the ideas
of the explorers of these new ways of life, the experimental
anthropologists one might call them, would change. I'd expect,
from some experience of testing new products one-at-a-time,
that initial reactions to the prospect of life in some proposed test city would be no guide at all to opinions of those
who had tried it out for a year or two. But how, I ask myself
now, would people ever get into the relaxed and confident state
of mind to permit such experiments to take place, at public
expense, and as a replacement of the professional practices
which now control so much of human evolution, under such
names as architecture, engineering, industrial design, planning,
market research, investment policy, and many kinds of legislation? For without some collective equivalent of the gifted

and inventive person's mind no such experiment can be expected to discover anything new. Collective inventiveness, and intelligence: that seems to be the quality most needed in design, a quality without which the new design methods are ineffective. The ability to act upon an intuition, with suspended judgement. To risk, to enjoy, to learn from, the finding out of the extent to which one's picture of reality can change.......that's not something one can do an a drawing board, or by computer simulations of behaviour. You have to live it. As the pioneers of alternative technology, and alternative lifestyles,are beginning to do for themselves without any encouragement from the rest of us who, one day, may be thankful for what they are finding out.

> 5 December 1978
> It looks as if the idea of beginning a design by writing specifications of the performance requirements needs revision so that one can be sensitive, especially at the start, to the interdependancy of problem and solution. Probably this is the entry-point to 'mind' in designing, the bridge to real thought, and away from cumbersome design systems and procedures that swamp one, or get abandoned.

My note, made at a computer conference, was written in a state of both encouragement (at the intelligent interest which the designers and engineers of computer software are showing in design methods) and alarm (at the rigid way in which the designing of this most expensive and influential new design-product is being carried out). I was surprised to discover, when I recently got a little involved in the designing of software, that it is far more like craftwork than design-by-drawing and that software designers, unlike most designers, can seldom make a fresh start, most of their work being tied to the adaptation of large pieces of existing software. Under this circumstance it is hard to see how anyone can get the room for manoevre that is essential if anything new is to emerge....how designers and users can recover presence of mind?

A story. Once the environment was considered as everything outside the body of a human being. The environment was the place where things happened. A stone was pushed off a log and it fell and the falling was a new piece of information that could be compared to what a stone did when it was still. Slowly it became interesting to think of all the other things the stone could do and what this reflected was an awareness of the doing that human beings were capable of. Then the action of the stone and the activity of pushing it became laws and experiments. Later the entire process was made into a small and comprehensible model and all the states of the stone that were possible were considered as either "yes" or "no" states. Then the process of describing created the thing described although the stone and the log were still there. Later the model and the description and the stone and the log and the activity of pushing and the environment disappeared and the people disappeared and what remained was a dynamic description and series of events without the divisions and nominal relationships.

The history of science? And a criticism, perhaps, of the concept of "environment" if it is taken to mean something that excludes ourselves, our thoughts and action? The words come from Edwin Schlossberg's letter to Gregory Bateson and were written for a book about Bateson's work, and particularly his concept of "an ecology of mind". When I took leave of design I was reacting against what I called the 'inhuman' use of abstract functional language to describe and fix life in the dreary and numbing formulae of design methodologists, environmentalists, ecologists, and others. Somehow, I felt, my friends, those with the good intentions of improving life, had become the enemies of mankind, of ourselves as persons. Then, at a conference, I met Edwin Schlossberg, and was amazed to find that, though he seemed to share my distrust of concepts like 'environment', he was using what I called 'machine language' (abstract terms) to describe people. And, when I eventually began to understand something

of what he was saying and writing on this topic, I was even
more surprised to discover that he had more or less invented
a way of using words, abstract or concrete, that really
seem to correct the error of mistaking abstractions for
things.....Even now I cannot put into any adequate phrase
the sense I have that he has developed a way of talking and
writing about 'mind', and all lesser entities, which evades
the traps of unreality to which philosophy is prone, and
which, in our world of design, seems to have driven design
methods out of its right place as a practical way of
enlivening design and into the sterile function of being
a vehicle for some pretty useless and fruitless academic
nonsense.   That's how I saw it in 1973, when I was driven
to compose the first of what became a series of 'conference
plays' written in protest against the inhumanity of the
language of design conferences. Plays in which characters
like Immanuel Kant speak a far better kind of abstract
thinking than we designers seem to be capable of, and in which
others, like Walt Whitman, speak, as antidote, about their
feelings and of more everyday concerns.

What IS the context of design? I seem to have two answers:
it is our minds, our lives, as persons, as beings able always
to imagine, to perceive, to remember,and to be,beyond the
range of whatever others who may try to serve our needs or
control our behaviour can foretell: it is also 'evolution',
the so slow, and seemingly mindless evolution of all things,
natural and artificial, which so often seems to exclude the
'most rational' or 'most intelligent' actions and to encourage
what looks like sheer stupidity. But again, when we attend
to what exists in an open state of mind, free of intention,
or the will to control, 'evolution', or 'nature' seems the
sweetest thing, the marvel of existence, the source of all
delight? Mind and evolution, each a terror but a joy in unison.

> I......became aware how much your writing allows for
> evolution in the context of thinking. As you suggest,
> what evolves is the context and not the entities.......

> This letter evolves because of its relationship to the
> writer, to the reader......and so on, and not in and of
> itself. Perhaps if I rewrite it some day it will change,
> but it will be rewritten because the context in which it
> exists has changed and so requires alteration.

More of Edwin's letter to Gregory Bateson. I like so much that little jolt to my thinking by the notion, new to me, that 'things' do not evolve but context does. Is evolution, then, the process of seeking to re-establish harmonies with context, a context that spontaneously changes? And is design this same seeking, or should it be? Intention, in designing, according to this view of things, would then be appropriate only as the means to get to the state of accord with context, the state of harmony, bliss perhaps, which intention destroys?....Is designing, then, a dangerous weapon to be used only when things have got into a mess, and something to be avoided when life is going well? The context of design, according to this apparent reversal of the usual view of it as positive, is 'problem', life gone wrong. And, in particular, the splitting of mind from matter, persons from nature. The underlying problem of modern times? In this light, 'bad' design is that which perpetuates this fundamental split, or alienation, between each of us, as persons, and 'the world', as we so destructively describe our situation. And 'good' design is that which tends to heal the split, and, in doing so, to make designing unnecessary........achieves a state which intentionality would destroy?

I did not expect my simple question "what becomes of design if we try to make it operate in time?" lead me so far. At last I feel I am understanding some of the impulses which led me to retire from design and to busy myself with the seemingly useless activities of musicians, poets, artists and philosophers.......But the variety of these thoughts, arising from the decision to let this article be guided by some chance quotations, seems, for the moment, too much for me. As a reader, of the writing, I am getting lost. Time to go to bed.

Next day:
I awoke disturbed, but soon, making some notes of what was in

my mind, I found my thoughts returning to the quotation from my notes at the computer conference, and to the idea that to begin a design by writing specifications of 'what's needed' is to close one's mind, to lose the room for manoeuvre that you must have if you are to discover anything new. Computer software designers, if they are tied to the adaptation of existing designs, may well find clear specifications a real help in trying to design in muddled situations. But obviously they lack, at present, the freedom to rethink the whole idea of 'why are we using computers anyway?' or 'what are we doing to life?'. My thoughts this morning let me see that, as with the term 'system design', I have been in the habit of using the technical language of design in a far wider sense than is commonly meant. I remember now that I have often advocated a version of 'specification writing' that is not at the scale of 'needs' as felt by existing users, who are adapted to the status quo, but at the scale of 'why are we doing it anyway?', the scale of what today I'd call creative disturbance: the letting-go, of our immediate self-interests, that reveals our larger selves.

> Arriving at Austin (we were met at the airport with gifts of Texas wild flowers) I visited the city dumps and found they were hardly suitable for a conference. There is no rubbish to be seen, only bulldozers moving the earth to cover everything as soon as it arrives. Then we found a more romantic dump, such as I must have had in mind, one in which unwanted objects are just left alone under the trees. But the owner of this dump would not let us meet there as he is being criticised for having it. I was about to give up when I realised why it is that I like dumps so much and the reasons why I'd felt them related to the conference theme: the theme of applying the principles of living organisms to dead buildings. I realised that what I like about dumps is that they consist of man-made things released from the bondage of purpose, that, once in the dump, the things have no function, they've lost their names. We are free to use them in new ways, or to ignore them, as we are with natural objects.

My contribution, to that conference on 'environmental evolution', was the suggestion that we try to hold it on a dump, where we would be obliged to survive, to improvise shelters etc, for the three days of the conference. As nobody wanted to join me in this I had to start on my own looking for a dump where I could live out the suggestion and see what happened. In the end, not finding the kind of dump I'd imagined, I stayed under an oak tree in the carpark outside the conference hall, arguing that a carpark is a temporary dump consisting of abandoned mobile architecture. Eventually several people joined me and some nice experiences ensued. They were some of the pleasantest days of my life. People brought me food, and a sleeping bag, and someone lent me a van to sleep in. And the organisers of the conference said, afterwards, that it turned out to be a nice extension of the conference as most people came out to the park where we had informal discussions and made some experiments in experiencing the friendliness, or the unfriendliness, of our reception when we visited nearby buildings. The results of these experiments went against our expectations, the big brutal-looking tower block being far friendlier than the small human-looking building, and the empty house we entered allowing a sense of freedom that one can almost never get indoors. A building, I realise now, is not just the material its made of, however beautiful that may be, or however 'well-designed', but the complete ensemble of building/people/their roles/the life being led inside it. And, as with objects on a dump, the empty building, nobody's territory, has a quality, shared with beaches, forests, and the like, that is very pleasant but is excluded from 'man-made-world' by our insistence that everything shall 'have a purpose'. Bad design includes, in this view of it, bad using of things, misusing of 'world', of what is given, by nature, by each other.

So what becomes of the idea that design is negative, a response to world gone wrong, misused, that designing is a disturbance, an opening of the door to chaos, creative chaos? In my note this morning I realised a reason why, perhaps, so many of what seemed to me to be constructive design proposals are rejected. It is that, in asking such broad questions as 'why

are we doing it anyway?' the person trying to apply the new
design methods in the spirit in which they were meant to be
used is threatening not only the existence of 'cars', 'schools',
'computers' or whatever, but is threatening the social relations,
such as those of family, or job, on which most people depend.
The destructive element in this approach to design is that it does
not acknowledge the right to stability in one's relationships.
But is there such a right? A right to hold everyone down to
the status quo so that you and I can continue, indefinitely,
our being, just as it is, together? Edwin Schlossberg, in his
book How I Learn How I Learn wrote

> I do not understand why the woods do not have walls.
> The section of the words that is most interesting is that
> part which sets you to some incredible flight of wonder.
> I am seriously (now you know) concerned with the act of
> posture which disallows growth. Like twisting to assume
> invisibility or familiar shape.

'I am responsible for you', 'I only work here'......are these
the postures he is thinking of......? Postures which recognise
that others exist, or that 'I' exist, at the reduced scale of
role but not, I feel, at the proper scale, the immense scale, of
'person'. The scale of 'mind', the largest scale of all, outside
the reach of all calculation, all measurement. The scale most
easily to be felt in myth, in dream, in fantasy, in fiction.
But everything IS fiction. That's just the point with which
these words began, the acknowledging that there is no stable
world, apart from the words we use to make it seem to be a thing,
a fixity, a fact. Human life, it seems, has, so far, been
organised around a diminished, and false, view of the size of
a person. And of our need, if we are to develop, to grow, to
really 'be', to change. Our constant need to keep changing
if we are to be free to adjust ourselves to 'context', to
'world', to 'reality', to unite mind with body, with all variety.

> ......I should not fail, even if the result were to make
> them resemble monsters, to describe men first and foremost
> as occupying a place, a very considerable place compared

with the restricted one which is allotted to them in space,
a place on the contrary immoderately prolonged - for simultaneously, like giants plunged into the years, they touch
epochs that are immensely far apart, separated by the slow
accretion of many, many days - in the dimension of Time.

The last words of Marcel Proust's last book Time Regained. Having
been inspired to begin with the last five of these words I chose
to end with their context, and to let chance decide their
position on the last of my pieces of paper. Which leaves me a
little space to think how this vast, compassionate, but perhaps
unedifying picture of 'a person' being the accumulating total
of his or her memories of life, relation, action, good or bad,
may disturb the peace I keep seeking, I think, in these thoughts
of extending the dimensions of design from those of space to
that of time. Not that I think time is in any way a 'dimension',
a line, a track of 'progress'. That whole idea seems wrong.
Time, I'll say for want of any worthwhile definition, is, as
Proust describes it (not as he names it in this comparison
with lines in space):'<u>simultaneously</u>, like giants plunged into
the years, they touch epochs......far apart'. 'It', 'life',
is, among other things, a process, not a progress, and so is
design, or it should be, can be. A process of re-membering,
re-making oneself, constantly, out of all one's past, one's
world, a world in which I am the contents of the worlds of
others, as they are of mine......?

But this is all so serious. And perhaps, like Proust's picture
of life, my view is coloured more by having lived than by
waiting to begin, without regrets......
What about the blonde who caught my eye, in that advertisement,
she was adjusting her bra, those two people, coming out of door
into the street, or the woman in blue, running after them, the
two children, leaning against the railings......

dear Mr Jones
During the past three decades there has been a growing concern
about the progress of technology and the......

SOURCES

The sources of the quotations are:

"Bruce asked..." is from <u>Dear Architects and Others Who Imagine How</u> a book I've written and published myself (Jones Family Editions, London, 1975).

"Any probing..." is from <u>Writings Remembered</u>, another book written and published by myself, as above, in 1976.

"I think..." is from the audio cassette <u>Aspects of Systems Designing</u> prepared by Robin Roy for the Open University, Milton Keynes, Britain (Side 2, Unit 32-34, T100 AC7), 1972.

* "THE AUTHOR:..." is from the prologue to the play The Shoemaker's Prodigious Wife in <u>Five Plays, Comedies and Tragicomedies</u> by Federico Garcia Lorca, translated by James Graham-Lujan and Richard L O'Connell, Secker & Warburg, 1965 and Penguin Books, Harmondsworth, 1970.

"......if we do go" is from Robin Roy's tape cassette, as above.

"5 December" is from my notes.

"A story" is from Edwin Schlossberg's letter For My Father in <u>About Bateson</u> edited by John Brockman, E P Dutton, New York, 1977.

"I......became" is also from Edwin Schlossberg's letter, as above.

"Arriving at" is from <u>Dear Architects</u>, as above.

"I do not..." is from the book <u>How I Learn How I Learn</u> written and published by Edwin Schlossberg, Chester, Massachusetts, 1977.

"......I should..." is from <u>Time Regained</u> (Volume 12 of Remembrance of Things Past) by Marcel Proust, translated by Andreas Mayor, Chatto & Windus, London, 1970.

"dear Mr Jones" is from a letter sent to me advertising a technical conference.

*Permission to reproduce this quotation in the United States, Canada and the Phillipine Islands is as follows:
    Federico Garcia Lorca, FIVE PLAYS. Copyright 1941 by Charles Scribener's Sons, © 1963 by New Directions Publishing Corporation. Reprinted by permission of New Directions.

Permission to reproduce it in the British Commonwealth excluding Canada is granted by Messrs Martin Secker and Warburg Ltd and is gratefully acknowledged. This is from their edition of Lorca's plays:
    Federico Garcia Lorca, "The Shoemaker's Prodigious Wife", from COLLECTED PLAYS (translated by James Graham Lujan and Richard O'Connell), Martin Secker & Warburg Limited, London, 1965.

continuous design and
redesign

This was written at the invitation of Les Belady of IBM who was organising a conference on long-life software (that is computer software which is re-used and modified so that it can match new generations of hardware and new situations and systems). The paper was reproduced in the pre-conference book Long-Life Software, The Sixty-Seventh Infotech State-of-the-Art Conference, London, 10-12 December 1979, Infotech International Limited, Maidenhead, Berkshire but the proceedings were not published subsequently. An edited and typeset version of the paper appeared in Design Studies, volume 4, number 1, in January 1983.

As this is another essay that was written camera-ready on prepared pages the original typescript is reproduced here as that is the form in which it was composed and is intended to be read: as a trace, or record, of a process of thinking and writing.

PART ONE   What can be learnt from other fields?

In planning this part of the paper I have chosen eight kinds of evolution or designing from which I am hoping to learn something that may be relevant to the special problems of continuous design, & re-design, that occur in the making, and remaking, of computer software. (I say 'making', not designing, because a programmer, unlike a designer in other fields, is himself both designer-and-maker; the medium of design is not a symbolic model of the product, it is the product itself.)

In preparation for thinking how these eight kinds of planned or unplanned change may relate to the process of changing, modifying, maintaining, updating, large software systems I have limited myself to one or two examples of each and to a page of comment. The examples have been pre-positioned on each page, leaving me to find words, fitting both my thoughts and the spaces left between the page-titles and the examples. Thus, my process for writing the paper resembles, to an extent, the process of re-thinking and re-designing within the limits of something that already exists, turning what might seem to be constraints into sources of inspiration.

Continuous design and re-design is a concept new to me. My previous thinking and experience has always been of design as 'the initiation of change, or newness, in man-made things'. So I have very little idea of how this rethinking, from a seemingly very different conception of design, is going to turn out.

NATURAL EVOLUTION

The term 'survival of the fittest' is not of much help in trying to understand how natural evolution occurs. Its not the organism that evolves, its the context. When a change in the environment decreases the chances of survival of the normal, or 'fittest', members of a population, some of the more freakish, or 'unfit', members may find they can survive better than they did. Thus, in response to evolution of context, the freaks become the norm and many of the 'fit' have fewer descendants, who thus become rarer, more freakish.

> ......a classic case of evolution has been the appearance over the last hundred years of black ('melanic') moths in areas where the vegetation is blackened by industrial pollution. It has happened independently in England, Germany, and Japan...... (J Z Young.)

This process, the slow adjustment of living activities of populations to meet varying conditions, as J Z Young called it, is completely different from the conscious deliberate planning and designing that we are used to in the evolution of the man-made. There is no conscious plan, no teleology, no sense of purpose, no way in which an individual can itself evolve. Change is accidental, occurring between, not within, generations. Yet it has such subtle and 'well organised' results.

What, if anything, can we learn, from this form of continuous change in the shapes of incredibly complex organisms? 'Watch the context' seems to me to be the lesson, the common ground between the otherwise incomparably different processes of natural selection and intentional design. Paying attention to changes in conditions, and being in readiness to respond to them, may not be as easy as it sounds when one is perceiving the world through eyes that have become adapted to seeing only what fits one's aims and objectives, which may themselves be a function of the kind of design one is paid to think about. The irrelevance of a change to the way one is designing now may signal its relevance to how one ought to be designing.

ADAPTATION OF ORGANISMS

Each of these elderberry leaves, though of recognisably the same 'design', is different in both shape and size. The large leaf is seemingly 'malformed' along one edge and each leaf was, before I cut the stem and flattened the leaves for xeroxing, curved differently in three dimensions, probably to reach the light. This variation of one design to fit differing conditions is even more evident in animals than it is in plants. A sparrow, such as the one which came near as I was planning this paper, changes the whole of its shape, moment to moment, redesigning itself by its power to move about and to twist, turn, swell, shrink, according to its sensing of what's all around it, food, threat, or whatever. Not to mention flying. How, I asked myself, are organisms able to adapt individually, and so variously, to differing circumstances while retaining, so precisely, the form they share with others of the same species?

Elderberry leaves

I arrived at what is perhaps a partial answer by noticing that the sparrow changed its size quite drastically, every second or so, by moving its feathers outward or inward all over its body. Each sub-unit of all of its apparently homogeneous surface being, I guessed, free to react independently to external conditions such as cold, or threatening movement. The adaptive units are at a different scale from that of the organism, the design.

THE EVOLUTION OF LANGUAGE

Owen Barfield, writing about poetic language, gives this example:

> Thlee-piecee bamboo, two-piecee puff-puff, walk-along inside, no-can-see.

It is Pidgin English for a three-masted steamship with two funnels. This foreign, and original, choice of words enables us, though familiar with both dictionary-english and the normal view of steamships, to "shed....civilization like an old garment", as Barfield puts it, and see the world, for a moment, through experience very different from our own. Is this a bizarre example of the normal process through which languages evolve: through the re-using of words, in almost total disregard for previous meanings, to name experiences and phenomena previously nameless? Barfield notes that Shakespeare was the probable author of the modern meaning of several of the key-terms in the abstract thinking of our time. 'Function' is one:

> Dark night, that from the eye his function takes
> (Shakespeare, 1590)

> Let us take a function a little more complicated, $u=ax^2$
> (Babbage, 1779)

Two examples taken from the history of the word in the Oxford Dictionary. Before 1590 the word apparently meant only the function, role, activity, of a person or class, eg ruling : the function of a king. Shakespeare is noted as the first to write of a bodily organ in this way. Is that like calling a mast a bamboo? Every abstract term, Barfield implies,is 'petrified metaphor' deriving originally from description of natural events. The logician, he says, is obliged, to obtain obedience to his arbitrary 'laws' of thought, to reduce meanings of words to as near zero as possible. But the growth of language appears to disregard dictionary meanings and to use words according to accidental similarities outside those meanings. Why, in language, is this disobedience creative, not confusing; why are dictionaries so dead?

CRAFT EVOLUTION

The more I see of software designing the more I notice resemblance not to design in other fields but to craftsmanship. In each the designing, if such it can be called, is done by the maker, and there is much fitting, adjusting, adapting of existing designs, and much collaboration, with little chance of a bird's eye view, such as the drawing board affords, of how the whole thing is organised, though, in craft evolution, if not in software, the results have the appearance of natural organisms or of exceptionally well integrated designs. But there is an important difference: software is increasingly made by modifying the actual material of previous pieces of software, as a building may be altered for a new use, whereas a waggon-maker, for instance, modifies the form, but does not re-use the material, in making each small step in the gradual evolution of his product. As in natural evolution, each alteration is made without conscious intention, or plan, of what kind of artifact may later appear out of the seemingly blind process of making corrections, here and there, as and when lack of adaptation to the working conditions, or to the materials or the making process, become evident. But there is a tremendous respect for the form, as it has evolved so far, embodying, as it does, the otherwise unrecorded history of a thousand ways in which the artifact and its context can be attuned. Of course the context has to be stable, within limits, for centuries, for craft evolution to be possible. Is there any way, I ask myself, in trying to learn from these various modes of evolution, for the makers of software, and the users of it, to attain this almost magical accord with context when context is itself in flux?

> ......farm-waggons had been adapted, through ages, so very closely to their own environment that, to understanding eyes, they really looked almost like living organisms. They were so exact. Just as a biologist may see, in any limpet, signs of the rocky shore, the smashing breakers, so any provincial wheelwright could hardly help reading, from the waggon-lines, tales of haymaking and upland fields, of hilly roads and noble horses, and so on. (George Sturt.)

198

NEW VERSIONS OF EXISTING DESIGNS

My experience of designing began with industrial design, which, in the fifties, was a new design profession devoted to the re-thinking and re-shaping of existing designs of manufactured products. The typical design process was for a design consultant, (who did not work for one industry, but several, and was trained in art not engineering) to be given a brief to re-design the appearance, and to re-think how it is used, while retaining, to varying degrees, the existing interior mechanisms and the existing manufacturing plant. Although meeting much resistance, at first, from engineering designers, salesmen, and others, whose experience was limited to making and selling the existing design, the technique prevailed and now many manufactured products are designed this way by people of wider training and outlook than that of an industry geared to one type of product. Quite a revolution. What, in essence, was the process of this kind of re-designing? At its worst it was cosmetics, restyling, the imposition, via the introduction of an operationally separated cover-component, of a fashionable appearance calculated to increase sales while minimising costly disruption of the expensive tooling-up of the mechanical parts, which were hidden from view. Top-down designing, aided by a physical separation from the engineering, which had been designed bottom-up. At its best industrial design means the deriving of a fresh concept for the product as a whole from a radical appraisal of the relevance of both inner and outer components and of the operations of using it (now called ergonomics) so as to find a design that is noticeable better from every point of view. In this re-thinking stability is discarded, at the physical scale, and re-created at the scale of functions, costs, sales.

    stretched versions of a passenger jet
    successive revised editions of a popular textbook

In many cases these are less deliberate processes than industrial design, often they are completely unplanned-for, but they seem to produce astonishing meta-morphoses of existing designs while re-taining the original organization of parts, or classification of subject-matter. The underlying concept accurately reflects the context in a way that transcends internal conflicts of design.

COST REDUCTION

We used to say that an engineer is one who can make for sixpence what any fool can make for half-a-crown. The chief instrument of the astonishing cost-reductions of mass-produced goods, as compared to hand-made, is, of course, not ingenuity of design but investment in tooling-up for repetitive operations. I remember being told, at the Olivetti factory in the early fifties, that a hand-made prototype of a typewriter that would sell for £80 had cost £15,000 to build. But, within mass-production, there are still largish differences of cost and plenty of examples of big savings made by re-designing the product to reduce its use of materials, labour, or special-purpose tools. A formal technique for doing this, Value Analysis, was invented by L D Miles in the fifties and has been used with notable success not only to reduce cost but also to rationalize, and to improve, functional performance. The essence of his method, which is a lot more involved than this little outline description suggests, is, as in industrial designing, to focus on function:

>   Value Analysis: define element
>   define function
>   consider alternatives
>   evaluate alternatives
>   select best

The strength of the method is that, given that the functions of each part _can_ be predicted, and held stable, everything extraneous to their achievement, using the absolute minimum of resources, can be identified and discarded. But there is a hidden cost, a severe one, which has only recently become evident. It is that of inflexibility, over-specialization, the realization that this 'plastic world' of homogenized, cost-reduced products is increasingly unalterable, un-repairable, and imposes upon us (from its stabilization at the larger scale of functions) a life, an obligatory way of _using_ what is made, that is felt as coercive, not satisfying, with decreasing outlets for individuality. The lesson is obvious, though how to apply it is not: don't stabilize functions!

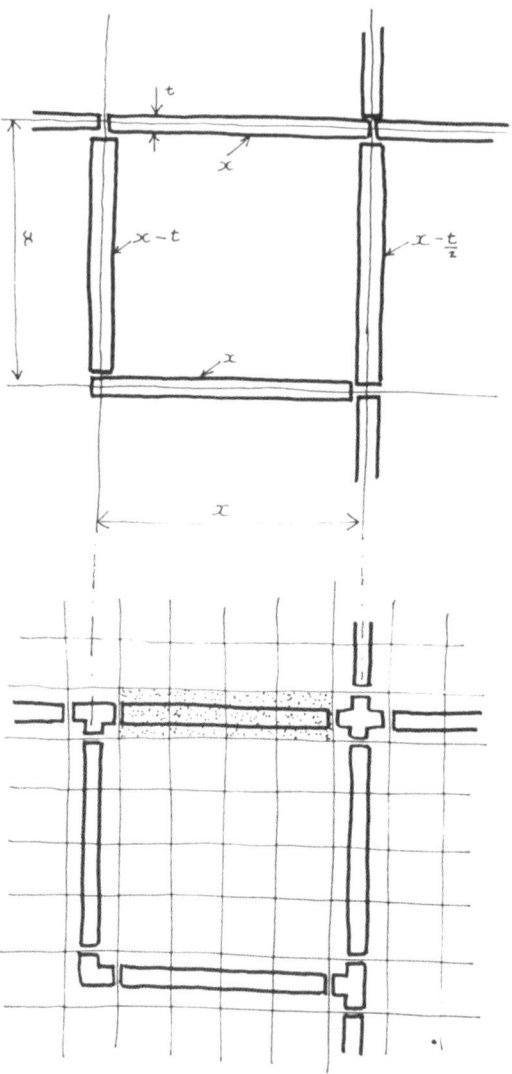

The logic of the components is separated from the logic of their use by shifting the dimensional grid from walls to joint-positions and by adding three standardised corner pieces. This change (analogous to the invention of zero or of the decimal point?) greatly reduces the number of component types needed and yet allows these to vary greatly in thickness, material, etc without upsetting the system.

MODULAR SYSTEMS

Increasingly I find this the most fascinating field of design
and the only one, perhaps, for which I see a long-term future.
Designing at the smaller, and less liberating, scale of products,
functions, seems ready for de-professionalizing. As was writing.

>   playing cards
>   plugs & sockets
>   a cassette
>   a brick
>   numbers
>   the alphabet

Under what conditions *is* it possible to discover such flexible
and ubiquitous units as these, each system opening up endless
possibilities most of which were unforseen? My own experience
of working with an exceptionally talented designer of modules,
Bernard Keay, suggested that there *is* an underlying principle:

> STANDARDIZATION versus FLEXIBILITY in industrialized
> building systems
>
> Our method of resolving this conflict is to maximise the
> standardization of joints and to minimise the standardization
> of components. This is done by applying modular dimensions to
> the *positions* of joints and by leaving space for *variation*
> in the sizes of components that fit into the modular zones
> between joint positions.

This was Bernard's way of getting round the fact that, if try to
standardise the sizes of wall sections so that they will join at
the corners of rooms, you need many 'specials' to make up for the
wall thicknesses, which themselves become very restriced. In
this solution, which accepts the use of only three standard
types of corner-piece (L,T,&+) walls can be of any material or
thickness and no specials are needed. The principle, in both
this building system, and in the other examples, seems to be to
separate the logic of the modules from the logic of their use.
Easier said than done. But its not impossible, sometimes.

ADAPTABLE DESIGNS

There is a principle, quite different from that of designing modules, evident in the type of exceptionally adaptable desk lamp which is mounted on a spring-balanced jointed arm in which arm-pieces and springs are positioned much as they are in the human arm, or leg. The point about this lamp (made in Britain by Anglepoise) is that the effort to adjust it is less, not more, than the effort of adjusting your own posture, or eyes, to continue reading with the light in the wrong place. Many systems of adjustable components, or so-called flexible designs, fail at this point. The adjustments they offer are seldom used because the effort-of-adjusting is greater than that of adapting, personally or socially, to the worse conditions of leaving the thing unadjusted. Does this happen with software too?

My last example, and perhaps the most relevant to software design, is the street, and the street-pattern of a city. Its relevant because, in both cases, street and software, its the actual thing itself which is re-used, adapted. A beauty so obvious its invisible.

> Now, after the great war, life goes on in our ruined cities, but it is a different life, the life of different or differently composed groups, guided or thwarted by new surroundings, new because so much has been destroyed. The great heaps of rubble are piled on the city's invaluable substructure, the water and drainage pipes, the gas mains and electricity cables. (Bertolt Brecht, writing of his theatre in Berlin)

The services beneath the streets are, of course, only extensions, invented millenia later, some of them, of the ancient excellence of the pattern of streets, and of the so basic idea of arranging for public space to reach, in this so accessible way, to every house, no matter how many. A similar example, which is quite obviously present also in the differnt ways in which computer storage, and access, is provided, is the library, and the book. Together they provide equal access times to every book, and to every page, line, word, letter, by the principle of 'pages', of splitting an enormously long string of symbols into units each with access both in series and in parallel.

PART TWO   What can be learnt from the study of design methods?

The formal study of design methods, and the conscious invention of new methods, such as Value Analysis, Morphological Charting, Man-Machine System Designing, Brainstorming, Pattern Language, has been evident for the last twenty years or so. During the same period there have been new methods, and with them a larger scale of aims and objectives, in many other fields of industrial life eg market research, operational research, work study, and new accounting methods. The common feature of all these endeavours is, I believe, to enable larger groups of people, specialists and sometimes non-specialists, to work and think together on the evolution of industrial life, as a whole, or in larger chunks than is possible with the more solo methods they replace. In the case of designing, the typical solo methods are the back-of-the-envelope-sketch (for the chief designer at the stage when he keeps the whole problem to himself, before it is farmed out in pieces to the designers of details) and the scale drawing (for the detail-designer, working with a smaller perceptual span but with greater accuracy, geometrically at least). The new methods imply a less hierarchical way of subdividing the work than do these two solo methods, or tools. Often there is group thinking <u>before</u> the 'concept' appears.

What I am doing here (using the same technique of writing to prepared pages, each with its title and example pre-typed) is to think, not about individual methods, but at some of the recurrent questions of design procedure that seem to be particularly relevant to the business of trying to make software that is easy to modify, or of modifying software that isnt easy, perhaps is muddled by the inevitable unpredictabilites of this new field of design, with its enormous complexities at the scale of thought (the largest scale there is?).

In reviewing the new thinking about design I am attending not so much to specific methods as to the mental and organizational difficulties that arise when designing reaches outside the range of experience of any one person, and of everyone.

DESIGNING IN A CHANGING CONTEXT

Imagination, I realised after writing that about 'designing outside the range of experience', has no bounds. That is why the seemingly impossible, eg to try to design software that <u>is</u> easy to maintain and modify, is a reasonable thing to attempt. My first move, when faced with designers or students who feel overwhelmed by 'the problem' is to ask them to release their imaginations by attempting not one design, but three: 'A', an immediate improvised answer, doable this week, or month, or

> What IS the context of design? I seem to have two answers: it is our minds, our lives, as persons, as beings able always to imagine, to perceive, to remember, and to be, beyond the range of whatever others (who may try to serve our need or to control our behaviour) can foretell;
>
> it is also 'evolution', the so slow, and seemingly mindless evolution of all things, natural and artificial, which so often seems to exclude the 'most rational' or 'most intelligent' actions and to encourage what looks like sheer stupidity.

(I forgot the example was coming up: but it seems to fit what I'm thinking) 'B', a design at the normal time scale, and 'C', a far-out design, for say ten years hence, assuming that people, as well as technology, are going to change. The essential point, in this way of releasing one's mind, is that of seeing how temporary, and subject to the existence of what is already designed, are 'reqirements', 'functions', and the like. For instance, in designing a school building, its folly to tailor the whole thing to present teaching methods and problems when its obvious that , in say fifty years of the building's life, education is going to change quite a lot. What kind of school will make it easier, not harder, for tomorrows teachers, and pupils (if those categories still exist) to reorganize according to how it is then? 'It' being their minds.

PARTICIPATION OF CUSTOMERS & USERS IN DESIGNING

One of the main adavantages of the newer design methods is that they make the process of designing sufficiently visible, and discussable, for customers and users to contribute to it the experience and insight which can only be got at the receiving end, but not in the design office. However, in the case of software, the designers are not only the makers too: they are much more able than are designers in other fields to experience for themselves, at a terminal, the effects of what they are doing. But the professional designer of software, despite this immediacy of trying out his work, lacks the experience of being adapted to the design he is testing and of being able to perceive it in relation to the life-activity of which its meant to be a part. This can be an advantage, for it is just this condition of being over-adapted to what exists that makes it difficult, sometimes impossible, for users to help designing very much. They are adapted to accepting, not to imagining.

> As soon as John Suter told me his ideas for leaving a lot of the designing of houses to the builders, and to the people who will live in them, I felt he'd begun to do what seems to me to be most needed in architecture now : to get beyond functionalism.

John Suter is one of the first architects to have the courage to attack this difficulty head on. I wrote that note after being inspired by his account of how, after much encouragement from him, the family and friends of his client had gradually begun to take real advantage of the freedom he'd given them to do for themselves the things that everyone believes 'only a professional can do'. His role, once he'd given up part of the design function to his clients, became, as he said, that of professional encourager. You can do it. Just try. But he was disappointed to find how hard it was to shake them from the ideas of functionalism, the accepting of the activity-names given to spaces and rooms at the start as final, for the life of the building. Its so hard to unlearn, and unlearning is the essence of designing. To share the design process with users is not as easy as it sounds. It needs a change of roles, of self-images, on both sides.

DESIGNING AS PROCESS

The difficulty which we all face, as users of all the things, products, or whatever, that are provided by professions other than our own, is that we are tied by our experience as consumers of products to accept them, and not ourselves, as the starting points of our thinking when asked to define our needs. And, as professionals in the provision of software, or of some other product, we are equally tied to thinking of the product as central and the users as existing only in relation to what we provide. 'We are here to help the others : what the others are for I've no idea'. That is product-thinking, the not always laughable weakness of industrial life. The alternative view, to be found in the recent developments in design, as in all the arts and sciences of this century, is process-thinking. To see process not as a means but as the end, a purpose in itself. To take the product alone as the criterion is to deny that we exist.

> at a break in a concert a most un-announcer-like voice, presumably a member of the orchestra, sitting some way from the mike, says "we will play the finale - opus one, number two"

That was the first occasion, in years of listening to the output of professionally organised radio, when I have felt the existence of the musicians as persons, as one of them improvised that announcement, presumably in a rare failure of the official announcer to keep track. That tiny lapse, in the almost totally impervious homogenaity of a planned professional service, is I believe the clue for getting out of the trap of means-ends thinking that makes us blind to our needs outside those of serving the system. The essential first step is to accept the roughness, the un-professional character, the reaction 'that's not design, anyone could do it' of improvised initiatives by users themselves, by us as we are as persons, unspecialised. Once this big jump is made then the way is open to becoming able to making this new life that is so rapidly coming into being as a result of our efforts, into something worth while in itself. In computing, more than in other technologies there is the opportunity to drop product thinking, to let the process come alive to us all.

DESIGNING WITH CHANGING REQUIREMENTS

The instability of requirements is perhaps the biggest difficulty in trying to design, and re-design, computer software as it grows in scale and in length of life. How does it arise? Hard to say, difficult to predict. My strongest impression is that the direction in which requirements are going to change, both during initial design and later, is not predictable from what either the customers or the clients know at the start.

> The sponsor's brief is treated as a starting point for investigation and is expected to be revised, or evolved, during divergent search....(but not without the sponsor's agreement).

That quotation is from the central chapter of my book on design methods in which I was describing how the new methods differ from the traditional ones. The main difference is that the new methods begin with formal ways of researching the problem more widely than the client's brief suggests so that the interdependancy of problem and solution can be properly explored and understood. It is far from easy to perceive, in any instance, why and how the initial requirement-statement can be so misleading and that the actual requirements, if the design is to be good, must reflect what is learnt as designing proceeds. But it easy to see that, in principle, designing is a highly informative process (essentially one of unlearning what we thought was the case, but is no longer true when we have changed the situation by making something new which interacts with what was there before) and that it is wise to act always on the latest available information. 'If we'd known at the start what we've learnt while designing it, we'd never have done it like this'. The practical point, in using the newer design methods to make possible collaborative divergent search, before the reqirements are fixed, is to change the basis of the contract between designers and clients. Both parties have to give up the use of the requirements as a semi-legal basis for control and measurement and to agree to work together in the continuous meta-process of evolving the brief and sharing in the eventual decision as to how the problem is to be seen and solved.

CONTROLLING THE GENERALITY OF SPECIFICATIONS

In teaching design, at the wider scale we are discussing here, I have always been surprised to see how difficult it is to write specifications in a way that helps the design process rather than hinders it. It is hard to keep in the background of one's thoughts some wider stability which might enable you to find the level of generality that would be useful.

GENERALITY	VERIFICATION
Ontological	By agreement, negotiation, perhaps force.
Logical	By logical consistency or inconsistency of statements.
Scientific	By objective observations ie independent of who makes them.

This little table is one such background-thought. It reminds us that differnt kinds of statement, and context, require different kinds of verification and warns of the folly of confusing these categories. Ultimate objectives, eg is it good or bad?, are always in the first category and we cannot expect any certainty of proof that they are rightly chosen. Instrumental objectives, contributing to these, may involve the seeking of a consistent logic between means and ends. They may also involve getting out of one's armchair and looking closely at the relevant aspects of the world. It is always tempting to concentrate on whichever of these categories one is used to working with and to neglect the others. Often one's job-description does not permit one to operate freely at all three. I dont believe that designing, at the wider scale, can be done well until everyone is free to think and act at all three levels. But, at a more practical scale of actually finding the words in which to specify something, there is another background-thought that may be useful to many. If you want to know if a given statement is at the level to be useful to the persons for whom its meant, ask two questions: does it give them enough room for manoevre to be imaginative? and do they have the means to know if this requirement, as stated, has been satisfied?

SPLITTABILITY OF DESIGN PROBLEMS

The essential difficulty, and the attraction, of designing, is that the problem cannot be split, while it is at the formative stage, because of the underlying interdependancy of problem and solution. Each way of stating the problem, no matter how abstractly, implies some range of solutions, and each solution creates a different world, different needs. At this most challenging level of designing the process requires conceptual integrity, wide awareness, detailed knowledge. Yet, for such collaborative and quick-changing activities as software design, this has often to depend on many minds, not one. My picture of the degree to which design problems can be split between many people is this:

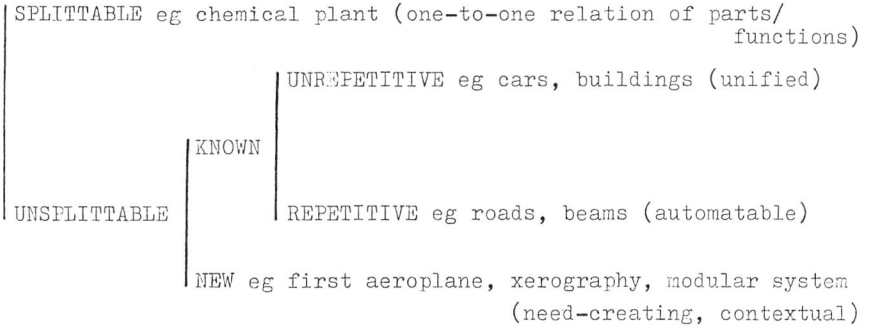

```
|SPLITTABLE eg chemical plant (one-to-one relation of parts/
|                                                       functions)
|             |UNREPETITIVE eg cars, buildings (unified)
|      |KNOWN|
|             |REPETITIVE eg roads, beams (automatable)
|UNSPLITTABLE|
             |NEW eg first aeroplane, xerography, modular system
                                           (need-creating, contextual)
```

Splittable problems, and those known types of unsplittable problem for which an algorithm exists, can be solved by what are sometimes called glass-box methods, wholly rationally, needing no imagination to discover the right form. Of the other two types of problem, unrepetitive known problems require some degree of black-box method, relying on the imagination as well as on reason, while new problems require not only both of these faculties of the mind but also a meta-ability, that of being able to design the design process while also designing the design. Software designing, I guess, can be of any of these types. Splittable, in this classification of mine, means shareable between several people who are working largely out of communication with each other. Unsplittable means they are acting with one mind.

COLLABORATIVE DESIGNING

It is our tradition, in modern life, to believe that creative work cannot come of several minds, only of one, and only then if the person is specially gifted, a genius as we say.

> Men and months are interchangeable commodities only when a task can be partitioned among many workers <u>with</u> <u>no</u> <u>communication</u> <u>between</u> <u>them</u>. (Frederick P Brooks, Jr.)

Our other common assumption, as Frederick Brooks implies here, is that the rest of us, not being geniuses, are fit only to work on farmed-out sub-problems and that, when we do so, the problems of keeping in step are either non-existent or can be dealt with by informal communication which need not enter seriously into our planning and logistics. If we are to solve the large and increasingly interactive problems of today, both of these assumptions, patently wrong as they are once you think about it, will have to go. One has only to look back to the remarkably coherent results of the highly collaborative, and unmanaged, process of craft evolution to see that, when opportunity for communication is ample, and when the effects of each action can be made evident to all concerned, then it is possible for creative work to come from a group. There are plenty of examples in modern life, too, both in computing and outside it, of amazing achievements which owe more to collaboration than to genius. The secret is to organise the process so that each person is acting as much as possible adaptively, creatively, and that we minimise the need to work to rule, shutting the mind to the evident effects of what one is doing. Where a top-down concept has, at some stage, to be accepted, it should, together with its reasons, be debateable at length by all who will have to act on it. Frederick Brooks gives a vivid account, in his book, of how such 'debating the bible' can be organised when designing an operating system. But I feel myself that, sensible as his account sounds, there is probably a better way to be found, one that owes something to the accepting of the incredible results of unplanned local adaptiveness that is evident in both natural evolution and in such human processes as craftwork and the finding of new ways to use modular parts, words, etc.

ERRORS AND TESTS

Perhaps the most important ability to develop in designing is that of being exceptionally sceptical of one's own ideas, especially those which occur at the start, while not losing the capacity to proceed with the problem despite the initial absense of an organising idea of what the solution is likely to be. This is where the new methods are particularly helpful, in that they provide many different ways in which one can find enough confidence, in what lies outside the problem-as-set, to be <u>able</u> to proceed in a state of creative doubt. The purpose of the initial stage of divergent designing, common to many of the new methods, is of enabling many to collaborate in this process of discovering what <u>is</u> open to change as the work proceeds, and what is <u>not</u>. Thus it becomes easier to find ways of adapting to, instead of obstructing, the aspects of the problem which must be left undecided for as long as possible if disastrous errors and back-tracks are not to be forced upon everyone at a later stage.

> When all is said and done, however, I still advocate building a pilot system whose discarding is planned.
> (Frederick P Brooks, Jr.)

That our experience of what existed before the new design was made, and our capacity to imagine in detail how its going to operate, are never equal to the complexity and unexpectedness of what evolves from our designing, need not stop us if we hold both to a right scepticism of our initial ideas and to these wise words of Frederick Brooks in which he recognises the need to <u>formally acknowleuge</u> our awareness of the incomplete nature of the thinking that precedes the making of a new design. Our rationality is always bounded by what we have already known, needs always to be doubted, put to test, when we are attempting to create the new. Allowing time for this, and money, is a start. Enabling all who are concerned in the process, and its effects, to themselves learn to use this caution, this imaginative conservatism, is more difficult. It is something we have yet to do.

PART THREE   How does this apply to the designing of software?

My first thoughts of how this little journey through some of
the possible precedents may help the process of designing,
and re-designing, software, are these:

Contexts
Context (a name I prefer to environment, because it sounds less
like a separate thing from ourselves) is the hardest thing to
perceive, because it includes us, our ways of thinking. The
fish cant see the water. 'It' is the source of change, of
unexpectedness, the real generator of newness, design, of
evolution. Aims, purposes, requirements, functions: these
are words for how we see what's needed. But when we name
them we tend to exclude the main part, the least predictable:
ourselves, our minds, and how they change, once we experience
something. Its ourselves, not our words, that are the real
purpose of designing. The biggest mistake is to take the
product alone as the aim. Its always secondary. Always a
means, to process, to what we're doing now or will be doing
later. Dont compromise the process : get it right.
The best kinds of evolution we know, natural, linguistic, hand-
crafted, are planless but highly responsive to change of
context. With astonishingly coherent results.
The first step to attempting something similar in design, in
continuous designing, is, I think now, to acknowledge publicly
from the start that when we design our knowldge is of necessity
incomplete. And to design the design process to reflect that
modesty, that expectation of learning what the problem is as
we try to solve it, discarding first thoughts. To make the meta-
process sensitive to what is learnt in the highly informative
process of designing.

Functions and parts, ends and means
Functions, statements of requirements, are essential but temporary.
Without them we cannot begin, but unless we can change them we
cannot finish, cannot discover. The essence of natural and
linguistic evolution is to adapt parts, existing parts, to new
functions, disregarding the old ones. This almost miraculous

process is possible only when the context is mobile, is sensitive
to the new functions of existing parts and is not tied to the
old functions. This, the largest scale of change there is,
supposes fluidity, not fixity, at its most abstract level, at
the scale of aims, ends.

So, for continuous designing, dont stabilise functions. To fix
the functions inhibits the human adaptiveness, present in
everyone, but inhibitable, upon which longlife designing depends.
Hard words. Its difficult to see how, in software designing
it can be done. In the short term its expensive because function-
fixing is the basis of cost reduction. But in the long term
mobile functions should be the real economy, the way to enlist
the efforts of everyone to smoothing the way.

How to fix the concept, how to get clarity, conceptual integrity
as its sometimes called? Imposed top-down is useless, unless
one can design a break between the concept and the parts. The
right concept has to embody a true perception of what is
mobile and what is relatively stable in the context, and it has
to embody this insight in a way that is independant of internal
design conflicts. Thats the challenge to ingenuity.

How, in practice, to cope with changes in requirements and
specifications? First, recognise that the 'right' requirements
are in principle unknowable by users, customers, or designers
at the start. Devise the design process, and the formal agreements between designers and customers and users, to be sensitive
to what is learnt by _any_ of these parties as the design evolves.
Organise collaboration so that each person concerned has (a) the
liberty to experiment and improvise and (b) the means to test
his or her improvisations to the operation of the whole. The
extent of (a) and (b) may vary much from person to person but
must always be such as to prevent destructive change, or the
making of blocks to other changes.

Built-in adaptiveness, is it possible? Yes. But its the most
difficult kind of designing there is. Designing modules is a
process very hard to describe and theorise about : its mind
operating close to limits. There seem to be a few guidelines.
Separate the logic of module-combination from the logic of
use (which may require the invention of extra parts eg the
decimal point). Let the sub-parts be capable of independant

adaptation to context changes. Ensure that the energy needed to adjust the design is less than the energy needed to adapt oneself to a worsening situation of using it unadjusted.
Make access routes equal regardless of size or number of things to be accessed.

Collaboration and communication
Creative collaboration is perhaps the main challenge of our time. Before computing it was not possible, in principle, at the scale at which we now operate and organise. The scale of billions and at the scale of everyone's minds. Its bound to be difficult but it is, I believe, the hidden question behind the quest for longlife designing. The attempt to act together as if all the things we make comprise one thing, a unity. As we do ourselves. But a unity that leaves us incredibly free, to make or mar. What are the blocks to collaborative design? What stops us acting together as a context for our works, adapting freely to what we discover in doing what we do? The blocks are product-thinking, function-fixing, role-fixing, cost-reducing, and our identification of ourselves with these things instead of with our thoughts, feelings, minds, common-sense awareness of what is needed but what we're not paid to do. All this leaves us over-adapted to the status quo (which we identify with self, with security, when in fact its what destroys the self, the being, the joy of living). Thats why, I believe, we seem to lose the adaptiveness, the biological adaptivness, with which we are born. The first practical step to unblocking, to being free to be inventive, and collaborative, is to widen, and to overlap, our job specifications, our roles. Once that happens the whole context begins to become mobile.
As larger groups begin to work together in design we need not only looser roles but more public ways of thinking aloud. More visible design processes so that everyone can see what is being decided, and why, before, not after, the main decisions are made. Collaboration before concept-fixing is perhaps the main strength of the new design methods. The other strength is to provide means of unlearning, publicly, with changing, not fixed, self-images.
Attentiveness to context, not to self-expression, is the

skill we have to foster, to encourage, to share. In natural evolution inattentiveness is death. So is inability to adapt to what we see happening. The context, not the boss, has to become the manager of what is done, and how. The bosses role becomes that of designing the meta-process, designing the situation so that designing collaboratively is possible, so that it flows.'It' being the interaction of what everyone is noticing with what everyone is doing. To find out how to re-structure the design situation so that the blocks are removed, so that initiatives are both encouraged and enabled to be self-correcting, given attentiveness, and the right tools, etc.
A first step is to change the contractual basis of collaboration between designers, customers, users, all concerned: make it independant of functions, requirements. Find some better level for agreements.
How, in principle, is the context, the design situation, to be organised if all this is to be possible? The general aim is to enable all concerned to take initiatives in the light of accurate knowledge of the effects of what they are doing. In practice this sounds very difficult. To make a start I'd suggest beginning by loosening specifications so as to allow 'unprofessional' degrees of roughness to be acceptable in improvisations from any quarter and to consciously drop pro-fessional standards wherever they seem to have local, not universal importance. Secondly I'd try progressively to do away with the need for 'forced communication', via manuals, meetings, memos, etc, and try more and more for the kinds of collaboration-without-communication that is possible in the evolution of language, in the use of modular systems, etc.

Now that I've finished these first thoughts about what are the main lessons to be learnt from other fields of design and evolution, and from design methods, I can see that they are a very tall order, a counsel of great perfection. And not at all easy to take in, expressed, as they are, in very abstract words and phrases. I hope that, in the course of the conference, after some other minds have had a go, that this line of thinking will become clearer, more concrete.

REFERENCES

J Z Young, <u>An Introductionto the Study of Man</u>, Oxford University Press, London, Oxford, New York, 1971.

Owen Barfield, <u>Poetic Diction, a Study in Meaning</u>, Faber and Faber, London, 1928. (still in print)

George Sturt, <u>The Wheelwright's Shop</u>, Cambridge University Press, Cambridge, London, New York, Melbourne, 1923. (still in print)

L D Miles, <u>Techniques of Value Analysis and Engineering</u>, Mc Graw-Hill, New York, 1961.

Bertolt Brecht, <u>Collected Plays, Vol 5</u>, editied by Ralph Manheim and John Willet, Vintage Books, Random House, New York, 1972.

Frederick P Brooks, Jr., <u>The Mythical Man-Month, Essays on Software Engineering</u>, Addison-Wesley Publishing Company, Reading Mass., Menlo Park, Cal, London, AMsterdam, Don Mills, Ontario, Sydney, 1975.

J Christopher Jones, <u>Design Methods</u>, John Wiley & Sons, London, New York, Sydney, Toronto, 1970.

The quotations not cited as coming from the above publications are from my recent writings some of which are published by Princelet Editions, 25 Princlet Street, Spitalfields, London, E1 6QH, and Postfach 780, CH 8025, Zurich.

The tabulation of splittable and unsplittable problems is a version of what is written as prose in Design Methods. The diagram of it was worked out by Juan Bonta and appears, slightly differently,in his article in a spanish language publication: El Simposio de Portsmouth, Editorial Universitaria de Buenos Aires, 1969.

Vte. MARTINEZ DAMIA
PUZOL (Valencia-España)
R. E. n.º 12.157. CAT. II

5

de 60 a 75 m/m

Cebollas LIRIAS

Linda

things

This was written in response to a letter from Th. Laffineur, editor of Neuf, a journal of architecture, urbanism, design and construction which is published in Belgium. Later I discovered that two of the co-editors, Monique Bucquoye and Georges Patfoort, whom I had met while teaching at the school of industrial design at Antwerpen, had suggested that I write it. It was published in Neuf, volume 4, number 87, in the summer of 1980, with an introduction in Flemish and French written by Monique. It is reproduced here by permission of Socorema S C R L, Rue de Merlo 28, O 1180 Bruxelles, Belgium.

dear editors of Neuf,

You asked me to write a text
for the special issue of Neuf
on the theme 'artefactica'.
I've not seen this word before
and note that you have chosen it
because
of the recent misuses of the word 'design'
and
'its close connection with the consumer society'.
(Is it bad to consume? Is it bad to eat?
Perhaps you mean that it is bad to be forced to consume
to satisfy the desires of others
to produce,
and to profit from producing,
from working,
from designing too?......)

I also have had objections to the word
design
feeling that it has become more a matter of control
than of trying to improve the world.
(Is it possible to improve the world?......
I'm reminded of what was written on this question
by John Cage,
from whom I've learnt so much in recent years.
He wrote:
'Our intention is to affirm this life, not to bring order out
of a chaos or to suggest improvements in creation, but simply
to wake up to the very life we're living, which is so excellent once one gets one's mind and one's desires out of its way
and lets it act of its own accord.')

So,
with these various objections
to the word design,

and with your new word artefactica in mind,
I am writing about 'things',
the things themselves,
rather than the intentions of their designers.
And I will try to complete this text
without using the word design
any more.
That will be a new experience for me
and I hope interesting to your readers.

You asked too for illustrations.
I have chosen eight 'things'
to be illustrated:
a room, a chair, a tv, a car, a book, a city, a phone, a brick.
I will now go and buy a film
and photograph examples of such things
the ones I find around me
here in London this July.
Then I will send you the photos
to be inserted into the text,
which will consist
of my thoughts
on being confronted
by these artefacts
these 'things'
that have somehow found themselves appearing
in this article.
Elements of this place,
of my life here,
little pieces of the world,
as we make it.

To take this photo of the room where I am writing this text
(you can see it on the typewriter)
I had to stand on the landing outside:
the room is so small.
Its small because I get cold when I write
and this is the cheapest room to heat in the daytime
when everyone else is out
and the central heating's off.
I suppose its the oil producers,
the OPEC countries,
who have forced me into this
the littlest room
in a big house.
My big working room is now unused
except for storing books and papers and things.
We call it 'the messy room'.
It is.

As I looked into the room
to take the photograph
I realised that
while writing at the window
I am almost unconscious of the room, as such.
What I'm aware of
is the view, the street, the house across the road,
the people passing by,
the trees, the clouds, the light......
and the items close to me:
the keyboard, the text I'm typing,
and what I'm thinking of.
And I'm conscious of the chair, the things I reach for,
pens, papers, books, etc.

I become aware of the room behind me
only if someone comes in.......

And when I adjust the heating, ventilation, light, or curtains,
to suit the continual slight balance-and imbalance
of my body temperature, and eyes, and posture,
and the changing weather and sunlight or cloud or rain or dark,
outside,
I become momentarily aware of this thing, this 'room'.
I like it very much,
this little writing-place,
this frontier,
between
the in-and-out,
the thoughts, the words, the pressing-of-the-keys,
as life goes by.

It was built as a dressing-room,
in 1900,
there are doors, unused, on each side of me as I write,
to the bedrooms on either side,
one of which is now a bed-sitting room, a studio, for Joanna,
a type of room they may not have known
when the house was built?

The bentwood chair.
Some kind of classic, rethought, brought up-to-date,
and trendy now,
obligatory almost,
for those of us who live
what we take to be the modern life?

Why the cushions?
I chose the chair because the profile felt right
in itself
without such extras
(having spent many years researching the comfort of seats
and being able, I thought,
to pick a chair that would be comfortable
in many hours of sitting).
But I was wrong.
This chair too is inadequate for that,
perhaps because,
in typing,
one is leaning forward such a lot?

(I notice, in writing this, that this having-to-comment
on my chair
is pulling me
out of the unconscious don't-bother-me-with-such-thoughts
attitude
of the active 'user'
into the aware-and-interested attitude
of ther ergonomist, the thinker, the 'observer'.
Its showing once again
how true it is
that
once you are involved in something
you lose sight of what it is.
'If I knew what I was doing
I wouldn't be here.')

The armrests,
I notice now,
are worn, bear the marks of use.
Yes. That's right. I use them a lot.
Not only to rest my arms but enable my arms to hold up my head,
not having a strong table-top to lean my elbows on.
(I prefer to put my papers on an inclining, adjustable, table
of the kind used in hospitals
for reading in bed.)
Its not good, I fancy, to be holding-up-your-head
all day long.
The neck should do that,
along with all the other things it does.

*

To take this one I sat in the best chair for viewing tv
in the room downstairs
a chair that's exactly the right distance
(the distance at which
each side of the screen
lines up with one's first and fourth knuckles
when one's arm is outstretched;
that's a figure I took from tv viewing research
done by the Ford Foundation
twenty years ago
but still true, I guess,
the eye and hand being 'things' that do not change).

But what am I saying?
The eye is NOT a 'thing', an entity,
and neither is the 'hand'.
Cut them off from the body
and they cease to work, to operate,
they die.
This whole idea of 'thing'
of artefact,
is wrong,
as is any 'naming', any treating of parts of the world

as seperable entities.
The whole purpose
of the new thinking of recent decades,
thinking about 'systems', 'environments', and 'integration',
was to recognise <u>that</u>:
the interconnectiveness of life,
that which is alive, not dead.

We've begun to forget
that great advance
of the fifties and the sixties.

On the screen as I watched: horse riding competitions.
Something I hate in actual life
but
when on tv
I watch it, often.
Why IS that?
Some strange compulsion of the screen,
a major element of modern life,
twenty hours a week for many,
equal to the hours spent in class
by a every schoolchild.
Do we know what we're doing?
If we did
would we be here?

The VW Beetle.
The German 'people's car', of 1933 or so,
still going very strong
a real classic,
advanced thinking when it was conceived,
and now loved for itself,
as 'a thing'
as something worthy in itself?

This one is my daughter Sarah's car,
parked outside the house,
her first,
she has a degree in philosophy
and is unemployed
finding it hard to get a job.
Nobody wants a thinker,
so it seems.
Why is that?
A philosophic question?

230
What is a car, what IS a car?
Do we know what it is?
I'd say it is MOBILITY,
the freedom to move,
at will,
without planning,
over a wide area,
the area of 'the city', 'the country', 'the continent',
no longer tied to walking-distance,
to village, farm, or tribe.
The freedom to exist,
as an influence, a person in touch,
over half the world.
A real magic carpet. One wish, and you're on your way!

John Cage's life
described in a book
by Richard Kostelanetz
(published by Allen Lane, London, 1970).

The book from which I copied the quotation at the start,
photographed here, just as I'd put it down,
on my tilting table-top.

What an influence, this book, all John Cage's books,
as far as I'm concerned.
The books which have REALLY influenced me, or so I think.
(For the last ten years I've been working quite largely
along lines learnt from John Cage,
with his idea of composing as being 'not control'
but 'letting things happen',
and I've also been following the example of his friend, and mine,
Edwin Schlossberg, from whom I've learnt much else,
too much to mention here,
of what he calls 'as is',
and living in the present,
or trying to......)
THE BOOK,
sometimes, I think,
the prime technology,
the most dangerous of all,
the medium through which we channel all our public thoughts
before they are allowed
to be realised in other forms,
as for instance objects, broadcasts, systems, or whatever.
Time we forgot the book a bit, I'm sure,
and trusted once again to word-of-mouth,
and the look in the eye,
and stopped requiring signatures, certificates, credentials,
and all this 'education',
meaning years-and-years,
of reading-and-writing what our elders thought and did.
What's so good about that?

How to photograph THE CITY?
Looking round the room, and into the street,
and thinking 'do I have an air photograph of London?
no I don't,
and besides
the air-view is not the city as we experience it,'
I realised that there is no place,
no single place,
no THING,
you can truly call the city.
The city is what's happening,
simultaneously,
in so tight-packed an area,
involving so many people,
all operating as one thing,
one inter-connectivity.
Its the connectiveness that is the value of the thing,
that's the reason for the high rents for city space,
and why,

if you want to live cheaply,
'for a song' as we say, so beautifully,
you'd better find a cottage in the wilds
far from any road, or water-main, or drain,
and far from any neighbour,
let alone the city lights......

Once I got downstairs I saw the answer:
photograph the Evening Standard, the London daily!
Which I did,
noticing the headlines:
£10-pound-a-night lure for tourists,
LONDON BARGAIN HOTEL DEAL
(which refers to a new scheme for airlines to help standby passengers
to book cheap beds
in London hotels
provided they are willing
to leave their holiday plans
to the very last moment).

I like that:
'the last moment'.
Isn't it just what we need, now?
To drop all this planning for a bit more action
and excitement?
(What an incredible hotel,
its not what I'd have chosen,
but who knows?)

SAVE OUR CITY
says the slogan also visible.

This moment,
as I write,
four men are moving a piano
out of the house across the road
and into a van
which is called Tiger Trucks.

The lady I've seen living there for years,
but whose name I do not know,
seems to be moving out.
Where is she going? I expect I'll never know.
City life.

*

The telephone. My favourite technology,
the only big communications-medium that is decentralised,
in which the messages,
unlike those in newspapers, or in broadcasts,
or in most of the big systems of which modern life consists,
are not planned from a central office.
(Mail is of course decentralised too,
but I'm thinking chiefly of electrical systems.)
And what messages! So trivial, so important,
who can say which,
and so personal, so improvised, so close to life-as-lived,
as-loved,
and so far from regimented, planned, dragooned,
unconsidered-in-advance.

Twenty years ago,
in my articles on Automation and Design

(I've had to break that promise not to use the word)
which appeared in the magazine Design
(there it goes again)
I was amazed, and very glad,
to find,
in the elements of the telephone-system,
a prototype
of the elements of automation
(invisible <u>central mechanisms</u>, not controlling the functions,
and operating <u>automatically</u>,
visited only by <u>craftsmen</u>, when things go wrong,
and widely distributed <u>in-out devices</u>,
the telephones as we see and touch and listen to them,
each <u>adapted well</u> to human body and action
and
despite operating <u>via</u> a mechanical flow of impulses
imposing <u>no mechanical constraints</u> upon the things you say
and listen to....).
Writing those articles taught me a lot
taught me to reverse my opinions of the new technology
the technology of complexity
and to see that it is no longer inhuman
in any inherent way.
Only the old technology of simplicity-and-power,
the coal-and-iron machines, and factories, and such,
are things to fear.
In the new machines and systems
the fear,
if it remains,
comes not from the machinery
but from ourselves. Our distrustful uses of things.

I notice also in the photograph
that I felt impelled
to include what stood beside the phone:
my index cards of phone numbers and addresses.
These remind me that perhaps the most novel element
of 'the telephone'
are the numbers which we get,

and take as almost-names,
in order to be able to communicate.
And I'm reminded that
in the more rigidly ruled countries
its said they do not issue directories to everyone,
the majority of numbers being unlisted, secret,
ex-directory as we say.
I'm also reminded that John Cage,
though beset,
like many celebrities,
with midnight calls from freaks who only want to hear his voice,
insists on keeping his number in the public book.
'The book'. That's the way to use it, openly,
and why, no doubt, its feared:
the power of the book,
the accessible word,
made semi-permanent.

*

My last 'thing', the brick,
or rather several bricks comprising now a piece of wall,
by the kitchen door.
I'm hoping that the photo will show the irregularities

of the bricklaying
which reveal how
in this craft
unorganised by any mechanical control-system
there is a subtle process
or errors-compensating-for-errors
as each brick is laid
'deliberately wrong'
in its position and direction
so that the resulting wall
(not itself so much a 'thing' as an ideal concept of flatness)
is accurate, within narrow limits,
while the bricks themselves
are none of them in their 'true places'.
This is only one small example
of the subtlety
the essence of life-human, life organic,
which in our earlier industrializations
is lost.
But resurrectable,
if we look for it,
and rethink our later, more flexible technologies,
on the same lines.

The brick by itself is,
I believe,
the most easily conceived example
of a type of product, artefact,
which,
unlike so much of what we make,
opens up possibilities
instead of closing them off.
Think of all the buildings
and uses of bricks
there have been in the world so far.
And think of all the other uses of this unit, this 'module',
which are yet to come.
We cannot.
The variety is too great for any single mind, or life.

And so it is with the other 'modules' that we use each day:
the words, the letters, the numbers, the plugs-and-sockets,
the nuts-and-bolts, the microchips, the lightbulbs, the
canisters, the tyres, the envelopes,......
These,
I believe,
are the models
for how,
in our present doubts about design,
to re-invent 'the thing', the artefact, the world.

* a slice of these photos was removed to fit page-format of Neuf.

I

never say oh dear said Mrs. Reynolds because there is no use in saying oh dear and said Mrs. Reynolds if there were any use in saying oh dear, oh dear said Mrs. Reynolds and she said how do you do and good-bye to Andrew Ell, and she knew she said she knew and she did know just what it would do. Every month makes it just that much earlier that is makes the night come just that much sooner. Mrs. Reynolds could always believe everything there was to believe.

Mrs. Reynolds went away and then she went home.

Gertrude Stein
Mrs. Reynolds

4
THINGS OF AUGUST

is designing a response to
the whole of life?

Wolfgang Preiser wrote to me in 1973 asking if I would present
a paper at the conference of EDRA (the Environmental Design
Research Association) at Blacksburg, Virginia. The story of
how I reacted against the abstract language of such conferences
by writing a conversation of different voices appears in two
earlier essays (How My Thoughts About Design Methods Have
Changed During The Years and "......in the dimension of Time.")
The chance process by which it was automatically composed consisted of taking a random number to find which of the five
voices would speak next and then typing the next sentence from
a text written by that voice (for the texts by Stevens and
Jung, which were being copied out consecutively) or else by
taking another random number to find the page and an imperfect-
ion on that page to find a spot on it (for the texts by EDRA,
Kant and Whitman, which were being copied out in random sequence).
Nothing was left to the decision of the writer once the choice
of the voices and texts had been made. The role of writer, or
composer, becomes, as John Cage says, that of "a listener" no
different from that of anyone else. Christopher Crickmay has
provided an account of his listening, or interpreting, which
includes several points which I would never have thought of,
as might the interpretation of anyone else. I like very much
this removal of the originator, or professional, as a screen
between the composition and those may attend to it or "decide
what it means", to them.

Graham Stevens, whose account of inventing 'inflatables' appears
in the play, came with me to the conference and brought it to a
standstill with his demonstration of 'walking on water' (inside
a large plastic balloon on a nearby lake). Graham's inflatables,
more so than those of others, are the closest to being works of
pure art. Some of them, the most beautiful and fleeting, last
only for hours or minutes as vast enclosures and surfaces of
transparent film float on water or in the atmosphere, making
visible the winds, the currents, the pressures and continuities
of the medium in which we breathe and move. I asked him to
re-enact his story of how his inflatables came into existence as
his straighforward account seemed the best thing I could find
to contrast with the abstract behaviouristic theories of design

against which I was reacting at the time. At the performance of the play I invited various people (who seemed to me to in some way resemble the writers of the texts) to read the voices. Graham read his own, Tom Regan read for Walt Whitman, Ada Esser read for Kant, Wolf Hilbertz read for Jung, and I read for EDRA. Each of us stood at different points in the audience as pictures of the writers and of Graham's inflatables appeared on the screen.

I am grateful for the permission of Graham Stevens to reproduce his account, which appeared first in Art and Artists of May 1972, and for permission to reproduce the photomontage, to Christopher Crickmay for permission to reproduce the text Dreams and Reason, and to Messrs Dowden Hutchinson & Ross Inc for permission to reproduce the essay which first appeared as "Is Designing a Response to Life as a Whole?" in ENVIRONMENTAL DESIGN RESEARCH, Volume 2, edited by W. F. E. Preiser, Copyright © 1974 by Dowden, Hutchinson & Ross, Inc., Stroudsburg, Pa. Reprinted by permission of the publisher.

The phrase 'reason can dream what dreams cannot reason' which Chris Crickmay quotes comes from the poem 'I have all the time in the world, my world' by Nicholas Snowden Willey in his book The Green Tunnel, published by Signals, London, 1965.

The essay was published in Spanner 17, Aloes Books, London, 1979.

IS DESIGNING A RESPONSE TO THE WHOLE OF LIFE?

An imaginary conversation between EDRA, Graham Stevens, Immanuel Kant, Carl Jung and Walt Whitman.

Composed automatically by a chance process at the request of

J Christopher Jones
The Open University
Bletchley, Bucks, England.

Abstract

When EDRA told me that I was to speak on "Design Languages and Methods" I remembered having once written that

> "methodology should not be a fixed track to a fixed destination but a conversation about everything that could be made to happen. The language of this conversation must bridge the logical gap between past and future but in doing so it should not limit the variety of possible futures that are discussed nor should it force the choice of a future that is unfree."

This conversation is hardly possible while the language of design theory remains so narrow and machine-like so I have employed a chance process to compose a wider but imaginary conversation between five voices: EDRA, an artist-designer, a psychologist, a philosopher and a poet.

Introduction

The voices in the conversation are as follows:

EDRA speaks some randomly chosen titles from the Conference program,

Graham Stevens tells, in his own design language, how the

idea of making inflatable environments came to him in a flash,

Carl Jung[2] speaks a paragraph he once wrote about method,

Immanuel Kant[3] speaks sentences randomly chosen from his "Critique of Pure Reason",

Walt Whitman[4] speaks randomly chosen lines from "Song of Myself".

I chose Kant because there is such a similarity between the language of design theorists and that of his philosophy. (Someone once said Kant's writing is illuminating but difficult: it should be read first for the fourth time.) I chose Whitman because I love his exuberant American vision and because it contains so much of what is missing from our own writings.

The chance process, which decided who should speak next, and which chose statements at random from the texts, is adapted from the way John Cage[5] composes his lectures.

EDRA Implementation of strategies leading to environmental change.

STEVENS During 1964-65, I spent a year with other students organising a movement to change our educational system, culminating in the Stockholm Students' Symposium passing a resolution that students should have full participation in all aspects of their education: selection, assessment, course content, lectures, etc; it also passed a resolution that exams should be abolished.

EDRA Gaming and simulation

STEVENS With all these negative aspects it seemed necessary to start from the beginning - from nature, the body, and people's behaviour; investigations into what was needed and how it could be done.

JUNG: An ancient adept has said: 'If the wrong man uses the right means, the right means work the wrong way'.

STEVENS: The relevant aspects of the course being studied were given by Professor Page on environmental physics, which also included the physics of the body; G. Broadbent on the theory of design, including the creative process and kinetic art.

EDRA: Design languages and methods

KANT: I shall, therefore, restrict myself to the simple and equitable demand that such reasoners will demonstrate, from the nature of the human mind as well as from that of the other sources of knowledge, how we are to proceed to extend our cognition completely *a priori*, and to carry it to that point where experience abandons us, and no means exist of guaranteeing the objective reality of our conceptions.

WHITMAN: I have instant conductors all over me whether I pass or stop,

WHITMAN: At the cider-mill tasting the sweets of the brown mash, sucking up the juice through a straw,

WHITMAN: And peruse manifold objects, no two alike and everyone good.

KANT: Now, as every principle which imposes upon the exercise of the understanding *a priori* compliance with the rule of systematic unity, also relates, although in an indirect manner, to an object of experience, the principles of pure reason will also posess objective reality and validity in relation to experience.

WHITMAN: Divine am I inside and out, and I make holy whatever I touch or am touch'd from,

WHITMAN: Approaching Manhattan up by the long-stretching island,

WHITMAN: There is no stoppage and never can be stoppage,

KANT: It is evident from the remarks that have been made in the preceding sections, that an answer to this question will be far from being difficult or unconvincing.

JUNG: This Chinese saying, unfortunately all too true, stands in sharp contrast to our belief in the 'right' method irrespective of the man who applies it.

STEVENS: These studies, coupled with experience in painting, meditation, rock music, slum housing (I was deeply dissatisfied with the current architecture, its limited concern with small sections of the environment, its rigid unresponsive, immovable demand that people might adapt to their environment instead of having it adapt to them) led to the Spacefield project.

KANT: But this representation, I think, is an act of spontaneity; that is to say, it cannot be regarded as belonging to mere sensibility.

JUNG: In reality, in such matters everything depends on the man and little or nothing on the method.

EDRA: Implementation of strategies leading to environmental change

WHITMAN: The connnoisseur peers along the exhibition-gallery with half-shut eyes bent sideways,

KANT: We cannot even cogitate time, unless, in drawing a straight line (which is to serve as an external figurative representation of time), we fix our attention on the act of the synthesis of the manifold, whereby we determine successively the internal sense, and thus attend also to the succession of this determination.

WHITMAN: This the touch of my lips to yours, this the manner of yearning,

STEVENS: Spacefield assumed immediate importance in the way in which it brought together and unified all the other isolated experiments and interests, at the same time answering the dissatisfaction with architecture.

JUNG: For the method is merely the path, the direction taken by a man.

WHITMAN: Adorning myself to bestow myself on the first that will take me,

EDRA: Decision making tools

WHITMAN: I will go to the bank by the wood and become undisguised and naked,

KANT: For, granting that certain responsibilities lie upon us, which, as based on the ideas of reason, deserve to be respected and submitted to, although they are incapable of a real or practical application to our nature, or, in other words, would be responsibilities without motives, except under the supposition of a Supreme Being to give effect and influence to the practical laws: in such a case we should be bound to obey our conceptions, which, although objectively insufficient, do, according to the standard of reason, preponderate over and are superior to any claims that may be advanced from any other quarter.

KANT: Transcendental freedom is therefore opposed to the natural law of cause and effect, and such a conjunction of successive states in effective causes is destructive of the possibility of unity in experience, and for that reason not to be found in experience - is consequently a mere fiction of thought.

JUNG: The way he act is the true expression of his nature.

KANT: For if they are to have something more than a mere logical significance, and to be something more than a mere analytical expression of the form of _thought_, and to have a relation to _things_ and their possibility, reality, or necessity, they must concern possible experience and its synthetical unity, in which alone objects of cognition can be given.

JUNG: If it ceases to be this, then the method is nothing more than an affectation, something artificially added, rootless and sapless, serving only the illegitimate goal of self-deception.

WHITMAN: Give me a little time beyond my cuff'd head, slumbers, dreams, gaping.

JUNG: It becomes a means of fooling oneself and of evading what may perhaps be the implacable law of one's being.

STEVENS: Its particular form was mainly derived from a piece of tactile sculpture made in 1965, designed to express the idea of containment - fullness, emptiness, filling and emptying, texture, weight, volume of content, etc.

KANT: For, as in the former case the cognition (conclusio) is given only as conditioned, reason can attain to this cognition only under the presuppositions that all the members of the series on the side of the conditions are given (totality in the series of premises), because only under this supposition is the judgement we may be considering possible _a priori_; while on the side of the conditioned or the inferences, only an incomplete and _becoming_, and not a presupposed or given series, consequently only a potential progression, is cogitated.

EDRA: Quatitative techniques in environmental analysis

JUNG: This is far removed from the earth-born quality and

sincerity of Chinese thought.

STEVENS: While considering these properties, the nature of toy balloons assumed greater importance.

(EDRA'S instructions were to complete the paper in 5 pages or less,* so I decide here to silence the other voices so that Graham Stevens has space for his story. JCJ)

STEVENS: The idea of the balloon as a flexible, tactile skin, completely expressive of containment, simply came in a flash while I was walking down a street.

Balloons were filled with water, soap solution, salt, beads, etc., and when air was used, one became much more aware of air as a material, with its own kinetic properties.

The whole exercise was immediately popular with the people around, with its range of sexual and humourous connotations – people squeezed, stretched, rubbed, poured, and ejected water and soap solution, swung, dangled, threw, made noises, sucked and passed around the balloons from one to another.

Knowing very little about the technical aspects of air structures and having seen photographs of warehouse-type structures, the Space Field project had to be worked out using models, discussions, contacting high-frequency welding equipment manufacturers and making up the structure in borrowed factory space over a weekend.

This was done by a process of trial and error for determining fan size, material thickness, amount of wind-loading, on-site repairs, anchorage, creep; until finally a week later, failure then success showed what kept the structure up or down, and anchored to the ground. Through this experience, the nature and

---

*This re-typing of the text, being more widely spaced, occupies more than 5 pages.

potential of the air structure, beyond that of storage function, became apparent.

References

1. Stevens, Graham, Blow-up, ART AND ARTISTS, May 1972.

2. Jung, Carl Gustav, THE SECRET OF THE GOLDEN FLOWER, (Translated by Wilhelm, Richard), Routledge & Kegan Paul, London, 1962, p. 83.

3. Kant, Immanuel, CRITIQUE OF PURE REASON, (translated by J. M.D. Meiklejohn) Dent: London, Dutton: New York, 1934.

4. Whitamn, Walt, LEAVES OF GRASS. New American Library of World Literature (Signet Classic), New York, 1954.

5. Cage, John, SILENCE, M.I.T. Press, 1966.

WALKING ON WATER

WATERBED 1966   TRANSMOBILE (Pat.'67)   WALKING ON SEA WAVES   PONTUBE (Pat.'67) with
WATERBOOTS 1969 HOVER PALLET IN HOVER TUBE (Pat.'70)   low and medium pressure.

(photos: forrest, kilburn, ogden, stevens, tweedie)

DREAMS AND REASON: an interpretation of the imaginary
conversation between EDRA, Stevens, Jung, Whitman and Kant.

C.L.Crickmay   30.3.73.

(In this note a writer attempts to find meanings new to him in
the spaces between the contrasting voices of a conversation
composed by chance. This interpretation is not meant to be
believed by others except as a record of what the writer (C.L.C.)
thought while reading the paper. The chance text is intended to
be open to different interpretation by each individual reader or
member of the audience.)

A first look at the text reveals how consistent are the statements of Jung and Whitman with the account of Graham Stevens.
Together they appear to invalidate the voice of EDRA altogether,
and reveal Kant as sterile. Stevens' story fits exactly Jung's
description of a method as "merely the path, the direction taken
by a man". His account of sources "painting, meditation, rock
music, slum housing", his integration of all these and other
experiences by starting with balloons, and his interest in the
experience for its own sake; "people squeezed, stretched, rubbed,
poured and ejected water and soap solution" fit exactly Whitman's
joyful assertion of total sensory awareness, "I have instant
conductors all over me whether I pass or stop", renders impotent
Kant's typically Western struggle to grasp totality via the
intellect.

A second look reveals a dilemma which I interpret from Kant's
statement "For, granting that certain responsibilities lie upon
us, which, as based on the ideas of reason, deserve to be respected and submitted to, although they are incapable of a real
and practical application to our nature, or, in other words,
would be responsibilities without motives, except upon the supposition of a Supreme Being to give effect and influence to the
practical laws: in such a case we should be bound to obey our
conceptions, which, although objectively insufficient, do,
according to the standards of reason, preponderate over and are

superior to any claims that may be advanced from any other quarter".

Our reason tells us, says Kant, that we have responsibilities which lie outside our personal motivation. Perhaps it is not practical to live permanently in a Stevens-Whitman-Jung-like world. The practical world is sustained by rational processes of which EDRA speaks. However, and here is the crux of it, we are not bound to reject the practical world as mere necessity, if we suppose that it contributes to a wider purpose than that of which we are conscious. I am reminded of one theme of Mailer's "Fire on the Moon" in which he speculates that the landing of men on the moon, a triumph of EDRA-like rational strategies, may still be a part of a total flow of things of which we are unaware.

Perhaps this is the meaning of Nicholas Snowdon Willey's paradoxical phrase 'Reason can dream what dreams cannot reason'.

I have one doubt about this second interpretation and that is to do with machines. There is a strong possibility that the practical life, of which Kant speaks, could one day become exclusively the realm of automatic machines. If this is the case, then the actions of Stevens and the words of Whitman and Jung refer to _our_ future and EDRA refers to the future of machines.

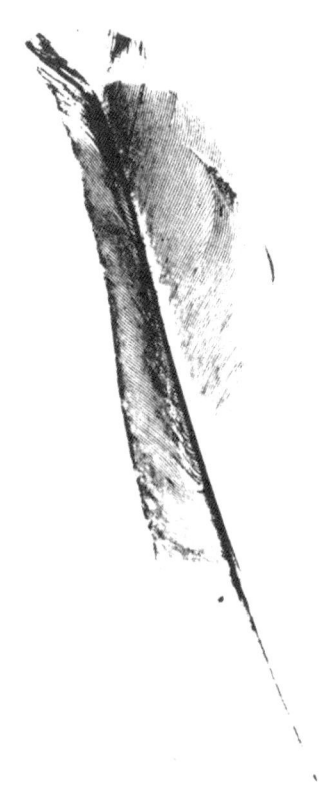

35 wishes

By 1976 writing conference plays had become a habit. This one
was composed by improvisation rather than by systematic chance
process, out of events, readings, phrases spoken by others or
heard on the radio while I was typing. I believe that the
experience of accepting words given by a chance process had
taught me to be much more accepting of words from any source,
including those from my own thoughts which formerly I'd have
rejected as unsuitable in some way. Below standard. Much of
the process of composing and performing this play is evident
in it. The whole thing is performed: title pages, instructions,
the initial abstract, everything.

About six months before the conference I was asked by Frank
Height and Christopher Cornford to send the abstract (the page
beginning 10.10 am Wednesday 14 April). A day or two before
the conference I visited the exhibition which was being got
ready for it and copied down 35 phrases from the captions to
photographs and other exhibits of 'designs for need'. Slightly
edited these became the recipie for Utopia with which the play
begins. The page beginning DESIGN FOR NEED ! was composed out
of words from the conference programme. The play itself,
starting at the page titled 'after 35 wishes THE SCHOOL OF NEEDS',
was composed by imagining what a typical day, or night, might
be like if all the promises implicit in the exhibition had
been kept and the world was freed of problems, as seen by designers. To write it I merely kept including in the text events
happening around me while referring to the theme of the conference and to lines from texts that were to hand. I imagined that,
in any Utopia, one would be completely unconscious of the problems
which had been solved by its designers and would be struck by the
similarities to ordinary life under any conditions, utopian or
not. One would still be preoccupied with such questions as when
to go to bed, what to read, where to go, what to eat, what to
say to someone, and probably unaware that the air was clean, the
housing shortage was solved, and poverty eliminated, etc.

The play was performed, or rather read, by Shiu Kay Kan and
Michael Poteliakoff (who were exhibiting 'the tin can house') and
by Vicky Cowell (the press officer and an amateur actor) and
myself. With music and props. And pauses. At chance intervals.

35 wishes

a performance
composed for the design for need conference
at the royal college of art, london, april, 1976

composed with the help of:

    chance processes
    the imaginary rock foundation
    the conference exhibition
    frank height and christopher cornford (persuaders)
    edward blishen's book,"the school that i'd like"
    muriel spark's book "the mandelbaum gate"
    kenneth koch's book "wishes,lies and dreams"

    and and many others particularly my family and and

©℗ j christopher jones 1976

DESIGN FOR NEED !
NEED !

a major international symposium
with supporting exhibition

to examine the present and the future
contribution of design
to
the satisfaction
of social needs

book now to be sure of a place

the numbers are strictly limited

10.10 am Wednesday 14 April   John Christopher Jones

35 wishes

As I write this note I am composing this paper (its not likely to be a lecture) and so far know only the title.
When Frank Height asked me to speak I replied with a letter saying that I'd much prefer to attend a conference at which designers did not display what they had done, or proposed, for those in need, but instead assisted users to say in public what their needs are. And perhaps helped them to design their own solutions. Christopher Cornford asked me to be more constructive than that, and to speak for 35 minutes. I was reminded of the book"The School That I'd Like"by Edward Blishen (Penguin, 1969) in which schoolchildren answer this question. Gillian,15,begins the book: "The school I would like would be perfect,glorious in every way...." and it ends with Nigel,14: ".....Let us rebel,us the opposed,and cast out those wage pulling civil critizers and form our own schools. The which teach us the beauty of all rough and tidy. Please excuse the spelling,no one will educate me."
Hence the title.   35 minutes to say what we want.

What wishes are implicit in the conference programme?
        THE EARTH: I wish I had a friend
        SEWAGE: I want to be food again
        THE HOUSE: I want to be autonomous
        INDIA: I wish I had no problems
What's missing? These don't seem to be the right wishes. What would life FEEL like if all these wishes came true? That's my question. 35 minutes: to see and hear what our utopia would be, a composition of our dreams.

UTOPIA

when somebody is hurt an ambulace comes
our fundamental needs (flirting, feeding the hens, cutting the
corn) have been satisfied (what do we do now?)
the population explosion is over
we no longer depend on ever more sophisticated techhnology
we have stopped exhausting our planet's resources (whose?)
design problems have ceased to be complicated
we are not noisy now
the anti noise campaign has succeeded
the old kent road flyover is used for roller skating on sundays
we have alternative transport systems
all planners use the symbol language
i live in an eco house
we have a bicycle made for two with better social disposition
(side by side)
bad management has been cured (by MORE management)
the oil boom is over
our community is fully developed
we have been rehabilitated
we have decimal housing (DECIMAL housing?)
we live in a tin can house
we have low energy houses
all domestic waste is saved
housing is available for everyone
alison has a wheelchair
i can hear the talking newspaper
we no longer need to search all bags and parcels
we are not committing future generations to problems we can't handle
we're not in this for the money, we're in it for life
neccessity is no longer the mother of invention
we have stopped using machine language (have we?)
there is no more pollution (none)
handicaps are no longer handicaps
we have agreed the future
everyone is taught design
people count
there are no more poor countries
there are no more rich countries either

after 35 wishes

THE SCHOOL OF NEEDS

sir !
this is a design
you mean the words
no   the time   35 minutes   that's how long it takes

ok   we'll do it

it hasn't started yet

THE SCHOOL OF NEEDS

would you like a cup of tea
mmmm
what's the matter have you got a headache
no my neck is stiff
i can't stand this
one moment you're prostrate and the next you're tapping away
i was waiting for an idea
a cup of tea
if i'd have known that i'd have brought you one
i didn't know i wanted it
I was waiting for something to happen
lights a cig
no need to say your wishes
reach for them
the audience waits
corrects typing errors
reach for them
22 spaces
you gave me one
he goes to get it
empties it
woman
eleven o'clock   the church clock strikes
i can   hardly hear
he was in bed   now he's typin
spark   muriel   what's she got to say
on a pilgrimage to the holy places
she clears her throat
of jordan, barbara vaughan, half jewish
it's up to the performers to decide which are the words
and which the stage directions
while performing
so it's different every time
barbara embarks on a pilgrimage
that becomes a rout
a desperate adventure of abduction and espionage

do you mind this tapping
no
a switchback of tragedy and farce
a love story, sacred and profane
cover photograph by van pariser
a woman with dark hair
the bes piece of furniture in the room was the camp-bed
and barbara lay upon it
cough
awake
gazing straight through the small window
and who DESIGNED IT
at the night sky
THE SKY
which
by contact with her emotional eyesight
was elated
with stares and lyrical energy   energy
that's what we're short of
who
that's an insult to the sun
S U. N
that would put an end to the gossip
pulling it to pieces
life
what was the point
what was the point
the point
oint
t   there's a t missing   the best piece
he rubs his chin again, nobody knows why
we know what our needs are
don't we
don't we
this is the school
the ideal
the ideal school
the ideal home   that's not a home   it's an exhibition
he stands up to look for something

the book
two minutes a pge   a page
that's a typing error
how much is error and how much is life
now you're being philosophic
why not   why NOT
it was underneath the other book
the unreal one
no, not unreal, it was a book too
but the wishes were unreal
wishes lies and dreams
in all the millions of words that are written annually
about education
one viewpoint is invariably absent
how does she know
that of the child
the client
its not at all difficult
to think of another sphere of social activity
a SPHERE
the earth
?
?
in which the opinions of the customer are so persos tently over-
                                                              looked
sis
who MAKES the errors
the unseen intelligence?
in a light airy room
i find chris, the lecturer, already seated
the stage directions
chris tells of research into the life of king george III
throwing light
catch
not to make fun   what we say is us
on the latter's fits of insanity
what a bore school is nowadays
no need to act it
i don't like it when the first few minutes tell you

what all the rest is going to be like
no tea left
she's sleeping
repeat page one[+]
and again[+]
no more[+]
what was the idea of this play   if it is a play
just to provide some composed experience
any
the words don't matter
but they're selected carefully
what about the wishes
thirty five
many thanks
for your 35 wishes
i want to be autonomous
not THAT   what is it anyway
this is a design   the play is a design
no
its the thoughts of those who watch it that's the design
and they are indeterminate
and much more extensive than what i'm writing here
here is not here
on the page
where is here
there
what ARE your needs then   what are they
your needs
all you can do in that building is what the designers expected
in the old one you can do many things
its time we danced
i have some terrible wishes
o that's not terrible   it's nice   don't we all
o
he wanted everyone to enjoy his wallpaper
as he enjoyed cycling in the country and looking at the leaves
utopia?
here's another cup of tea
do you want some toast

   [+]the page beginning 'would you like a cup of tea'

```
no     do you want some
no     i won't bother
did you need to buy that car
i don't want to talk about that
I'M GOING BACK TO BED NOW
are you coming
mmmmmmm
you need me
this could go on for ever
is this utopia
this
this
this is a committee meeting
what's on the agenda
for the future
the future can be perfect    perfect
come off it kid
we're living in the future   how's it feel
the royal college of the future
the conference
art'n'design
A'N'D
i need bringing up to date, i've had this hairstyle for tears
that's not a need
no
no
mmmmmmmmmm    mmm
she works as a secretary AND looks after her husband and junior
junior
yes, junior
you know
i know nothing
nothing
yes    i mean no
where's barbara gone
she went out
is that a need
all kids are equal
nobody is average thuogh    though
```

how do you pronounce that
there are moments when i wonder why i'm sitting here
but this is the conference of your dreams
our dreams
dreams, like wishes, are a frequent source of poetic inspiration
has the post come
there weren't any
none
but it's her birthday
he goes to look again
dreams, like wishes, are a frequent source of poetic inspiration
even the scary parts
ooooooooo
the planning of extraterrestial communities
the same problem
for instance
the navajo universe consists of mutual relations
between several types of beings
humans animals supernaturals ghosts and natural forces
ooooo
yes   that's a nice word
i'm thinking of using it
using it
yes
mmmm
yes
what for
o   i don't know
i like it
yes
in the US house most of the space is taken up by furniture
or by space
not much be people
the night chant dance of the navajo
takes nine days to perform
the step used throughout
used
yes used
is a type of trotting step, performed thusly

thusly
yes   it's a nice word
i hate it
hate, that's not a subject for us to discuss here
a thing of beauty is a joy for ever
why were you tapping in the night
typing
i was writing a play
you gave me the idea

pause*

that was a red pause

black pause

nobody nobody
has decided
what you are thinking what ARE you thinking
no need to apologise
for utopia
for you

NO MORE PROBLEMS:

ebeneezer (a shorthand writer): it is deeply to be deplored
        that people should continue to stream
        into the cities

        he invented the garden city

        how to combine the fundamental vividness
        the fundamental vividness
        of rustic life

* red ribbon

         with urban culture
         that is the main problem

         of the EVOLUTIONIST
         him
this is utopia
not a committee meeting
or a discussion
it's a slice of life
fiction
perhaps you came for something
yes
icame i came
thinking of your daughter
i cannot speak for her, let her say
this is the custom
if she is willing , there are no further formalities
in Zuni
it is never thought to be difficult
men are perenially willing
to aquire a new husband
she gathers his possesions   and places them on the doorstep
his skirt, his shoes, his precious feathers, his paint-pots

pause

music

he comes home
it is evening
he picks up the bundle   and returns to his mother's house
it is the subject of only fleeting gossip

bickering is not liked and most marriages are peaceful

the client speaks
the neglected client   the user
is ther a user
there

here
we are here to solve problems
we are here to help the others
what the others are for i've no idea
this IS th school of needs
the school
where we learn
social needs
not otherwise being fulfilled
this seems good   good

pause

these pauses can be inserted anywhere in the play

all the actions are very slow

this pause is timed
to make the play exactly 35 minutes long

the play continues
he looks at his fingers
she continues
distributing the wealth   that's ok

no more dissatisfied clients

have you any serious wishes
those are the context
35 of these are to made public during the performance
the wishes of the audience
noted beforehand

and presented   as faits accompli   as if they've happened

now i'm going
to look for her: if she sleeps   that's good   good
chopin piano music throughout   and liszt
off and on

the scene is composed to
the scene is composed
to be seen
with wishes incorporated
                              and perhaps the night chant
                              dance music (track 1 folkways
                              album fd 6510)
performers:
each marks his or her words in one colour in the text
some to be spoken   some to be acted   some both

wishes:
could be prerecorded on the tape with the music
could be indicated by slides notices or scenery or extras
 public needs, one's own needs, deep, superficial, constructive,
  destructive, any

what are extras
anything that is added
that's progress
progress is no longer a question of destroying the   present
to make room for the new
its just adding to what is here
extras

in the spirit of

the present

this is a present

it hasn't started yet   (end)

. . . .

Words, phrases, and occasionally lines from the following
sources are embedded in the play, here and there:

Edward Blishen's book The School That I'd Like, published by
Penguin Books, Harmondsworth, 1969.
Muriel Spark's book The Mandelbaum Gate, published by Macmillan,
London, 1965 and Penguin Books, Harmondworth, 1967.
Kenneth Koch's book Wishes Lies and Dreams, Teaching Children
to Write Poetry, published by Vintage Books, Random House Inc,
New York, 1970, originally published by Chelsea House Publishers,
1970.
Ruth Benedict's book Patterns of Culture published by Routledge
and Kegan Paul, London, 1935, and much reprinted.
Magoroh Maruayama's article Design Principles for Extra-Terrestial
Communities, in Futures, volume 8 number 2, April 1976.
The record sleeve of the American Indian music, Folkways Album
fd 6510.
A text by Ebeneezer Howard.
A play by Tedeuz Kantor.

voices at the
conference conference

Most of what I might say about this essay is included in it.
Of those written through a chance process this is perhaps the
only one in which I regretted or doubted some of the statements
appearing and edited them somewhat or expressed my thoughts about
them. I would like to thank Anthony Judge for inducing me to
make notes for a paper about conference design and to Barrie
Evans for persuading me to write the essay, long after the
conference at which I spoke had finished. Its first publication
was in the conference proceedings: Changing Design, edited by
Barrie Evans, James Powell, Reg Talbot, published by John Wiley
& Sons Ltd, Chichester & New York, 1982, pages 347-367.
The following note, written a year or so before the essay, was
prefaced to it.

. . . .

28 March 1977
Suddenly, after days, years, of worried seeking, planning,
and not finding: release.
I realised that, of the things done before, the ones that were
done with ease, lucidity, were not the ones that tried to achieve
anything, or to change the world, or to improve my lot, or anything like that. They were things like just writing out thoughts,
out of curiosity, to see how they'd go, and things like sculp-
ting, and attending to the thoughts and sensations, existentia,
while inspired or otherwise enthralled, by some artwork or
composition, some theory, or such.
They were not things like plans, ideas for how the world of men
could be improved, not even the lighthearted plays and stunts
made in protest. Neither were they any acts of protest or
rebellion or deliberate change of circumstance. Not factional
at all.
So?
A signal at last to just stop trying, to realise there is
nothing to be got or gained, only something to be free of:
anxiety and an obligation to do what "should" be done. If there
IS any necessity, of acting for others, eg to earn, it should
also be, if at all possible, a way to enjoy doing that, or doing
whatever is not chosen but brought by circumstance.
The middle-life change at last: the learning to accept, and to
be free in accepting. What is.
How fortunate if this indeed is happening.

NO SHOULD
ONLY IS

That poem, sent me by Edwin Schlossberg, he thought I needed it,
to whom my thanks, again, a gain.

VOICES AT THE CONFERENCE CONFERENCE

Earlier this year I was invited to speak at a conference about conferences but it never took place. Now I have been asked to write a paper about "context designing", a concept which I mentioned at the Portsmouth Conference but did not explain. Instead I gave an example of it by reading John Cage's Lecture on Nothing, a composed talk that is meant, like a piece of music, to be performed to a tempo and thus to be not so much a message, meant to control our future thoughts and acts, but an experience of the moment in which we are freed from the anxieties and purposes that often close the mind to all but self interest. A context in which our thoughts may be unexpected not only to the lecturer but to ourselves, the audience.

Today I do not want to repeat, in writing, that lecture which is better heard than read (and which is available in John Cage's book Silence) so I am trying to compose something in the same spirit to exemplify context designing and perhaps to explain the idea too, if that is possible. It seems to me that I can do this by bringing together some thoughts on the designing of conferences, thoughts of others as well as myself, as all such "softwares" as conferences, courses, computer systems, legal systems, political systems, public services, societies, groups, communications and the like are more contexts than products and all suffer the marks of neglect, total neglect, by the imagination, the artistic mind, the impulse to make life beautiful. These fine things, what are proudly called creative processes, seem so far not to have been applied to the shaping of industrial life itself but only to the shaping of the hardware and the artworks, the products not the processes. Is it possible to design, to make pleasant, beautiful, not only the results of industrial and human processes but the conditions in which these processes occur? To get rid of alienating ways of acting and communicating and rule-making and planning and instead to make new forms of industrial life in which the millions, and billions, of us who now exist can feel everywhere at home? That is the serious question before this play.

Who is to speak (at this conference-on-the-page, this account
of a discussion that never took place, this play in my mind,
and yours, as we read between the lines of what is said)?
The first to arrive is Shih Nai-An, Mr SHIH, a Chinese gentleman
from the thirteenth century, perhaps. He is not able to listen
to what the others are saying so long after he has left this life
so he will be speaking the words he wrote in introduction to
Water Margin, the book of stories that he wrote to entertain
himself and others in the absence of his friends. He came to
my mind because his description of friendly conversation seems
to me the best I've read, amusing and beautiful, even though
today he would be called an enemy of the people. This paper is,
I suppose, about the possibility that our enemy, as people, is
ourselves, as non-people, as ciphers, roles, as specialists
deaf to thoughts and feelings. Able to see that the system's
wrong but not free to put it right. We only work here. He
begins to speak by himself before the others come. He speaks
his mind. For anyone to read. He has the time, long past, to
think about the future.

MR SHIH:
A man should not marry after thirty years of age; should not
enter government service after the age of forty; should not have
any more children after the age of fifty; and should not travel
after the age of sixty. This because the proper time for those
things has passed.......

He is interrupted by the arrival of INTERNATIONAL MAN, a busy
fellow, expert at attending conferences, that is his life. He
is not happy to hear that the proceedings have begun without
mention of the agenda, the official programme of topics to be
discussed at this conference about conferences. He begins to
read from his list of 82 ideas for those unfamiliar with
international conferences so that they may become efficient and
satisfied participants.

INTERNATIONAL MAN:
Discretion is all very well, but timidity is useless and annoying. Remember that others are in the same position as you,

and may be even more isolated. Introduce yourself to other
people and make as many introductions as possible between other
participants.

MR SHIH does not hear this interruption and continues speaking.
We do not hear what he is saying as INTERNATIONAL MAN speaks
in a loud voice. Those who want to know what they missed can
read in J H Jackson's translation of Water Margin (The Commercial Press Ltd, Hong Kong, 1963) the words we did not hear.

MR SHIH:
..........Why talk about insects when the whole world is before
you? How can you count time by years? All that is clear is
that time passes, and all the time there is continual change
going on. Some change has taken place even since I began to
write this. This continual change and decay fills me with sadness.

He falls silent. It is the end of a paragraph. I wonder about
this old-fashioned dislike of change and for a moment hear the
ghost of Edmund Spenser flit by offering to speak his cantos on
change, Mutability as he called it, or was it her?, trying to
prove all things are subject to decay. But Mutability was
defeated, in Spenser's mind, by Mother Nature who, at the point
of defeat, argues that change is not decay but growth in which
each thing works its own perfection, approaches its true state
of being. At which she, Nature, vanishes and Mutability is seen
to be subject to perfection. The doctrine of progress, now so
discredited with us, how far is that a fallen version of that
hope of man, of Edmund Spenser, and of what was once the modern
spirit? But, sympathising a little with the desire to get on
with things, and to leave philosophy aside, I leave Spenser to
return to his time. For the present.

Others arrive, all ready to begin speaking, so I decide its time
for some order if everyone is to get a hearing. Order? Isn't
that, our idea of order, what's wrong, what's so ugly, what's
making progress (the life industrial) so unpleasant, unjust,
alienating? I feel that there is no official view of order that

permits anything but distrust to organise the lives of everyone
alive, now that we are so numerous. So, without asking if he
approves, I adopt a form of order preached and practiced by John
Cage, the order of chance, an attempt to get as near as can be
got to unintentional designing, not presupposing an aim except
that of "imitating nature in her manner of operation" while
trying to set aside self-interest. Is that possible? I don't
know but it seems adequate to me: to let a chance process
(letting a random number table decide who speaks and what they
say) be the organising principle. And thus to exhibit some
trust in what is outside one's conscious purposes. Numbers 1 & 2
will be the signal for MR SHIH to speak another sentence from
his book; 3 & 4 for INTERNATIONAL MAN to speak whatever of his
82 ideas is chosen next by random process; 5 & 6 will permit
THE WRITER (me) to speak, initially from a short piece I wrote
in 1973 about designing a conference and, if that source runs
out, to improvise some responses to what the others say; 7 & 8
will enable us to eavesdrop on JOHN CAGE reciting sentences
chosen randomly from his Lecture on Nothing; 9 & 0 will bring
quotations from what THE DESIGNERS (Nigel Cross, Robin Roy,
Reg Talbot and myself) wrote about in our report about the
future of confernces in 1969. MR SHIH, being the oldest speaker,
will have the last word. The play will continue until he has
reached the end of his piece. By which time I hope that whatever
can be learnt, by myself and other readers, about context
designing or about whatever else is said, will be evident.
(An impious hope, not in the spirit of the design, the play,
the unintentional process?) Who is going to open the proceedings, now that everyone is present?

JOHN CAGE:
Originally we were nowhere; and now, again, we are having the
pleasure of being slowly nowhere.
(He speaks slowly, with long pauses, to a tempo of his own.
The chance process favours him with a request to speak again.)

JOHN CAGE:
There seemed to me to be no truth, no good, in anything big in
society.

THE WRITER:
Henry Sanoff said something that begins to answer this question.
(The question was: what is a second generation design method?
That was the question in 1973.)

THE DESIGNERS:
How much money are people prepared to pay for better facilities?

INTERNATIONAL MAN:
Listen carefully, bearing in mind the aims of the congress, the
views of the speaker, and your own; make notes while listening.

THE WRITER:
He pointed out that the organisers of the EDRA Conferences have
each year tried to make it different from conventional conferences, less ponderous, more human, etc.

MR SHIH:
What excites pleasure in me is the meeting and conversing with
old friends.

INTERNATIONAL MAN:
Don't overstep your alloted time. This may annoy the chairman
and the other participants.

THE WRITER:
But each year it turns out just like every other conference.

THE DESIGNERS:
Delegates may not ask questions because (a) they are timid (b)
they don't know if the question would reveal their ignorance
(c) they don't want to make the author appear foolish in public
(d) they have no questions.

JOHN CAGE:
I myself have called it form. It is the continuity of a piece of
music. Continuity today, when it is necessary, is a demonstration of disinterestedness.

THE DESIGNERS:
We hope that better use can be made of the unique opportunity afforded delegates to technical conferences, the opportunity to interact with a large sample of co-workers gathered together in the same place at the same time.

THE WRITER:
"Why, he asked, can't designers design a conference?"

MR SHIH:
But is is very galling when my friends do not visit me because there is a biting wind, or the roads are muddy through the rain, or perhaps because they are sick.

THE DESIGNERS:
The main causes of the problem appeared to be as follows:
1. Inadequate information about delegates, papers, etc
2. Over-restriction of the conference schedule
3. Poor quality papers
4. Difficulty of recapitulating on the contents of technical sessions.

THE WRITER:
A good question.

JOHN CAGE:
(He rises to speak, remains standing for a few moments, and sits down.)

MR SHIH:
Then I feel isolated.

JOHN CAGE:
All I know about method is that when I am not working I sometimes think I know something, but when I am working, it is quite clear that I know nothing.

THE WRITER:
Since our conversation I keep remembering his words and at last

I have what feels like an answer: "Because they are IN IT"

THE WRITER:
Is it that design skills and methods as we know them are suited only to the designing of objects outside of ourselves and that a new kind of method is needed if the level of designing is raised from that of objects to activities?

JOHN CAGE:
I must say I still feel this way, but something else is happening : I begin to hear the old sounds - the ones I had thought worn out, worn out by intellectualization - I begin to hear the old sounds as if they are not worn out.

THE WRITER:
To design an event of which one is a part, an activity one is going to live oneself, sounds exactly like deciding what to do in life anyway.

MR SHIH:
Although I myself do not drink, yet I provide spirits for my friends, as my family has a few fields in which we grow millett.

MR SHIH:
In front of my house runs a great river, and there I can sit with my friends in the shadow of the lovely trees.

THE WRITER:
So designing becomes a way of ordering life, or re-making a culture while living it.

THE WRITER:
That's as much as I want to quote from what I wrote in 1973. Its time to renew my vehicle licence. How I hate having to search for all those certificates of insurance, log books, etc.

THE WRITER:
In an earlier version of this paper, now discarded, I realised that words and numbers are good examples, perhaps the best that

can be found, of what I mean by context design. Though having a purpose they are used in ways that are not predictable in advance. It is as if there is no separation of designing from using: just a process, or tradition, in which, each time a word, a letter, or a number is used, the user is free to reinvent its purpose, to a great or less extent, and also to reinvent its sound or shape, so long as it is decipherable.

THE WRITER:
New methods cannot force us to do good, nothing can, but they can change the context of designing. There is a morality in widening the scope of life; what was inevitable or impossible before becomes now a conscious choice.

JOHN CAGE:
It is and it isn't.

MR SHIH:
I have four old women to do the cooking and household affairs, and also ten small boys who act as messengers.

THE WRITER:
All those messengers? Is that your equivalent of having a postal service and being able to use the telephone?

INTERNATIONAL MAN:
Arrive punctually at meetings.

THE WRITER:
Its time I thought about what has been said. At a conference that would be difficult but here I have a printout of the proceedings as they happen and can halt them at any moment to review my thoughts and theirs......I read through from the beginning, much enjoying the diversity of views, but unable to digest it all just yet. I like the idea that one reading does not exhaust this text: that different meanings may emerge at different times, depending on the reader's state of mind, and how long he is prepared to ponder what is said. Just now I'm curious to go on and see what comes next.

MR SHIH:
If all my friends came there would be sixteen, but because of the weather there are seldom more than six or seven here.

THE WRITER:
I pause to do the last thing needed for the renewal of the vehicle licence: as the registration document was stolen I have to copy out the chassis number from the vehicle onto the form applying for a new one. I notice that, since vehicle registration has been computerised, the people seem much more helpful when you phone the office about any difficulties like this. That's just what, in the fifties, I predicted would happen as computers began to take the drudgery out of life. But many people seem to find that computer systems are making life more difficult. Why is this?

THE DESIGNERS:

	A	B	C
b) profit to venue organizers	=	(+)	(+)

(This is a line from a table showing how three proposed new kinds of conferences, A B C, affect the interests of the parties concerned. In this case Type A has no effect and Types B & C have possible positive effects.)

INTERNATIONAL MAN:
Take advantage of meals, receptions and excursions; change to another group instead of staying with your compatriots, or at the same table, or in the same coach.

JOHN CAGE:

JOHN CAGE:
However modern music still fascinated me

with all its modern intervals. But in order to have them the mind had fixed it so that one had to avoid having progressions that would make one think of sounds that were not actually present to the ear. Avoiding did not appeal to me.

THE WRITER:
I dont know what to say.

MR SHIH:
When they come they drink and chat, just as they please, but our pleasure is in the conversation and not in the liquor.

THE WRITER:
I still dont.

JOHN CAGE:
If anybody is sleepy, let him go to sleep.

JOHN CAGE:
A lady from Texas said: I live in Texas. We have no music in Texas. The reason they've no music in Texas is because they have recordings in Texas. Remove the records from Texas and somebody will learn to sing.

MR SHIH:
We do not discuss politics because we are so isolated here that our news is simply composed of rumours, and it would only be a waste of time to talk with untrustworthy information.

THE DESIGNERS:
Seating for only ⅔ of delegates
(Item from a list of hundreds of difficulties reported by people attending conferences)

INTERNATIONAL MAN:
If you do have to read a text prepared in advance, because this is more concentrated in substance than an improvisation try to avoid the temptation of reading it too quickly. You run the risk of not being understood by your colleagues or by the interpreters. In any case, you should always let the interpreters see the text beforehand.

MR SHIH:
We also never talk about other people's faults, because in this world nobody is wrong, and we should beware of backbiting.

THE DESIGNERS:
Effects of conference evolution on conference goals.

THE DESIGNERS:
Conference Type B is likely to have the benefit (to sponsors and employers of delegates) of increasing the speed of technology transfer and the penalty of higher cost.

THE DESIGNERS:
In formulating solutions, we have fitted the new types of conference into an "evolutionary pathway" along which conferences may develop from their present form to something like that which we envisage in perhaps ten to fifteen years time.

THE DESIGNERS:
One feature of Type B Conference is a transcript office which relays a continuous print-out alongside the TV of the proceedings, and from which transcripts may be obtained.

MR SHIH:
We do not wish to injure anyone, and therefore our conversation is of no consequence to anyone.

MR SHIH:
We discuss human nature about which people know so little because they are too busy to study it.

THE WRITER:
I'm having to edit the statements of the designers as the chance process keeps picking out inexplicable statements from long lists and tables of which the report is mainly composed. Writing in lists: what does that suggest?

THE DESIGNERS:
Disadvantages of large international conferences:

1) Standard format with little time for discussion, still less for exchange of ideas, comments and criticisms.
(10 items listed)

THE WRITER:
To abandon function, purpose. That could be the releasive step we've yet to make.

INTERNATIONAL MAN:
Remember that quite a few of those listening to you without listening to the interpretation are hearing a foreign language and that many dont know it very well. If you wish to be understood speak slowly and clearly, pausing before and after difficult words. Dont use uncommon terms and avoid quotations and colloquial expressions.

INTERNATIONAL MAN:
If you have any questions, address them to the appropriate authorities; if you do not know who the appropriate authority is, ask at the information desk.

INTERNATIONAL MAN:
If possible, prepare a condensed version of your speech in a few concise paragraphs. The person writing the account of the proceedings will be grateful to you and you will be surer of being reported accurately.

INTERNATIONAL MAN:
Mark on your list of participants the names of those whom you want to meet.

MR SHIH:
My friends are all broad-minded and well educated but we do not keep a record of our conversations.

MR SHIH:
The reason for this is (1) we are too lazy, and do not aspire to fame; (2) to talk gives us pleasure, but to write would give trouble; (3) none of us would be able to read it again after

our deaths, so why worry; (4) if we wrote something this year
we should probably find it all wrong the next year.

INTERNATIONAL MAN:
If the preparatory work of the congress is carried out by meetings of national committees or working groups, take part if you are invited to do so; get to know their conclusions and recommendations.

JOHN CAGE:
If one is making something which is to be nothing, the one making must love and be patient with the material he chooses. Otherwise he calls attention to the material, which is precisely something, whereas it was nothing that was being made; or he calls attention to himself, whereas nothing is anonymous.

THE WRITER:
Dear John, I expect you've noticed that International Man is intent on making a lecture on nothing even though I'm omitting most of yours?

INTERNATIONAL MAN:
Speak straight into the microphone without turning your head and keep the volume of your voice as even as possible.

THE DESIGNERS:
Delegates cannot store ideas about papers and listen to the paper at the same time.

INTERNATIONAL MAN:
Before leaving for the congress check to see whether any working papers are missing, in which case make a list and ask the congress secretariat for them immediately on arrival when completing the final registration formalities.

INTERNATIONAL MAN:
Keep an eye on your listeners and if you get the impression they havent understood you, repeat what you have said, if possible more clearly.

KEEP AN EYE ON YOUR LISTENERS AND IF YOU GET THE IMPRESSION
THEY HAVENT UNDERSTOOD YOU, REPEAT WHAT YOU HAVE SAID, IF POSS-
IBLE MORE CLEARLY.

INTERNATIONAL MAN:
before starting, state clearly and audibly your name and the
organization you represent or belong to, without using any
abbreviations. It is essential to those taking the minutes or
recordings to be able to identify you and to attribute what
you say to the right person in the report of the proceedings.

THE WRITER:
I can't stand much more of this. Why on earth did I invite him?

THE DESIGNERS:
The chairman may favour his friends (or people whose views,
or calibre, he knows) when selecting people to ask questions
during the discussion.

INTERNATIONAL MAN:
If a wireless installation is being used, obtain your earphones
before entering the hall.

MR SHIH:
I have written these seventy chapters of Shui Hu just for my
own pleasure after my friends had left, or when they had not
turned up owing to the weather.

JOHN CAGE:
Much of the music I love uses the twelve-tone row, but that is
not why I love it. I love it for no reason. I love it for
suddenly I am nowhere. (My own music does that quickly for me.)

MR SHIH:
I have had no preconceived plan, but have jotted these items
down just as they occurred to me, sometimes when sitting outside near the bamboo fence, or at early dawn when lying on my
couch in pensive mood.

THE DESIGNERS:
The principal evolutionary features of our solutions are facilities for: 1) improving and increasing the exchange of information, using the conference as a problem-solving device, individual or small group research and study, being able to re-cap on the proceedings, improving and increasing delegate enjoyment. All of these features incorporate or enhance the concept of multi-level participation.

INTERNATIONAL MAN:
Before leaving, check to see if evening dress is requested for the receptions.

MR SHIH:
But someone may ask, "As you did not write down your friends' conversations why have you written this book?"

THE WRITER:
I'm often advocating creative inaction: less doing and more perceiving. But a lot of this is neither.

JOHN CAGE:
Blackbirds rise from a field making a sound delicious beyond compare. I heard them because I accepted the limitations of an arts conference in a Virginia girls finishing school, which limitations allowed me quite by accident to hear the blackbirds as they flew up and overhead. There was a social calendar and hours for breakfast, but one day I saw a cardinal, and the same day heard a woodpecker.

INTERNATIONAL MAN:
(I've lost the list of 82 ideas.)

JOHN CAGE:
(He stands but does not speak.)

INTERNATIONAL MAN:
(I've searched again, not too thoroughly, but he seems to have dissappeared.)

JOHN CAGE:
The other day a pupil said, after trying to compose a melody using only three tones, "I felt limited." Had she concerned herself with the three tones - her materials - she would not have felt limited, and since materials are without feeling, there would not have been any limitation. It was all in her mind, whereas it belonged in the materials. It became something by not being nothing; it would have been nothing by being something.

INTERNATIONAL MAN:
When not using your earphones turn the control to zero so that your neighbours will not be disturbed by noises coming from your appuratus.

MR SHIH:
To which I reply (1) because it is just a hotchpotch, and cannot make me famous or even discredit me; (2) I have only done this to fill up my spare time, and give pleasure to myself; (3) I have written it so that the uneducated can read it as well as the educated; (4) I have used this style of composition because it was such a trifle.

MR SHIH:
Alas! Life is so short that I shall not even know what the reader thinks about it, but still I shall be satisfied if a few of my friends read it and be interested.

JOHN CAGE:
That forty minutes has been divided into five large parts, and each unit is divided likewise. Subdivision involving a square root is the only possible subdivision which permits this micro-macrocosmic rhythmic structure, which I find so acceptable and accepting. As you can see, I can say anything. It makes very little difference what I say or even how I say it.

JOHN CAGE:
Originally we were nowhere; and now, again, we are having the pleasure of being slowly nowhere. If anybody is sleepy, let

him go to sleep.

THE DESIGNERS:

MR SHIH:
Also I do not know what I may think about it in my future life after death, because then I may not be able even to read it.

INTERNATIONAL MAN:
Please speak clearly — however quick the reactions of the interpreters may be, it takes several seconds for them to absorb your idea and to express it correctly in another language.

THE WRITER:
The boy told the teacher what was wrong with his teaching. The next day he was teaching as the boy had advised.
(The writer pauses to think, conscious that some new principle, perhaps obvious once seen, named, but hidden as yet, seems to be sought and needed in this conversation, in the world of design, in the life we live......our context.)

JOHN CAGE:
I have a story: "There was once a man standing on a high elevation. A company of several men who happened to be walking on the road noticed from the distance the man standing on the high place and talked among themselves about this man. One of them said: He must have lost his favourite animal. Another man said: No, it must be his friend whom he is looking for. A third one said: He is just enjoying the cool air up there. The three could not agree and the discussion (Shall we have one later?) went on until they reached the high place where the man was.
One of the three asked: O, friend standing up there, have you not lost your pet animal? No, sir, I have not lost any. The second man asked: Have you not lost your friend? No, sir, I have not lost my friend either. The third man asked: Are you not enjoying the fresh breeze up there? No, sir, I am not. What, then, are you standing up there for, if you say no to all

our questions? The man on high said: I just stand."
If there are no questions, there are no answers. If there are
questions, then, or course, there are answers, but the final
answer makes the questions seem absurd, whereas the questions,
up to then, seem more intelligent than the answers. Somebody
asked Debussy how he wrote music. He said: I take all the
tones there are, leave out the ones I don't want, and use all
the others. Satie said: When I was young people told me: You'll
see when you're fifty years old. Now I'm fifty. I've seen
nothing.

(The Writer, noticing that he is to speak next, perhaps for the
last time, and that it is late, near midnight, decides to go to
bed......They wait, tireless, as he sleeps, confused, baffled
by this concept that he cant explain, suspicious of the whole
idea of designing, its too much like control, tired after a day
tied to the posture of a typist, but happy that, at last, he's
found something to replace that paper he'd abandoned.)

Wednesday morning.
He wakes to realise he dreamt of missing his place and trying
to catch up, never quite doing so, his family and friends
(is that who they were?) all of whom had to walk, as prisoners
just sentenced, in a long procession, ceremonially dressed,
after being tried in court, to some place assigned, not a
prison, quite friendly really, but which was difficult to find
because just as one reached it the destination changed.
That's not quite what the dream was like: it won't really go
into words. Do they ever?

While getting breakfast he remembers a fragment seen on TV
last night while resting from this bit of writing: a simulated
documentary film about miners rescuing other miners trapped
underground. The actors, who appeared not to be actors, were
all Yorkshire comedians.
Is there something missing, he thought, from this view of life,
largely learnt from John Cage, which is appearing in this
conversation? Is it the seriousness, the selfless bravery,
unquestioning and gentle, of the miners, once they see that

an accident's occurred and life's in danger? The play was
called The Price of Coal.
But I realise the title's wrong, untrue. Lives lost underground
are not the price of coal: they are the price of cheap coal.
One can conceive of a feasible way of getting energy automatically, by remote control, using robots or some such, in which
not a life would be put in much risk. But it would be expensive.
Probably much cheaper than the moon trip and using much of the
same knowhow.
That selfless bravery? Doesn't it sound very like the self-
forgetful manner of being interested in the sounds more than the
meanings, in the present rather than the future, that John Cage,
the zen buddhists, and all who believe that human life is not
the whole story, keep recommending as the way to live? To act
religiously. Not following any church but just because life is
so amazing.

A fresh start.
He remembers how he keeps finding, in a million ways, that the
enemy of doing what seems right is specialization: that strange
deformity that disables us all from acting on our perceptions
of what we can see needs doing and what is useless. What is
beautiful and what is ugly. Not that those are always the same?
And he asks himself: how came it all, this voluntary limbo that
we all are in. Except in emergencies, it seems, and International Man has surely got 82 ideas for those. Rules, he seems
to mean. The cause, it seemed to him, me, is the fact of being
middle class, or drifting in that direction. Wanting to be
safe, and comfortable all the time, and willing to accept the
price: to give up being present as a person? A society, we have,
in which most people have a place, not a very brave one, in
which to act in self-interest is to do the public good. Or so
its thought. But that is precisely what I doubt, he said to
himself. Surely the time has come already when what most people
do, for money, as "work", is no longer helpful to others: more
often it is harmful: the presence of you and I holding on to
our right to do this or that job could be just whats preventing
any evolution towards the social forms, beautiful ones I keep
hoping for, in which it would be possible for industrial life,

the life of this by now so numerous species, us, to go in trust
not alienation? What a sermon this is. No apologies.

What's needed then? (All this flashed through his mind as he got
together the cups and saucers and the marmalade etc)

Is it a different basis of organising social life? Not on self
interest but on plain interest, not in oneself but in life itself? Is that possible? A new kind of religious life, outside
the monastery, the convent, the ashram, the Buddhist temple.
Outside John Cage's world of music. He's left it himself. Left
it by so expanding his conception of "it", music, as to coincide
with life. Isn't that what we need to do with designing? To
widen it far, far, beyond the point where critics say "You cant
do that, its not designing, its not your business? Get back
to your drawing boards, and plans, fixed aims,.....get back to
doing what you're paid to do". Make designing non-exclusive.
Include what's now left out. What does designing leave out?
John Cage found that what music, Beethoven's kind, and even
Schoenberg's, left out was silence, noise, it made nothing of
them. What, in design, is the equivalent of silence in music?
Silence, he found, is not silence. There are always tiny noises,
sounds, and musicians trying to shut them out.

I switch off the electric typewriter for a moment. The sound
of it stops immediately. What a relief. I didn't realise that
in this task I'm fighting against that constant noise of the
electric motor. Why am I against it?

That was most of what he thought at breakfast. Time, perhaps
to go back to the theatre, to witness the ending of the play.

On the way I pause to read the mornings post: just an advertis-
ment and a bill. Looking like an attractive modern light fitting,
the MULTISUN unit is ideal for the bedroom. Suspend it over
the bed - and relax in comfort.....Get yours now - it gives
more than a great tan - it's a great tonic! As used in health
clinics.

The others are waiting, they've not heard my digressions, and
my dream, or read the advertisement. They do not seem very
real, just now, and my memory of what we said yesterday is faint.
I must be careful. If we are, in these last few words, to make
some progress (yes, Edmund, we've not completely lost faith in
progress, towards perfection: how are _you_ getting on?). To find,
even at this late hour, some way to make a start, a new start,
to CHANGE DESIGN, as it says in the title of the conference, to
which this is an extra. We begin where we left off.

THE WRITER:
What more is there to say?

MR SHIH:
So why think anything further about it?

TO INTERNATIONAL MAN, AND OTHERS, checking out of the conference
that is our life
(surely _that's_ going a bit far, Chris?, we're still alive you
know, most of us, and Mr Shih, he's become a classic, his
voice still speaks to millions, not to mention the TV series,
and isn't International Man, who seems to have come so badly
out of this, a picture of yourself, as you used to be, at least?
You've often said you were educated at conferences, and see them
as good things, a new social form that's free enough, despite
its faults, to enable the new life, the life of planetary man,
to find itself.)

OK, I agree. All I was going to say was that, for those who
want to read more, to trace sources, etc, here are the refs:

(the ones I didn't mention in the text)

John Cage, _Silence_, Wesleyan University Press, Middletown,
Connecticut, 1973

R J Talbot (in collaboration with J C Jones, N G Cross, R Roy)
_Conferences: a study of the possible future of technical
conferences_, published by The Design Research Laboratory, UMIST

Sackville Street, Manchester, MQ60 1QD, Britain, 1969 (and now obtainable, if at all, from R J Talbot at the Manchester Business School, Booth Street West, Manchester M15 6PB, Britain).

G P Speeckaert, <u>How to take part in International Meetings</u>, Union of International Associations, 1 rue aux Laines, Brussels, 1969

Anthony Judge has written extensively about conference design and new social forms in papers published by the Union of International Associations and, more recently, in the proceedings of Fondation Internationale de l'Innovation Sociale, 20, rue Laffitte, 75009, Paris. It was he who got me writing on the topic.

Are we still in context?

That's not all.

The story about Henry Sanoff, whom I thank for being one of the sources of this paper, was quoted by The Writer from an article that some of Henry's students asked me to write:

To be a Part, or what is a second generation design method?, appearing in <u>Designing the Method</u>, edited by David K Tester, The Student Publication of the School of Design: Vol 23, North Carolina State University, Raleigh, N C, 27607, 1974.

Readers who cannot quite place Mr Shih (Shih Nai-An) may like to know that, at the beginning of Water Margin, he prints a list of 108 heroes giving both their Chinese names (An Tao-ch'uan, Ch'ai Chin, Chang Chin.....etc) and their nicknames (Skilled Doctor, Small Whirlwind, Arrow Without Feathers, etc) and also a list of other characters (who did not join the heroes at Liang Po) eg Chang San (nickname Old Rat Who Crosses the Road), Ch'ao Kwan-hsi (Heavenly King), Cheng Kai (Bully of the Western Pass)......that's wrong: the last two are Ch'ao Kai and Cheng Kwan-hsi.

The conference over, I sit, a little sadly, at the typewriter
on which it took form, not wanting to leave the happy state of
mind it left me in. Soon I'll be sending these words to the
editor, Barrie Evans, who asked me to write them.......and then
what?........some of the libraries and bookshops and bookshelves
of the world will be expected to make room for this little
addition which becomes a place where others can retrace the
track of what we said. Not one place, as now, existing only
in the original composition, but as many identical copies,
waiting, in various places, for whoever may look and read.
For you.

A final question:
What do you consider the most important tool of genius today?
Answer:
Rubber cement.

Donald Barthelme speaks that from: Sadness (Bantam Books,
and Farrar, Straus & Giroux, New York, 1972)

Context design?

Nothing fancy. Just a willingness to include, not only the
designers but the sponsor, the makers, and the users, in IT,
in the process. Everyone. Included. Not as ciphers, but as
people, present. Not in roles. Not as designers, sponsors,
makers, users. As variables? Why not?

A fabrication.

. . . .

I am grateful to the authors and publishers cited within the
essay for permission to reproduce the words spoken by Mr Shih,
John Cage, International Man, and The Designers. The words
from John Cage's Lecture on Nothing are copyright © 1961 by
John Cage, reprinted from Silence by permission of Wesleyan
University Press. This lecture first appeared in Incontri
Musicali.

the design of modern life

responses by

Frank Quadflieg, Allen Fisher, Chris Jones, Alberto Carreto, Denis O'Brien, Pauline Amphlett, paul bas, Robert Wouters, Erwin van Handenhoven, Alwyn Jones, Edwin Schlossberg, G.Y. Solis (Erea Grillo), Jef Jannsens, Fionan de Barra, Alan Pinder, Necdet Teymur and Ranulph Glanville

This was presented at the conference of the Design Research
Society in 1980. It is a modest attempt at what I hope will one
day be done as a matter of course: the inclusion of everyone in
the process of shaping the life we live. Having decided to offer
a paper on this topic I realised that if I wrote it myself I would
be acting against the spirit of the idea - so I made the paper a
vehicle for the ideas of others. In the first page I attempted to
define a context (in time, and in the range of things to consider)
and left the remaining pages for the responses of anyone who wished
to reply. I wrote one reply myself. The invitation was sent to
delegates before the conference (thanks to the enthusiastic efforts
of James Powell) and it was seen by students and teachers of design
at Antwerpen (where I was teaching a week or two before). I sent
a few copies to friends whom I knew to have ideas on the subject.
The paper aroused criticisms which can be read in the conference
proceedings and in the newsletter of the Design Research Society.

The essay first appeared in DESIGN: SCIENCE: METHOD, Proceedings
of the 1980 Design Research Society Conference, edited by Robin
Jaques and James A Powell, published by Westbury House, PO Box 63,
Bury Street, Guildford, Surrey, GU2 5BH. It appears here by
permission of the publisher and with thanks to those who contrib-
uted to it. The last response, by Ranulph Glanville, arrived too
late for the conference proceedings. The next-to-last is his re-
writing of that response for this publication. The illegibilty
is intentional, as is the legibilty of some parts, but the original texts are a little easier to read, both being larger than what
is seen here and the last being in two colours. I am grateful to
Ranulph for giving his somewhat reluctant permission for this
publication and for encouraging me to go to the conference in the
first place.

an invitation to anyone who wishes to present proposals for the design of modern life as it could be in 1981, 1984 and the year 2000.

My paper for the DRS Conference is to consist of this page[1], plus six others, written by whoever responds to this invitation. In this page I am supplying a format, or context-design, which will I hope enable some of us to collaborate in making a picture of how modern life could develop, according to the ideas of those who study design processes.

I am inviting proposals for the design of the six starred items in this list of sectors of modern life. The six were selected by chance.

*00 broadcasting
 01 agriculture
 02 education
*03 central & local govt. depts.
 04 cars & road transport
*05 the design professions
 06 air travel
 07 manufacturing industry
 08 the unions
*09 post office & telephones
 10 computing & microprocessors
 11 housing & the building industry
 12 health services
 13 tourism
*14 leisure (sports & hobbies)
 15 parliament & political parties
 16 advertising & public relations
 17 banks, credit, investment, etc.
 18 law & order & the armed services
*19 anything not in this list

[1] The text has been retyped again with shorter lines as this book of essays is narrower than was the book of conference proceedings. The first "page" has thus become larger than a page of this book (it extends to to page 3). JCJ.

As a contrast to the sometimes dispiriting names of these
sectors, and as an inspiration to recovering a sense of 'life
as a whole', I seek a quotation from a source which I've often
found helpful on such occasions: The Collected Poems of Wallace
Stevens (Faber and Faber, London, 1955). A chance process
(random numbers) leads me to these lines on page 201-2 from
The Man on the Dump:

> ....the dump is full
> Of images. Days pass like papers from a press.
> The bouquets come here in the papers, So the sun,
> And so the moon, both come, and the janitor's poems
> Of every day, the wrapper on the can of pears,
> The cat in the bag, the corset, the box
> From Esthonia: the tiger chest, for tea.
> The freshness of the night has been fresh a long time.

If you wish to respond please choose (by preference or by chance)
one of the starred sectors. Then write your answers to these
questions:

1. Which sector have you chosen?
2. What do you think is most wrong with this sector?
3. How do you propose that it could be changed
   (a) immediately, e.g. in 1981, as a local improvisation in
       your area?
   (b) more slowly, e.g. by 1984, through existing procedures
       for change, and making a modest but noticeable
       improvement thoughout the sector?
   (c) even more slowly, e.g. by the year 2000, as a fundament-
       ally better way of organising this sector of modern life?

Please reply on one page to me care of DRS Conference Secretary
Jennifer Powell, School of Architecture, Portsmouth Polytechnic, King Henry I Street, Portsmouth, PO1 2DY, Britain, or give
it to me at the Conference by 16th December 1980. All replies
will be exhibited and six, chosen by chance, will appear in the
Conference proceedings. Please write with electric typewriter
OR IN CAPITALS WITH A FIBRE PEN within a text area no larger

than this. I will submit a response myself. Don't forget to add your name and address. - J. Christopher Jones.

NOTE: 16 responses were received, some from those at the conference, some from a dozen people (famous and unknown) to whom I mailed page 1. As many used less than a page the editor has offered more than the original 7 pages which were available for this paper so that all 16 can be reproduced. To make this possible we have retyped all the responses to more space-saving layouts, except where it seems that the original spacing is poetic or meaningful. The sequence of the responses is close to that of the list of sectors on the first page. J.C.J.

Broadcasting

problem: there's very few feedback between programm designers and
        consumers

        they absorbe formal programms without contents

1981: develop the criticism of consumers. By receiving broadcast products in full conciousness, they will feel the need to react. So, a taste will be created, which will improve the quality of programms.

1984: starting from this taste, design new concepts around broadcasting, where the consumer is more engaged. One should broadcast documentaries, where personal problems of certain groups are discussed, instead of american series.

the future: whatever technique will achieve considering broadcasting, the utopic idea will always be the same:
EVERYONE CAN EXPRESS HIS/HER VISION BY USING THE MEDIA.
it's the end of the creative spiral, where everyone CAN COMMUNICATE in perfect harmony.

During the total development we have only one purpose:
   TO SHORTEN THE FEEDBACKTIME AS MUCH AS POSSIBLE
   feedback during the expression is the utopic form of
   communication

Frank Quadflieg, Lange Brilstr.8, 2000 Antwerpen, Belgium.

THE DESIGN OF MODERN LIFE   From ALLEN FISHER of SPANNER
                                         85, Ramilles Close,
                                         London SW2 5Dg
1. sector chosen: 00 broadcasting

2. what's wrong with it? not enough included error.
   (too polished/professional/established/closed/determinded)
            wrong emphasis on audience ratings

3. could be changed: how?

(a) immediately by use of wider variety of reportage/enter-
    tainer and mediums. drawn sketches as well as films of
    events.
    hand-held slide viewers as well as carefully chosen photos.
    use more showing of errors in process of making.
    more local groups and specialised groups.
    Friends of Earth as well as Royal Society proceedings.
    Poetry readings as much as lab technicians describing in
    situ their research.

(b) more slowly introduce indeterminate rotas of local and
    specialised presentations.
    replace film re-runs with contemporary video and film
    makers in process of making as well as finished product.
    more live coverage in situ instead of sterilised "live"
    studio with personalities.

(c) Extend technologically into and out of home.
    video-telephone directly broadcast.
    immediate broadcast of conversations at a distance,

not necessary to use professional reporters for this.
welsh miner speaks to minister of housing by video-phone.
cut out intermediate "censor" "editor" for many programmes.
remove overall editorships replace with co-ordinators.
introduce indeterminate editor rota. all finance circulated freely to participants not power structure. those involved get paid, but also those not currently employed because of rota receiving guaranteed income. lower scale payments.
replace conceptual circuits/centres/lines of responsibility/power structure with FIELDS MULTICENTRED
replace public demand/concensus/audience rating ideals with all that wishes to be available is and whoever wants it receives it. allow one person to broadcast to an audience of one. create technology to make this possible.
multi-screens as catalogue of what's coming on.
the only "censor" for viewing - individual on/off switch.

A Chinese archaeologist, Professor So Te Sun, searching the dumps of pre-electronic government papers, has found a packet of office memos and other documents on the back of which a twentieth century janitor, Stanley Moon, had written poems over a period of 19 years. The poems are now illegible but it is thought that they were addressed to Catherine Pears, a pioneer of decentralization, as her name appears on every paper in the packet. Three of the papers are reproduced here as interesting evidence of the gradual process by which centralized government offices were transformed into the present system of open-access unstaffed government computers and real-time local decision-making.

- -

31 December 1981   to: Ms C O Pears, Secretary of the Decision Review Committee.
                    from: Mr B T Corset, Head of Department.

I am agreeably surprised by the results of the experiment, as described in your report of the committee's first year. I was, as you know, sceptical of the view that committees of the traditional type are intrinsically bad because, as you put it, 'their decisions are not made by the people most affected, but by others who are separated in time, place, and experience from the actual conditions'. And I was aghast at your proposal that we try out the giving of power to alter and veto our decisions to a local committee of laypersons and vested interests. But now that its happened I am surprised how safe and cautious are the decisions they made and how seldom did they go against what you, as the Department's representative, were instructed to set as limits of spending and public policy. I'd be glad of your views on how we can be more adventurous in phase 2. But for the moment my congratulations. A bouquet for you!

----

31 December 1984   to: Secretaries of all DRC's
from: Catherine Pears, Department Coordinator,
Local Government Nucleus.

Now the cat is out of the bag! Our first year of operating the department decentrally, with open-access on-site meeting broadcast on local radio and tv, has shown everyone that the new system is far cheaper, and much more acceptable, than centralization. But this good news is being hidden behind the active resistance and protests of the 45% of officials who have lost their jobs and by those who try to over-staff the shrinking nucleus. There are also growing protests against using so much of local taxes to pay and pension these groups. It seems that we will have to accept a slow-down of decentralization until there is agreement on the Carrington plan for a minimum unearned income, funded by oil revenue and by automation throughout the BritJap Common Market. Please let me have your proposals for DRC organization in the light of these developments.

----

31 December 2000   to: Catherine Pears, member of DRC 601 and
voter ZGBH 354 3
from: Government Computer Nucleus

dear Cathy

GOCON calling. I'm to remind you to vote today on the 24 questions from other DRC's over which DRC 601 has requested modification...... Your own proposal, for regrading pensions of government nucleus staff made redundant by the final stage of computerization, will appear in citizen viewdata tomorrow. Pre-poll suggest you are over-optimistic. ......Your old colleague B T Corset sends new year greetings.

(Document 03 Central & Local Govt. Depts. originated by JCJones)

"THE DESIGN OF MODERN LIFE"   Alberto Carreto

CARS

-"I travel in a widewalk, faster than cars in the traffic jam. I cross between the cars walking my fingers over its hot metal sheet. I see angry drivers with sweat in the face. I do not breath well, I have tears in my eyes, I can not see the trees neither the sky due to pollution."-

What is wrong?... The traffic light system? The lack of fly-overs? The materials used to construct car? Its dimensions?

-"I am in my car, moving terribly slow. I have to wait before reaching the spectators of a white blanket, that hides the face of a fellow creature. As I get along I see the lifeless foot exposed. The assassin car, some meters forward."-

What is wrong?... Brakes that do not stop the mass of metal in the wet road? The speed of cars? Cars and people using the same space, street?... or... THE CAR?

- I could spend thousands of lines describing sensations that we all have seen; splinter-proof glass covering like snow the dark pavement; red spots on cloths, then screaming sirens; pain of metamorphosed man in machine.

What do I propose?

More than a proposition this is a wish:

I DREAM in my not yet born child showing to his son an image of a car, and saying: "This was a car" while travelling on the...

...MOVING STREET.

Alberto Carreto, A mexican student of planning, Alberto Agustin Carreto Sangines, 20 Castle Hill, East Leake, Loughborough, Leicestershire LE12 6LX

The Design Professions

Denis O'Brien, 7, Sorrell Bank, Lynton Slade, Forest Dale, Addington, Surrey.

Whats wrong
:Professionalisation
:some are cut off from their users.
:Doing has been replaced by abstraction
:Increase in specialisation / professional demarkation
:Professionals are sometimes denatured by measurement

What to do now
 a. Get those who actually create products/systems to talk to one another about successes/failures. Get successful design practitioners to talk at a methodological level with each other and with their users.

1984 If a. has been successful, a formal organisation should now exist to actively influence the education and training of professionals both new and old.

2000 By now, the slow change over education and training should have reached the universities, Art colleges and professional societies. The best of the old should have been merged with the best of the new.

PERISCOPES IN THE DESERT.

FINDING THAT RESILIENCE
IS NOT STORED IN BOTTLES AND JARS
CAME AS A SURPRISE
TO A ONCE INNOCENTLY CORRUPT IMAGINATION.
THE PSYCHE WAS PLACED,
AS WERE THE SAMPLES,
IN TUBES,
TO BE CATEGORISED.
OBJECTIVE;
TO CLASSIFY THE INDIVIDUAL AND THE WHOLE
RELATIVE TO EACH OTHER.
AN ODD DESIRE
TO SEEK OBTAINING COMPLEXITY
IN A MORE MANAGEABLE FORM.

A TRAIN FLEW TO ANOTHER DESTINATION
HUMMING IN THE SAME KEY,
HUMMING IN THE SAME KEY,
AS SOMEONES HEARTFELT MESSAGE.

YOUR SAMPLE NUMBER IS .....
YOUR EGO HAS BEEN TRANSFORMED
TO A CATAGORICAL SYSTEM
EXPLAINED BY 'SCIENCE',
(WILL MR. SCIENCE PLEASE REPLY TO THE LETTERS
I HAVE SENT, IF ONLY AN EXCERCISE IN SOCIAL ETIQUETTE).
VERBAL PARADOX WINS ONCE MORE
WE HAVE FOUGHT A BATTLE
AND WON THE WAR ⎫
AND LOST THE WAR ⎬ CHOOSE ENDING

1. Catagory 05 the Design Professions.
2. The notion of "wrongness" is an inappropriate one as it
   suggests shortcomings and imperfections, a perfectly 'normal'
   state of affairs if we are all imperfect. If everything has

relative perfection then there is nothing "wrong".
3. The situation will not change, only individual perceptions of appropriateness.

Pauline Amphlett, c/o 128, McKean Road, Oldbury, Warley, West Midlands. B69 4BA. Dec 16, 1980

---

post office & telephones; thoughts on the subject, born in a train compartment.

problems concerning the subject,
* it's difficult to remember a lot of adresses and/or phone-numbers, therefore one is obliged to carry a notebook.
* one always needs coins for stamp-automates or phone-boots.
* there aren't enough public phone-boots, mailboxes or stamp-automates available.
* phone-boots or stamp-machines are usual out of order when you urgently need them.
* there is an overall shortage of higher mentioned devices.

proposals towards improvement,

a. raise the number of stamp-automates, letter-boxes and phone-boots. maybe combine the first two items into one machine.

b. this proposal is based on a kind of credit card with a magnetically coded strip for identification of the user. In order to use the public phone or mail-box and stampautomates, which are now combined, one has to insert the mentioned card and form a certain number-code (which is the only thing the owner has to remember). after dialing the code, which is a protection against unallowed use of the card, one can dial an information-number which gives him acses to a databank where everyone has a certain space for storing away phonenumbers and adresses. after this he can make his phonecall or post his envelope. the charged taxes are automatically credited on the user's personal account. the card can be combined with the identification-card.

c. the base of this system is the same as in proposal "b". but this time everything, except inserting the creditcard and dialing the code, is fully computerised. the acses to the databank also is, the information automatically appears on a screen built in. the phone and letter-box now also are combined. the person one speaks to on the phone appears on the screen. if the addressed person isn't home, the call is automatically recorded on tape, together with the video-image. letters can be sent by inserting a manetical strip. a computer combines the letter with the image of the main or the woman who sent it... etc.

paul bas, ambtmanstraat 7, 2000 antwerpen, belgium.

MODERN LIFE AND DO-IT-YOURSELF:

A response to the invitation to present proposals for the design of modern life as it could be in 1981, 1984 and the year 2000.

The do-it-yourselfsector becomes more and more important. For some people it is a hobby; for others a way of saving money because a garage keeper or a paper-hanger is too expensive.

I think that the do-it-yourselfsector is the beginning of a change of our society and economy in a positive way. What is wrong in our society is that a lot of people don't understand anymore how most of the products they use every day do function. Why should it stay that way? We should be able to act more independent and to influence our surroundings in stead of being told what we should buy (and throw away after a while). Happily more and more people are starting to realize that (e.g. the succes of do-it-yourselfshops; powertools;...).

So, immediately (in 1981) the change has already started and I believe that this sector is still becoming more and more important. The reason for this growth is partly because of the economical depression (since 1973). Manufacturers and do-it-yourselfshops can influence this growth by e.g. publicity, service.

More slowly (by 1984) I think that this change can be stimulated by manufacturers by designing new products (nnovations) for the do-it-yourselfsector. This should not only be in our western society but also in developing countries.

Concerning the future (by the year 2000) I think that it is a change that will have to grow slowly. It can't be stimulated by one manufacturer or one designer. The mentality of the people is very important. It is also very important that a lot of manufacturers and consumers are aware of the problems of our society and of the change which is necessary. The consumer should become mature. I think that almost everybody wants to live in a comfortable way but that does not mean that we should have a second house and a luxurious car which will be replaced by another even more expensive car every two years.

Stimulating this new mentality can be one of the tasks of the designer of the future.

(Robert Wouters. Lelienstraat 26 2610 Wilrijk Belgium - dec. 1980)

LEISURE

Personally I think leisure is one of the more important problems nowadays. Most of the people equate leisure with no-activity, rest. Activity means the job they are doing, the daily duty. If we only look at the big part of retired people living for the rest of their lives very unhappy because they just don't know what to do, the problem becomes clear: society does not know how to use leisure. Or better, society does not know how to use leisure anymore! Indeed, it used to be better. Let us look where it went all wrong.

When economical systems were invented for the prosperity of society, productivity became very important. As every system it has fixed aims and finally it becomes the purpose to maintain the system itself. Productivity means working and nowadays keeping everybody to his 8 hours a day, 5 days a week job is the aim of the system. Obviously this is an artificial situation. People are tired out by this system and invention is killed.

Future should create a change in mentality. Less daily-duty-work does not mean less productivity; today we have the technical possibilities for this. So, we can create more leisure! Because we are not able to use our leisure, people should be taught how to use it (the same way it is perhaps better to teach people how to design their own environment than designing it for them). But finally, having more leisure will start society to think about it and create their own, new ways of using it.

Is this now how it used to be before productivitiy became so important? Folk tradition was different in each village and was the product of leisure from the total society of the village, young and old. Folk tradition is history today, no such thing exists anymore. More leisure could switch this situation. More leisure will be a renaissance of invention!

Erwin van Handenhoven - Lepelhoekstraat 35, B-2700 Sint-Niklaas, Belgium

---

1. SECTOR CHOSEN (by random process)   Leisure and Hobbies

2. WRONG
   The 'dictatorship' of public T.V.

3. CHANGE?

   (a) <u>Now</u> Fourth channel to be used for and by the community. Think how local 'leisure centres' (although far from perfect) serve as a model of how policy can produce concrete results.

   (b) <u>1984</u> Draw up a new Act to make 'TV literacy' (as viewer and actor) part of education - as sport is, for example.

   (c) <u>2000</u> A society with a complex structure of mutual entertainment channels. The ability to act out leisure any level down to the very local and be able to share it as entertainment right up to national level.

Alwyn Jones, City University Business School, 23 Goswell Road, London EC1M 7BB

EDWIN SCHLOSSBERG   JOHNSON HILL ROAD, CHESTER, MASS. 01011, 413-354-6541

INSTITUTIONS EXIST TO PREVENT ABUSE BETWEEN PEOPLE
EVERYTHING ELSE TAKES PLACE IN A SPIRIT OF LOVE

CULTURE EXISTS TO ENHANCE INTERACTION AND TO PERSERVE IT

NOTHIN IS LESS LIKE THE TRUTH

WITHIN NEXT TO BY ABOVE AROUND ARE THE DIRECTIONS

YOU ARE STANDING IN A ROOM, AND THERE ARE OTHERS THERE AND YOU OFTEN
FORGET THAT YOU CAN TALK WITH THEM THAT THERE ARE SUBJECTS OF
DISCOVERY THAT ANY MEETING CAN PROVOKE

IMAGINE A WORLD SO FILLED WITH INTELLIGENT OBJECTS THAT MEMORY CAN
BE FILLED WITH THE PERFUME OF SIGHT

[signature]
December 6, 1980

THE DESIGN OF MODERN LIFE

G. Y. Solis - Gabriela Yazmin Ladron de Guevara (Erea Grillo)

Subject chosen : 19 Anything not on this list

'THE DESIGN OF INDUSTRIAL WORK

What is wrong:

a. Job redesign effort has been heralded as the solution to discontent with routinised, meaningless and dead end jobs. But in reality there is little agreement concerning the applicability of any particular theory of work satisfaction across even a modest range of tasks, organisations and work setting.

b. Technology has been used within industry as an instrument of control, manipulation and subordination by those in positions of power and authority.

c. Workers are seen as merely instruments that generate a valuable commodity called 'work'.

d. The alienation of mass production workers with repetitive and unskilled tasks seems to imply not only lack of interest in the job but also decreases the interest in the change process that otherwise would make possible the influence of the worker on his/her working life.

Change proposals:

a. Immediately. Members of society in different positions and at different levels should be taking more active steps to make work likeable. For example more advanced equipment should be designed to reduce the stress and fatigue of the operator.

b. More slowly. The automation of repetitive manipulative tasks should relieve the workers in asembly lines. As machinery and equipment improves performance new goals could be set.

c. Even more slowly. Machines could be designed to do all the drudgery and dangerous work in the world. The wealth produced by automation would be able to provide every family with a critizen's right to a good basic standard of living. The number

of unemployed could increase substantially, yes but instead of
thinking of job design we could think of providing suitable
leisure activities to replace work, or, restraining people for
new jobs where human technical skills and intelligence could
be used for maintenance, organization, creativity and any job
where human emotion is an essential ingredient of the work.
In the future, work could be designed to become a tool for
better livingand not as the end in itself.

Gabriela Yazmin Solis Ladron de Guevara (Erea Grillo), 20 Castle
Hill, East Leake, Loughborough, Leicestershire, LE12 .6LY

THE DESIGN OF MODERN LIFE - ANSWERS TO THE QUESTIONS-

Question I : I have chosen no 19 (anything not in this list)
according with my final year's theoretical examination essay.
I have chosen for life as a whole and "the system" today.

Question II : In design and in all circumstances where decisions
are taken concerning the future, MAN WITH HIS REAL NEEDS should
be the focus, and NOT THE CONSUMER as in marketing, or THE WORKER,
as in politics. About the real needs, I have selected (at random)
and translated quotations taken from a book I was reading the very
moment I received your request. The title of the book is "THE
EXTATIC MAN". It's author is Steven De Batselier (1977)

p.19 (middle) : "Yes, you are definitely a child of the Cosmos.
But "the System" wants clear agreements, predictable certainties,
well defined instructions and tasks, clearly described duties.
And you feel down-cast and frightened, because you have seen
into the game and you feel defenceless, with empty hands and
stripped of your Self. The course of your life - that should not
worry you - it is programmed and assured : studying - working -
earning money - securing a safe job and then ... then you can get
married, rejoice sex, build a house with borrowed money, secured
by an insurance company ... And you are pinned down; but "the
System" is at east for a least twenty years."

p.64 (middle) "Visit these sacred temples of nature : they are like gothic cathedrals raised by the Invisible Hands of the Creative Ghost. There you will find rest and peace, joy and gladness while you are listening to the morning song of the nightingale. The rays of sparkling sunlight, dwelling on the cristal beauty of the morning dew, will broaden your chest and make your body grow until it meets the very sun."

Question III : Man's real needs SHOULD be focused in 1981; about 2000 the real needs (conscious of surviving and cosmos) WILL be the focus of all activity, thanks to man's evolution of consciousness.

> "If mankind only caught a glimpse of what infinite enjoyments, what perfect forces, what luminous reaches of spontaneous knowledge, what wide calms of our being lie waiting for us in the tracts which our evolution had not yet conquered, they would leave all and never rest till they had gained these treasures." SRI AUROBINDO

Jef Janssens - Bredabaan 926 - 2060 Merksem - Belgium

THE DESIGN OF MODERN LIFE

Answers to Chris Jones's questions by Fionan de Barra, 3 Church Building, Main Street, Arklow, Co.Wicklow, Ireland.

1 Sector 19 - "Anything not in this list" - religion.

2 The values that underly people's decisions and determine their actions, can be explained by their religion - or set of beliefs. What I see wrong here is not that there is so little religion but that there are so few believers.

3a) Why not concentrate on what cannot be changed for a change? - the bedrock of values that determine man's respect for the dignity of his fellow man, for the human person. The quality of peoples' lives, their values, goals, aspirations etc are not determined, nor could they be, by the levels of technical and scientific achievements, but rather by the great living traditions of art, literature, philosophy - the study of man himself, his errors, discoveries, failures, successes, fears, beliefs....

b) The introduction into systems of education, legislation, government, employment etc. of some means of alleviating the tension between those who see human knowledge and experience as intrinsicly valuable, and those pragmatists who continually ask of all knowledge, "what use is it?"

c) Continual affirmation of faith in God.

Questions

1. Which sector have you chosen?
2. What do you think is most wrong with this sector?
3. How do you propose that it could be changed,
 a) immediately, e.g. by 1981
 b) more slowly, e.g. by 1984
 c) even more slowly, e.g. by 2000

Answers

1. Anything that is not on this list.
2. Its not on the list.
3a) By adding it to the list at a rate of $1\frac{1}{4}$ letters per month.
 b) By adding it to the list at a rate of $\frac{1}{4}$ letter per month.
 c) By adding it to the list at a rate of 1/30th. of a letter each month.

'Anything' shall be in Optima, which is a letterface with a timeless quality. It shall be in lower case only as the begining is of no greater significance than the end. 3a shall be in primary yellow and proceed from bottom to top. 3b shall be in primary blue and proceed from right to left. 3c shall be in primary red and proceed from left to right. By 2000 'anything' will be in black, but with a multicoloured history.

(This is not intended as a flippant response. What I propose is a work of Art that can only be perceived by an efficient mind's eye. Neither this subject nor this skill has had that attention at this conference that I had hoped they would have).

Alan Pinder, Department of Landscape Architecture, Gloucestershire College of Art & Design.

The "DESIGN" of "MODERN" "LIFE"
    (What?)   (Which?)

1. The life is not so much about chioces, but combinations.

2.(a) 'Wrong' implies 'right' prescriptions which involves choice, which involves denial of chance....

    (what was the question?)

(a) A good question is better than the most brilliant answers.

(b) Everything is both part of some problem(s) and part of some solution(s).

    (what is the problem?)

3. Has our highly 'sophisticated' 'civilization' got so desperate that it needs one-page 'solutions' for its undefined problems?

CONCLUSION

*A GOOD QUESTION IS BETTER than the MOST BRILLIANT ANSWERS.......

HISTORICAL CONJUNCTURE: 16.12.1980

Slavery papers sold at auction for £115.000 / Hunger strike joined by 23 more Maze prisoners. /* The Archbishop of Canterbury sitting for his portrait by Michael Noakes (and pictured in The Times while doing it). /* Rents for council houses (that is, whatever is left of them) to rise £3.25. /* £455 million trade surplus confounds pessimists. /* Iran and Iraq continue to cut each other's throat. /* Report on virginity and bone tests of immigrants published. /* The last day of the DRS Conference.

Necdet Teymur, University of Dundee, Dept of Architecture, Perth Rd., Dundee DD1 4Ht

PORTSMOUTH POLYTECHNIC, SCHOOL OF ARCHITECTURE.

[Printed text, heavily overwritten by handwriting:]

an invitation to anyone who wishes to present proposals for the design of modern life as it could be in 1981, 1984, and the year 2000. This page is a conference paper, one of a set which is being written by whoever responds to this invitation. In this page I am supplying a format, or context - in which it is hoped that a central selection of topics will build up a picture of how modern life could develop, according to the ideas of those who study design processes.

I am inviting proposals for the design of the six starred items in this list of sectors of modern life (*selected to be like so many frozen food packs to be sampled whenever...what you ask for (when the details allowed to slip away) down the drain) is the kind of thing that...

*00 broadcasting   10 computing & microprocessors
*01 building   *11 housing
*02 education   12 health services
*03 central & local govt. depts. 13 tourism
 04 cars & road transport   *14 leisure (sports & hobbies)
*05 the design professions   15 advertising & public relations
 06 the countryside   16 ...
 07 manufacturing industry   17 banks, credit, investment, etc.
 08 ...   18 ... & ... services
*09 post office & telephones   *19 anything not in this list

As a contrast to the sometimes ... inspiration to discovering a sense of 'life as a whole', I seek a quotation from a ... of Wallace Stevens (Faber and Faber, London, 1955). A chance process (random numbers) leads me to these lines on page 201-2, from The Man on the Dump:

> The dump is full
> of images. Days pass like papers from a press...
> And so the moon, both come, ... and the janitor's poems
> Of ... We ... appear ... cans of pears.
> The cat in the bag, the corset, the box
> From Estonia: the tiger chest, for tea.

If you wish to ... please choose ... or change one of the stated sectors. Then write your answers to these questions:
1. Which sector have you chosen?
2. ... do you think is most wrong with this sector?
3. Does your proposal show that it could be
(a) immediately; e.g. in 1981, as a local improvisation in your area?
(b) ... by 1984 ... making a modest but noticeable improvement throughout the sector?
(c) even more slowly ... by the year 2000, as a fundamentally better way of organising this sector of modern life?

Please reply on one page to me (care of DRS Conference Secretary Jennifer Powell), School of Architecture, Portsmouth Polytechnic, King Henry 1 Street, Portsmouth, PO1 ... or bring it to me at the Conference by 16th December 1980. All replies will be exhibited and six, chosen by chance, will appear in the Conference proceedings. Please ... electric typewriter OR IN CAPITALS WITH A FIBRE PEN within a text area no larger than this. I will submit a response myself. Don't forget to add your name and address. — J. Christopher Jones.

[Handwritten response overlaid across the page:]

DEAR CHRIS,

SOMEHOW, YOU ARE ASKING TOO MUCH OF ME — OR, PERHAPS, TOO LITTLE. AND YOU ASK IT IN SOMETHING THE WRONG WAY! YOU SEE, IT'S NOT THAT YOUR INITIAL SELECTION OF TOPICS — AND OF TIME SCALES — IS WRONG, NOR IS IT THE RANDOM SELECTION FROM THEM. IT'S THE WHOLE APPROACH, PARCELLING OUR-SELVES UP LIKE THAT. WHENEVER WHAT YOU ASK FOR IS FINE, BUT THE WAY YOU WANT IT REDUCES ITS RELEVANCE. I MEAN THAT.

ALL YOUR TOPICS SEEM TO BE THE SAME, AND SO, IN A FUNNY WAY, ARE ALL YOUR TIMES. BEHIND IT ALL, WHAT YOU'RE TALK-ING ABOUT IS COMMUNICATION, ABOUT WHICH THIS TO SAY:

WE CAN ALREADY GENERATE TV PICTURES, AUTOMATED WRITING, THE (PERVERTED) RE-REPRESENTATION OF OUR THOUGHTS, PATTERN RECOGNITION, EVEN DEEP HOLOGRAMS (HOW LONG TILL THEY GENERATE THEM, TOO) ARE HERE, AND THAT MEANS THAT INFORMATION HAS CHANGED, AND WITH IT, THE STATUS OF THE FIXED, THE STABLE, THE XEROXED WORD (DIRECTLY GENERATED BY COMPUTER OF COURSE). WE ARE ENTERING THE AGE OF THE INTERACTION OF THE CONSTANT RE-WRITE, THE CONSTANT FADE OUT. HERE I AM, IN MARACAIBO, THE AIR CONDITIONER (WITH A "SAVE ENERGY" NOTICE ON IT) RE-WRITING MY ATMOSPHERE. THAT'S WHAT'S HAPPENING, AND LIKE ALL REWRITES, IT'S DOING IT ITSELF. COMMUNICATION: THE IMAGE, FADING, REWRITES ITSELF. DOES IT SHIFT? IS IT THE SAME AS IT WAS? THE STATIC PREMONITION IS DEAD, ALREADY, LONG BEFORE ITS CURRENT BIRTH. YOUR STATUS IS WHAT MUST BE CHANGED. DESIGN QUESTION IS LIVE TYPE ALREADY, WILL SO BE BEING WRITTEN OVER BY CONSTANTLY REWRITTEN INFORMATION.

WHAT WE HAVE TO DESIGN IS THE REWRITING. YOU KNOW THAT.

GOOD LUCK, LOVE,
RANULPH.

Utopia and Numeroso

Ralph Jones and Neil Stamper, editors of Futures, asked for an essay of 3000 words about the idea of 'experimental city'. By the time the essay was written (1981) they had left the journal and it was never published. It has however appeared in Spanish in the art/life magazine El Porteno of Buenos Aires, volume 1, number 2, february 1982 and it will appear in the proceedings of the Design Policy Conference held at the Royal College of Art, London, in 1982, to be published by The Design Council. A short version of it was performed as a play-reading-with-video at the conference. The words of Utopia, Numeroso and Unesco were spoken by Erna Ragnarsdottir, James Powell and Phil Roberts and their actions were represented on video by Marie Haenlin, Patrick Harrison and Michael Harrison. The video camera was operated by Richard Layzell and Simon Clifford. In the discussion which followed a second Numeroso came forward to take the place of the performers who had by that time left the platform. His action was, I like to think, the next step in a fiction that may continue.

With apologies to Unesco.

(Utopia is the voice of perfection, Numeroso the voice of us all. They are quite fond of each other, though of differing tempraments. Utopia has ideas for the improvement of twentieth-century life while Numeroso is suspicious of attempts to set the future into a mould, however good it may seem. Unesco, who has suddenly come alive, has invited the two of them to plan an experimental city in which new technologies, and new ways of living, can be explored more fully than they can in the real world. The new city is to be built as a film set and life in it is to be broadcast as a tv spectacle. Utopia and Numeroso are camping on a deserted airfield where the city is to be built. They are having breakfast.)

Numeroso: Honey.
Utopia: Mmmm?
Numeroso: Honey on toast. Is there going to be honey in the city? What will people eat? Perhaps we should begin by asking that?
Utopia: I think they should decide that for themselves. The whole idea of this experiment, as I see it, is that everyone in it is going to decide, and carry out, much of what is now decided by experts and provided by big organisations. This honey you're eating. Did you decide to eat it, or are you just taking it because its there?......It was my idea to bring it along. Remember?
Numeroso: I've no idea, Utopia, I just like the taste. If we are going to get this philosophic about every detail we'll never have any plan at all......But I like it here. I don't care how long it takes us. I hope the inhabitants enjoy it as much. Utopia.
Utopia: Its nice. Nothing's decided. Everything's possible. But we're forgetting that Unesco has a definite purpose. He wants us to plan a city in which the inhabitants will be expected to explore new lifestyles, to discover new ways of life appropriate to our time. It won't be a holiday. More of an adventure, a risk, a new kind of danger sport, a new form of work. Applied anthropology you might call it. Something that's not been tried

before. I believe that Unesco got the idea when he saw that tv series about some people who lived for a year in a simulated stone-age village, cut off from the world. This is going to be the same thing, only it will be set in the future. What we have to do is to decide what kinds of technologies they are to be provided with, how far into the future they are expected to go, and how the whole experiment is to be organised. All we have to do is to propose a few initial targets, and guidelines, to get it launched. I imagine that, once its going, even that role will be gradually taken over by those who are carrying it out. The ones who run the risk. As we know, it could be dangerous. And there's the question of how much of it is to be real life, for those in it, and how much will have to be some kind of fiction, or simulation, where the risks are too great or the technologies not yet available.

Numeroso: Very good. That's the first time I've heard it put so clearly. You seem to have thought it out already, more so than Unesco has himself. Whose idea was it?

Utopia: Its been around for quite a time. But until now its been ignored. Our scribe's had a hand in it.[1] Soleri too.[2]

Numeroso: That's interesting. And now its being put into effect, on quite a grand scale. Its becoming fashionable. The experimental city is about to become one of the idea that everybody knows about, thinks about; and a few actually do it, make it happen......Whatever it is that decides when such changes in fashion, in culture, come about - I'd say *that* is the real futurology, the thing to try to predict......But I dont believe in prediction at that scale, the scale of history, you might say. I dont believe that this city of ours was pre-ordained, or was entirely a function of the recent past. It need not have happened. And we two might not have been here now, trying to set it going. But I'm glad we are, Utopia. I'll never forget this. Our moment. Or one of them. I can't believe its really happening.

Utopia: I dont know what to say. No need to say anything, I guess. More coffee?

Numeroso: OK. What are we doing, do you think - trying to improve life, or just enjoying it?

Utopia: Well I'm pretty sure we're doing both. It took a lot

of effort by some strongly motivated people to get to this point. But now that the experiment seems bound to happen, one way or another, its becoming part of life, something to enjoy, if one can, or to suffer, if things go wrong. The whole thing could go very wrong. I expect you've thought of that.
<u>Numeroso</u>: No I hadn't. So far I've not given it much thought. I came because I was asked. And to be with you. You know that. But I suppose you're right - we could have some sleepless nights. What happens if the people living here get violent? If they start killing each other. Is that on the cards, or has Unesco got some rules that he is going to enforce after all?
<u>Utopia</u>: That's for us to decide. He said its to be as realistic as we dare to make it. He'll accept what we say.
<u>Numeroso</u>: Perhaps he will, but if I was one of the people coming to live here I'd want some kind of security I think...... or would I? This sounds like the most difficult question we have to decide. If the thing's to be more than a game there'll have to be some real risks. But I'm forgetting. Its to be a semi-fiction. When it gets too dangerous it will be a matter of simulating what's supposed to happen so that it looks real to the tv audience, but not to those involved. But what about its political effect, on the viewers? Are there any limits there?
<u>Utopia</u>: No. This is to be one bit of tv where the only censor is to be the channel selecter. Unesco is going to beam it worldwide from sattelites. Of course, with the present technology, each country can decide for itself whether to re-transmit on their own networks, but there'll be videotapes too which will reach some people, at least, in most countries. But its not our job to think about that, its outside our influence. Its up to us to make it as perfect as possible. To give the future a chance.

Numeroso smiles.

<u>Utopia</u>: Shall we go outside? Its getting hot in the van.
<u>Numeroso</u>: You're quite fragile, aren't you, when it comes to realities. Yes. Lets go outside. Its a beautiful morning. Its perfect.

Next day. Unesco arrives. The conversation continues.
<u>Unesco</u>: Don't let me interrupt. I'm only here to listen. There's a meeting tomorrow and I have to make a report.
<u>Utopia</u>: Perhaps you'd like a summary of our thinking so far? We've discussed a lot of possibilities and it would help us both, I think, to describe them in brief, and to hear what you think. We could be losing sight of the goal.
<u>Unesco</u>: The goal, Utopia? I remember you lecturing about goals. You said that fixed goals are over: things of the industrial past. If the process is informative we should be open to act on what it teaches. Isn't that what you said? Or somebody did.[3]
<u>Utopia</u>: Yes of course. I should have said 'we can learn from your reactions'. But its hard to shed that reductionist jargon, the vocabulary of the narrow path.
<u>Unesco</u>: That's a nice way to put it. But I don't pay so much attention to the words people us. I listen more to the tone of voice.
<u>Numeroso</u>: Before we go on, Unesco, could you tell us what you really had in mind when you proposed this experiment?
<u>Unesco</u>: Yes of course. I had two very clear reasons. Firstly, I am tired of hearing from experts that so many of the world's problems are insoluble: poverty, malnutrition, pollution, road accidents, bureaucracy, illiteracy, inflation......there are literally hundreds of such problems, and most of them getting worse. So why not make a fresh start? Try to clear our minds, to rethink the possibilities in a less restricted context? The conventional planning methods seem to be too limiting to make real difference. And my second reason is that I've come to doubt the futurologists, the people in the think tanks. Too much thinking and too little practice. They seem to forget that technology is not just an idea: its action. Its the making of physical changes to the world, its altering nature, to an extent at least. And such changes, such actions, create a <u>re</u>-action. A social reaction, when we see for ourselves what the changed world is really like. Seeing it, and experiencing it, changes our perceptions. I'm sure of that. It tells you things you didn't know about yourself and leads you to act in new ways. Ways that are not predictable from a

theoretical model, or concept.[4] That's my belief. That's why you're here. Ideas are essential to generate something new. But I don't believe that they can predict its effects. That's my theory!

<u>Utopia</u>: That's not a theory, Unesco. Its a morality, an ethic. A theory is meant to predict. To control. To create certainty. But what you're saying is that ideas, if acted upon, do the opposite. Your belief, as I understand it, is that we should accept not knowing what the future will be like and that we should trust in the abilities of ourselves, and of everyone else, to be surprised by what happens, to be changed by it, and to be able to react in new ways that at present we do not know? To seek to fix the future into a predicted form is, by this ethic of yours, a wrong thing to do. Its to deny us our humantiy, our ability to <u>be</u>.[5] Life will change beyond our expectations.[6]

Numeroso is silent. He looks surprised. A little embarassed, perhaps. Its getting dark. The scribe knows that they have a lot more to say and wonders how it is to be fitted into 3000 words. Most of them are gone.

<u>Numeroso</u>: Its time we spoke of the details, the kinds of new technology to be tested in the city and the precise questions that the experiment is meant to answer. But what we've just been saying makes me ask if even that is going too far. Its hard to see how to begin with enough reality to generate action while leaving space for genuine doubt.

<u>Unesco</u>: What specific proposals have you discussed?

<u>Numeroso</u>: Many. Here are a few. Not in any special order but just as I remember them. Education: very largely without books, perhaps without literacy, even. The paperless office. No jobs. Everything is to be produced automatically, without workers or managements, or else is made by hand by those who need it. No cash, just credit cards, and a guaranteed unearned income. At first all structures will be temporary - mobile homes and the like. Public access to all information, personal files included, no copyrights, no privacy of information, public or private. Each profession is given the task of translating its specialised services into a mixture of computer aids and do-it-yourself.

Private cars and buses to be replaced by automated minicars and minibuses accessible by credit card, and free of accidents, congestion, and parking problems, being computer controlled. Walking and cycling facilities to have top priority in city design. Private ownership of space to be limited to the times when the persons concerned are actually present, each person's territory being a mobile entity in law. Law-making, and law-changing, being a public responsibility to which everyone has to give a lot of time. Referenda, by tv viewdata systems, every day. Have I said enough to let you see what we have in mind? Obviously its going to call for very different motivations, and ways of living, than those we are used to. To discover those is, I imagine, the main question.

<u>Unesco</u>: All this sounds like technology and western culture carried to the extreme. What about the poor countries?

<u>Utopia</u>: We propose that it begins, as you say, with the most advanced technologies we know, but with a new factor that changes the picture completely: negative growth, or rather planned economic decline. The aim of the imaginary economy is to gradually approach the levels of income that are common in the majority of the world, a fraction of western incomes now. Why not try to close the gap from the top down? That's the idea we'd most like to see tried. Why not? Its no more astonishing than was the growth of industrialisation in the first place. The alternative technology people have in many cases shown the way.

<u>Numeroso</u>: You dont have to argue with us, Utopia. We agree I'm sure. But, where its a proposal that seems to call for <u>persuasion</u>, shouldn't we be thinking of letting the inhabitants of the city decide for themselves? I don't think I understand the politics of this experiment. Who's in control?

At this point my story becomes the introductory scene of a fiction which could be continued.

<u>References to the real world</u>:

1. Jones, J. Christopher, "Trying to Design the Future", <u>Design</u>,

September 1967, <u>225</u>, page 35 ff.

2. Paulo Soleri is the architect and initiator of the ecological micro-city Arcosanti in the desert north of Phoenix, Arizona, USA.

3. Jones, J. Christopher, <u>Design Methods, 1980 Edition</u>, (New York, Toronto, Chichester, Brisbane, John Wiley & Sons, 1981), page xxii.

4. As I was typing this I switched on the radio to hear the voice of my friend, J.K. Page, speaking the second reason in a broadcast for the Open University course T101, Living With Technology. (Open University, Milton Keynes, Bucks, Britain)

5. Heidegger, Martin, "The Question Concerning Technology", in <u>Martin Heidegger, Basic Writings</u>, edited by David Farrel Krell, (London and Henley, Routledge & Kegan Paul, 1978), pages 284 to 317, and throughout the book.

6. I was visiting Welsh villages, asking people to write their impressions of how they expect their village to be in the future. Mrs Clarice Mary Allen, of Llanwrtyd Wells, wrote "I think it will be changed beyond any expectations.". I dont think I have ever read a more intelligent comment on the future. Quoted from <u>25 Views of Wales</u>, edited by Jones, J. Christopher, (London, Jones Family Editions, 1980).

afterword: john chris jones at 90

John Thackara's afterword was first written as retrospective review of Jones's The Internet and Everyone *(2000) and then republished on the occasion of Jones's 90th birthday. It provides a suitable coda for this book.*

For Jones, *writing and living are still intertwined* in a sublime but grounded way.

I've been rereading The Internet and Everyone by John Chris Jones.

I've been astonished once again by the sensibility of an artist-writer-designer whose philosophy – indeed his whole life – first inspired me when I was a young magazine editor more than thirty years ago.

Like another muse of mine, Ivan Illich, John Chris Jones was decades ahead of his time. The time is ripe now for a wider readership.

He wrote about cities without traffic signals in the 1950s – sixty years before today's avant-garde urban design experiments.

In the 1960s, Jones was an advocate of what today is called 'design thinking'; (then, it was called design methods).

He advocated user-centered design well before the term was widely used. He began by designing aeroplanes – but soon felt compelled to make industrial products more human. This quest fuelled his search for design processes that would shape, rather than serve, industrial systems.

As a kind of industrial gamekeeper turned poacher, Jones went on to warn about the potential dangers of the digital revolution unleashed by Claude Shannon.

Computers were so damned good at the manipulation of symbols, he cautioned, that there would be immense pressure on scientists to reduce all human knowledge and experience to abstract form.

Technology-driven innovation, Jones foresaw, would undervalue the knowledge and experience that human beings have by virtue of having bodies, interacting with the physical world, and being trained into a culture.

Jones coined the word 'softecnica' to describe 'a coming of live objects, a new presence in the world'. He was among the first to anticipate that software, and so-called intelligent objects, were not just neutral tools. They would need to adapt continuously to fit new ways of living.

In time Jones turned away from the search for systematic design methods. He realized that academic attempts to systematize design led, in practice, to the separation of reason from intuition and failed to embody experience in the design process.

After watching the rapid wing movements of a flying duck, Jones compared 'the beautiful, unconscious and ever-changing complexity of natural control systems with the stiffness and self-conscious centrality of all forms of government, management or social control'.

Jones called for the re-introduction of personal judgement, imagination and aesthetic sensibility into the design process. He came to believe in 'reversing the reversal' – by which he means the Renaissance 'and its antecedents in ancient Greece and at the end of Stone Age thinking when masculine gods and values displaced feminine ones, and notions of dominance replaced those of receptiveness'.

The Internet and Everyone is the opposite of a how-to textbook. But at one point, in a passage on contextual design, Jones lightly introduces a manifesto that calls on designers:

> To begin with what can be imagined
>
> To use both intuition and reason
>
> To work it out in context
>
> To model the contextual effects of what is imagined
>
> To change the process to suit what is happening
>
> To refuse what diminishes
>
> To seek inspiration in what is
>
> To choose what depends on everyone.

A character in the book (who I 'think' is Jones) attributes this sensibility to being brought up in an old culture – in Wales – where 'the renaissance never happened' and 'pre-Cartesian thinking is in the language'.

John Chris Jones's real enthusiasm, throughout the years, has been for a kind of social designing that did not even have a name when he started writing and teaching about the subject.

He decided that he would not try and change the system from within. So, thirty-six years ago, Jones resigned from institutional life – from having a job, material security and a neat job label – for the life and economy of an independent writer, researcher and artist.

Since then Jones has written 'design plays' and other fictions, many of which are included in *The Internet and Everyone*.

'I've been drawn to study ancient myths and traditional theatres for decades,' he writes, 'unless we can rid modern culture of its realisms there is no getting out of the grim realities of commercial engineering and the way of life built on it.'

With its multiple voices and formats, this is not a book that I would presume to 'review' in a linear way. The best I can do is tell you how much I have been inspired by its 560 pages and urge you to explore the book for yourselves.

Jones writes, 'There are two kinds of purposes. The purpose of having a result, something that exists after the process is stopped, and does not exist until it has stopped … and there is the purpose of carrying on, of keeping the process going, just as one may breathe so as to continue breathing. The purpose is to carry on.'

Long may John Chris Jones carry on.

His public writing site is http://www.publicwriting.net/&#8217.

John Thackara